LITERACY MYTHS, LEGACIES, & LESSONS

LITERACY MYTHS, LEGACIES, & LESSONS

New Studies on Literacy

Harvey J. Graff

With a Foreword by Shirley Brice Heath

Transaction Publishers
New Brunswick (U.S.A.) and London (U.K.)

Library of Congress Catalog Number: 2010030806
ISBN: 978-1-4128-1475-1
Printed in the United States of America

Library of Congress Cataloging-in-Publication Data

Graff, Harvey J.
   Literacy myths, legacies, and lessons : new studies on literacy / Harvey
   J. Graff.
          p. cm.
   Includes bibliographical references.
   ISBN 978-1-4128-1475-1 (alk. paper)
      1. Literacy. 2. Literacy--Research. I. Title.

LC149.G65 2010
302.2'244--dc22
                                                              2010030806

To My Students

Contents

Foreword

International and national commissions, along with publishing com-
panies and independent booksellers, keep up a steady chorus of cautions
to the public sector about drastic changes in the nature, appreciation,
and expectations of literacy. Ironically, however, most of these warnings agree that uses and types of written texts have exploded since the
opening of the twenty-first century. At the end of the last century, literary
scholars could confidently name and describe the majority of written
genres that could be found in nations with advanced economies. In
classrooms throughout these nations, teachers taught and tested students
for their competencies in producing and interpreting specific genres
(such as the essay, laboratory report, etc.), believed to be central to the
academic enterprise.

We now know that into the foreseeable future, neurologically sound
individuals with reasonable access to role models who use technology
both to produce and receive information and to network socially will learn
to read and write more through goal-driven trial-and-error and practice
than through formal instruction. Individuals will read and write a host of
brief genres (ranging from word-limited texts to notations associated with
visual images). Choices of timing and purpose for reading extended texts
(such as how-to manuals and guidebooks, collections of short stories,
biographies, or film scripts) will depend almost exclusively on stage of
life, roles, and layers of identity. Different timescales, as well as definitions, will henceforth apply when we talk of "learning" to read or write.
Many individuals now in their sixties have just begun to learn to read text
messages from their grandchildren or the reports of medical test results
emailed from their physicians. In the future, a perspective on life-long
learning has to guide us to expect that multiple temporal dimensions,
along with roles and needs, will shape individuals' engagement with the
extended texts generally associated with being *literate*.[1]

Sooner or later, those living in the midst of change want to know the
history of specific phenomena for which strong feelings, both negative

and positive, remain. Literacy is no exception, and Graff has stepped in to offer an overview of the historical development of not only the myths of literacy, but also some central tenets of the protean shapes of its past. This is not a volume that attempts to detail how technological demands will continue to multiply the shaping and learning of reading and writing. Instead, Graff looks at intersections of academic valuations and occupational realities, acknowledging the consequences that follow when high-performance workplaces, outsourced labor, and low-service consumer sales owe relatively little to either the literacy instruction or concepts of *literate* we have known in the past.

Readers of this volume will surely recall their own histories with literacy. Few of us can remember precisely how or when we learned to read or write, though we all have our high moments of history with written texts—our own and those of others. Graff's volume suggests that such moments are less likely in the future to be characterized as mountain peaks but more as dunes—rolling, shifting, linked to specific shores of exploration and discovery. But this is not to say that the multiplication of technologies for producing and receiving written texts will eliminate the thrill and challenge that mountain peaks give us in terms of both new perspectives and widened horizons. Many of those whose occupations keep them climbing dunes—engaging with short uneven bursts of texts for most of each day—are highly likely at some point to find the time and means to take on the peak experiences that result from fiction, autobiography, history, and poetry. Publishers keep bringing out these established genres, as well as specific extended texts that relate to visual representations (e.g., film scripts and case studies of film and television stars). The social networking the internet makes possible generates interest not only in those directly involved in one's immediate social network. Also much desired are insights beyond this network into the lives of the famous who recount their paths to success (or colossal failures) in the worlds of business, culinary arts, entertainment, finance, and politics in their autobiographies, novels, confessionals, annotated cookbooks, etc.

Such texts, whether between the covers of a book or transmitted via technological devices that give readers easy access to multiple extended texts, travel with readers into those periods of time when certain types of forced leisure or "away-from-work" chunks of time are either chosen or imposed (e.g., in long airplane flights or travel by train or bus). Whether novels, narrative histories, or how-to books, these texts share a key quality with those volumes of literature that literacy instructors have for generations held up as the ultimate reward of engagement with extended pieces of writing: *truth*. The writer John Updike often spoke of this quality of fiction. Readers and writers want texts that "ring true," and this quality overtakes others that suggest mere instrumentalism or functionality. The "point" of truth never stands still, and it is toward that point that each new generation heads in their reading as they reach young adulthood and move through the lifespan. Readers and writers of long texts seek the privacy of self-reflection, psychological insight, thrill of the mystery, or seductive power of narrative that stimulates inner dialogue.

Sought most frequently in extended texts are narratives of human life. The animated characters of cartoons and videogames, as well as the actors within (auto)biographies, seven-step advice books, confessionals, and novels, repeatedly tell stories of the capacity of individuals to overcome problems, to rise to challenges of the human spirit. Even in the multiplying social webs that technology makes possible, most of us are likely at some turning point in our lives to seek some sense of what is *true* for us. This realization leads us to step away, even temporarily, from the seductive bliss of alternatively drifting and navigating the vastness of the Internet sea. We are drawn to stop for a longer look at the direct human truth of the lived experiences of others and hence of ourselves.

Knowing the history of literacy with its "myths, legacies, and lessons" enables us to look at the changes and new directions of reading and writing ahead with some sense of "truth." Sooner or later, that which is vital in extended texts will come into the lives of most of us. Books give a permanence not tied to changes in either hardware or software but to our own personal histories, timescales, and physical spaces. When we carry or move our books around with us, memories come with them, whether in the textbook of a beloved class once taken or the gift of a now-forgotten lover. Books remind us not only of where we have been (museums, bike trips, vacations, family reunions), but also of where we may yet go in our travels, careers, or roles as parents, worshippers, citizens, or healers (of ourselves or others). Through books as our most permanent artifacts of literacy, we have the privilege of holding not only the past and present but of contemplating the future.

The intellectual and social history embedded in this collection will stir readers to reconsider the dire warnings of the "end" of the book (or of literacy, reading, and the like). Though the young and technologically enamored, addicted, and dependent may seem not to give great hope of their turning toward sustained pursuits of leisure time with books or other extended texts any time soon, history suggests that they will not do away with books. As they mature, questions will remain that cannot be answered in the quick bursts of instant wisdom the Internet spits out (along with "matched" marketing). The young will, in the main, come to need more in-depth trusted and faithful stories and explanations. This volume helps us believe in this characteristic of what it means to be human. As did Graff's earlier volumes on the history of literacy, this volume asks us to see beyond what may seem imminent. Graff leads us to take the long view and to know that we gain nothing by believing the world today reveals a gaping divide between the magnificent promise we would wish literacy to hold forever and the miserable decline we may fear it suffers at the hand of the demons and angels of technology.

Shirley Brice Heath
Stanford University

Note

1.   Wortham, Stanton. 2006. *Learning identity: The joint emergence of social identification and academic learning.* Cambridge: Cambridge University Press.

Acknowledgments

Special thanks to my graduate assistants Shawn Casey, Karin Hooks, and Seth Reno, and my Literacy Studies colleague Susan Hanson for their work on this book and to the Department of English, the former College of Humanities, and the College of Arts and Sciences, The Ohio State University, for research support. At Transaction Publishers, I thank Irving Louis Horowitz—for his interest in and support of my work over many years, Mary Curtis, Maureen Feldman, Andrew McIntosh, Mindy Waizer, and Aileen Bryant-Allen.

The many people and institutions that contributed to the specific chapters are acknowledged with gratitude in the chapters themselves.

The author gratefully acknowledges below the publishers who granted permission to use previously published material, and the institutions and audiences for whom several of the chapters were crafted and presented.

Chapter 1. New introduction to the studies draws, in part, on "Introduction," in *Literacy and Historical Development: A Reader* (Carbondale: Southern Illinois University Press, 2007), 1-9 and "Introduction to Historical Studies of Literacy," *Understanding Literacy in its Historical Contexts*, ed. Harvey J. Graff, Alison Mackinnon, Bengt Sandin, and Ian Winchester (Lund, Sweden: Nordic Academic Press, 2009), 14-22.

Chapter 2. "Many Literacies: Reading Signs of the Times," unpublished public lecture. Presented to audiences at Ohio State University 2004, Western States Rhetoric and Literacy Conference 2004, University of Illinois, Urbana-Champaign 2005, Arizona State University, 2006, Miami University, Ohio, 2006, and elsewhere.

Chapter 3. "Literacy Myths," with John Duffy, *Encyclopedia of Language and Education*, 2nd ed., Vol. 2 Literacy, ed. Brian V. Street and Nancy Hornberger (Berlin and New York: Springer, 2007), 41-52. Reprinted with permission.

Chapter 4. *"The Literacy Myth* at 30," *Journal of Social History*, 43 (Spring, 2010), 635-661. Presented at Kent State University 2009; Expanding Literacy Studies international conference for graduate students 2009. Reprinted with permission.

Chapter 5. "Assessing the History of Literacy: Themes and Questions," in *Escribir y leer en Occidente*, ed. Armando Petrucci and M. Gimeno Blay (Valencia, Spain: Universitat de Valencia, 1995), 5-46; revised slightly for reprinting in *Understanding Literacy in its Historical Contexts: Socio-Cultural History and the Legacy of Egil Johansson,* ed. Harvey J. Graff, Alison Mackinnon, Bengt Sandin, and Ian Winchester (Lund, Sweden: Nordic Academic Press, 2009), 243-264. Plenary Address, Conference on Writing and Reading in Western Europe, Valencia, Spain, 1993; Conference on "From Woodblocks to the Internet: Chinese Publishing and Print Culture in Transition," Ohio State University, keynote address, 2004, and elsewhere, revised for republication.

Chapter 6. "New Introduction" to *National Literacy Campaigns and Movements: Historical and Comparative Perspectives*, co-editor with Robert F. Arnove, new edition (New Brunswick, NJ: Transaction Publishers, 2008), xi-xvi. Reprinted with permission.

Chapter 7. "Literacy Studies and Interdisciplinary Studies: Reflections on History and Theory," in *The Scope of Interdisciplinarity*, ed. Raphael Foshay (Athabasca: Athabasca University Press, forthcoming). Presented to the Scope of Interdisciplinary Conference, Athabasca University, Edmonton, Alberta 2008.

Chapter 8. "LiteracyStudies@OSU as Theory and Practice," unpublished presentation/lecture. Presented at Ohio State University 2008, Conference on College Composition and Communication 2008.

Chapter 9. "Bibliography of the History of Literacy in Western Europe and North America," in *Literacy and Historical Development: A Reader*, ed. Graff (Carbondale: Southern Illinois University Press, 2007.), 417-439; reprinted in *Understanding Literacy in its Historical Contexts*, ed. Harvey J. Graff, Alison Mackinnon, Bengt Sandin, and Ian Winchester (Lund, Sweden: Nordic Academic Press, 2009), 265-300.

1

Introduction*

Literacy and history have much in common. Both are prone to perceptions of crisis and decline–precipitous declines that are sometimes claimed to threaten civilization as we know it. Both literacy and history attach themselves to discourses of legacies and lessons. Both are susceptible to mythologization and are hard to define and measure. With attention to the calls for "many literacies" and the long reign of "the literacy myth," Chapters 2 and 3 introduce some of these threads. Subsequent chapters develop them.

New interdisciplinary histories of literacy challenge those charges, among other presumptions about literacy that have been influential in many academic disciplines, in public debate, and among policymakers (see Recent Emphases in Historical Literacy Studies and Chapters 4 and 5, below). (For example also compare Hirsch, 1987 with my own work cited below and Gagnon, 1989; Stearns,1991, 1993; Kaestle, et al., 1991; Barton, 1994; Barton & Hamilton, 1998.)

The study of literacy is prominent among both historical and contemporary subjects that have attracted significant interdisciplinary attention (see Chapters 7, 8, and 5 in this book). For example, it is an established interest of social, economic, cultural, and demographic historians, their colleagues in fields of contemporary studies, and other interdisciplinary scholars across the disciplines (see for example my own work, listed below and in the Bibliography). At the same time, historical studies have influenced research and understanding—including great debates over literacy's impacts—well beyond the boundaries of the discipline of history. This collection of studies reflects and speaks to those relationships from a number of perspectives and with special attention to literacy myths and interdisciplinary research and interpretation (see also Vincent, 2003; Graff et al., 2005).

The history of literacy is an instructive example of interdisciplinary history with respect to its founding and the course of its development. Chapters 7 and 8 tell this story, each amplifying and complementing the other, first in general terms of both disciplinary and interdisciplinary dimensions of literacy studies, and second in the specific case of Literacy Studies @ Ohio State University (LiteracyStudies@OSU), a university-wide interdisciplinary program that I developed beginning in 2004.

Literacy Studies followed a path common to new social science influenced histories of the 1960s-1980s (see New Historical Literacy Studies, and Chapters 7 and 8 below). (See, in general for what follows, Graff, 1987, 1995a, 1995b, 2001; Graff et al., 2005; Kaestle et al., 1991.) On the one hand, pioneering social science historians of the 1960s and 1970s confronted a diffuse historical, and more general, literature that made easy (if poorly documented) generalizations about the distribution of literacy across populations and also (even though vaguely) the great significance of literacy's presence, absence, or degree of diffusion. On the other hand, they confronted a social science literature, some of it with theoretical aspirations, generally derived from modernization approaches that placed literacy squarely among the requisites for progress by individuals and by groups.

The historical writing rested on a thin base of mainly anecdotal evidence, with little concern about its accuracy or representativeness. The social science writing included modernization theories with stages and threshold levels, macrosocial correlations from aggregate data, and, occasionally, contemporary case studies. Taken together, the studies that constitute this book explore complicated, confusing, and very important aspects of this history and its continuing legacies and consequences, from the life and times of the literacy myth, to reading "signs of the times," and matters of conceptualization, theory, institutions, expectations, and policies.

Writings in both areas treated literacy uncritically and as unproblematic, whether conceptually or empirically. Literacy's key relationships, they assumed, were simple, linear, and direct, and its impact was universally powerful. At the same time, most scholarly writing neglected the subject of literacy even when it was highly relevant. These were among the characteristics, indeed hallmarks, of common views of literacy, elements that I identified collectively and designated "the literacy myth" in my book of that name, published in 1979, and whose more critical, often interdisciplinary study an international group of scholars, including myself, promoted from the 1970s on. Chapter 5 tells that story in broad strokes, Chapters 3 and 4 probe the literacy myth. Chapters 2 and 6 reconsider outcomes and expectations. Chapters 7 and 8 probe the interesting relationships among disciplines and interdisciplines in the pursuit to understand literacy.

Critical of earlier work, the new literacy studies that emerged in the 1970s and especially the 1980s questioned the received wisdom that tied literacy autonomously and directly to individual and societal development, from social mobility (+) and criminal acts (-) to revolutions in industry (+), fertility (-), and democracy (+) [+=positive relationship; -=negative relationship]. Skeptical about modernization models and with at least some of the conclusions taken from aggregative data, researchers from an impressive number of nations, disciplines, and specializations were wary about imprecise formulations, levels of generalization, and their evidential basis.

Critical and revisionist in intellectual orientation, a generation of scholars sought to test old and newer ideas, hypotheses, and theories with reliable and relevant data (see Recent Emphases and New Historical Literacy Studies, below). This included my books, *The Literacy Myth: Literacy and Social Structure in the Nineteenth-Century City* (1979), *The Legacies of Literacy* (1987), and related work.

Initially, this meant identifying measures of literacy that, ideally, were direct, systematic, routinely generated, longitudinal, and comparable—mainly quantitative indicators—and building databases to promote their use and enhance their accessibility to other researchers. In Sweden, this meant church registers; in France, marriage and military records; in Britain, marriage and census records; and in North America, manuscript census records. As research matured, the challenge became to interpret this material, increasingly in combination with other primary sources in its social, cultural, political economic *and* historical contexts (see Chapter 5 in particular; also Chapter 4).

The goal of a fully critical and comparative history of literacy remains elusive, despite the advances in research to which demographic and social databases contribute. Literacy studies have taught us to make comparisons and assessments more carefully, often restricting their range. As a recognizable field of literacy studies emerged, literacy's significance as an important variable for many subjects across the realms of social science, cultural studies, and other interdisciplnary histories became accepted (see Chapters 6 and 5 in particular). Its relevance expanded just as expectations of its universal powers were qualified and contextualized. That is a lesson which the chapters of this book explicate. Equally importantly, as our understanding of the past has changed, so too has that of the present. That set of connections is an important part of the story of the literacy myth told in these pages.

Earlier expectations (and theories) that literacy's contribution to shaping or changing nations, and the men and women within them, was universal, unmediated, independent, and powerful have been quashed (see Chapters 2, 3, 4, 5). Literacy–that is, literacy by itself–is now much less often conceptualized as independently transformative. To the contrary, we now anticipate and recognize its impact to be shaped by specific historical circumstances as context-dependent, complicated rather than simple, incomplete or uneven, interactive rather than determinative. Literacy's influences are mediated by a host of other intervening factors of a personal, structural, or cultural historical nature rather than universal. In other words, literacy is a historical variable, and it is historically variable.

The Chapters

The chapters in this book confirm this point. The seven wide-ranging and diverse essays speak to each other's central concerns about the place of literacy in modern and late-modern culture and society, and its complicated historical foundations. They are supported by a final chapter, a Bibliography of the History of Literacy. The essays reflect different origins; for example, several saw first life as public lectures or keynote addresses: Chapters 2, 5, and 7. Four were invited presentations. All were drafted for interdisciplinary audiences. Together, they reconsider central questions related to literacy, and are critical, comparative, and historical. The collection is noteworthy for its attention to my critical reflections on the path-breaking identification of "the literacy myth" as well as my recent work in developing the LiteracyStudies@OSU initiative.

The studies also deal with fears about literacy, or illiteracy, that are shared by academics and concerned citizens. The nonspecialist essays speak to both academic and nonacademic audiences across disciplines and cultural orientations.

Selected from my recent writing, the chapters draw on my recent academic experiences. As a body, they reflect and are influenced by my relocation in 2004 to Ohio State University as the first Ohio Eminent Scholar in Literacy Studies and Professor of English and History, and my building LiteracyStudies@OSU as an experiment and a model for university-wide interdisciplinary programs. That story is told explicitly in Chapter 8 "LiteracyStudies@OSU in Theory and in Practice," but in various ways, it touches all the pieces of the book. This represented a shift in my academic interests back to literacy studies, a return to my concentration in graduate school and the first decade and a half to two decades of my academic life. In the late 1980s my interests had shifted more to the history of children and youth and the history of cities. More recently, my research focuses on the social history of interdisciplinarity.

Together, the chapters are the reflections of a scholar who has influenced the understanding of literacy for more than 30 years. Landmark essays, they are interdisciplinary, critical, and historical. They are also new, different, and timely perspectives on an important subject of widespread interest and concern. My studies represent a variety of relevant topics, approaches, styles, and genres exploring the meanings of literacy and alternative ways to understand them. And as mentioned, my critical reconsideration of my fundamental identification of "the literacy myth" and recent work in developing the university-wide, interdisciplinary LiteracyStudies@OSU initiative are special features of this collection of accessible, nontechnical, and nonspecialist essays.

Introducing the Chapters

Chapter 2 "Many Literacies: Reading Signs of the Times"

Every now and then, I look up and out from the past (where, as a historian, I live more or less comfortably much of the time) to ask if matters relating to literacy, its condition, relationships to lives and to its lessons, and our understandings, have improved or changed? Have we learned from our own experience?

In asking such questions, I try to read "signs of the times"—which typically tell me that the answer(s) is not much, not enough, not as much as we need. Many implications follow, that we might theorize or historicize, or both.

Among the many relevant questions, consider these:

What is the state of play between *practices* of literacy and *talk* about them? How do matters of discourse and ideology shape practices? What are the *limits* of current conceptualizations?

What are the *new literacy myths*? What is their relationship to social, cultural, economic, and political change … and to historical change?

Literacy or Literacies? What's wrong with these terms and the conceptualizations on which they stand?

Literacy's *place(s)* in American culture and society—ambiguous and contradictory, sometimes surprisingly so.

Chapter 3 *"Literacy Myths,"* co-authored with John Duffy

Literacy Myth refers to the belief, articulated in educational, civic, religious, and other settings, contemporary and historical, that the acquisition of literacy is a necessary precursor to and invariably results in economic development, democratic practice, cognitive enhancement, and upward social mobility. Despite many unsuccessful attempts to measure it, literacy in this formulation has been invested with immeasurable and ineffable qualities, purportedly conferring on practitioners a predilection toward social order, an elevated moral sense, and a metaphorical "state of grace." Such presumptions have a venerable historical lineage. Taken together, these attitudes constitute what I have called "the literacy myth." Many researchers and commentators have adopted this usage.

Such attitudes about literacy represent a "myth" because they exist apart from and beyond empirical evidence that might clarify the actual functions, meanings, and effects of reading and writing. Like all myths, the literacy myth is not so much a falsehood but an expression of the ideology of those who sanction it and are invested in its outcomes. For these reasons, the literacy myth is powerful and resistant to revision.

Chapter 4 *"The Literacy Myth at Thirty"*

This chapter reviews the thirty year history of *The Literacy Myth: Literacy and Social Structure in the Nineteenth-Century City* (1979). I reflect on *The Literacy Myth* and the critical concept of "the literacy myth" that it proposed on the occasion of the book's thirtieth anniversary, a special and also a sobering moment. On the one hand, I speak to its broad influence in a number of fields of study. I also consider some of the criticisms encountered. On the other hand, I discuss what I think are its principal weaknesses and limits. The success of *The Literacy Myth* may be determined at least in part by the extent to which it stimulates new research and thinking that begin to supplant it. After considering the relevance and value of its general arguments for both persisting and newer questions and issues, I reframe my conclusions about social myths and in particular "the literacy myth."

Chapter 5 "Assessing the History of Literacy: Themes and Questions"

The history of literacy is well established as a regular, formal, significant, and sometimes central concern of historians of a wide range of topical, chronological, and methodological inclinations. The active thrust and exceptional growth in historical literacy studies over the past two decades have propelled the subject to new prominence. Highlighting increasingly the spheres of reading and of writing, stimulating searches for interdisciplinary approaches (methods and interpretive frames), and probing relations of past to present stand out among the impacts. The maturation of the historical study of literacy has been enormously beneficial, inside the academy and on occasion beyond its walls. Nevertheless, this significant body of scholarship demands attention more broadly, both in terms of what it may contribute to other researchers, planners, and thinkers, and in terms of its own growing needs for inter- and intra-disciplinary cooperation and constructive criticism.

Chapter 6 "New Introduction" to National Literacy Campaigns and Movements: Historical and Comparative Perspectives, with Robert F. Arnove

Reflecting on the publication of the first edition of *National Literacy Campaigns: Historical and Comparative Perspectives,* we find that the lessons learned from surveying comparatively four centuries of literacy movements are as important today as they were two decades ago. The UNESCO Institute for Lifelong Learning announced on September 6, 2007 that "International Literacy Day provides an occasion to put the spotlight on the neglected goal of literacy which is crucial not only for achieving education for all but, more broadly, for attaining the overarching goal of reducing human poverty." Despite major international initiatives spanning over five decades to reduce illiteracy and provide basic education to all, current data indicate that more than 860 million adults lack minimal capacities to read, write, and calculate. Two-thirds of this number are women. Within regions, such as sub-Saharan Africa, over 50 percent of the population is illiterate.

Chapter 7 "Literacy Studies and Interdisciplinary Studies: Reflections on History and Theory"

This chapter brings together my current interests, including the social and cultural history of interdisciplinarity and the building of a university-wide interdisciplinary program or set of integrated programs in Literacy Studies at a large and disciplinary-ordered public university (LiteracyStudies@OSU, my Ohio State University endeavors since 2004). Taken together, they embrace and interrelate conceptually and theoretically both intellectual and institutional articulations, and social and cultural criticism: the history of interdisciplinarity from the late nineteenth century to the present, and the delineation of an interdisciplinary field of study with attention to its critical, comparative, and historical foundations.

In this chapter, I explore the development of literacy studies in terms of the history of interdisciplinarity. It also compares that narrative to the principal explanations of interdisciplinary developments in higher education. At the same time, I argue, our general understanding of interdisciplinarity over time and across "disciplinary clusters" needs new critical, comparative, and historical approaches and understandings.

Chapter 8 "LiteracyStudies@OSU as Theory and Practice"

Question: What happens when you cross a 50-some-year-old social historian who is a recognized authority on the history of literacy and who has long pursued interdisciplinary programs and their development, with a faculty position as Ohio Eminent Scholar in Literacy Studies (and professor of English and history), a huge Department of English, an Institute for Collaborative Research and Public Humanities, and a mega-university in the middle of Ohio in the early twenty-first century?

Answer: You get LiteracyStudies@OSU, a campus-wide interdisciplinary initiative and an experiment in university-wide interdisciplinarity. You get a series of remarkable transformations, challenging relationships, and complicated questions. And a potentially unique case study in the sociology of interdisciplinary knowledge and organization, with some general lessons to draw. All in a few years beginning in 2004.

Lessons: Literacy beyond Myths and Legacies

Literacy's students now understand that the equation or synonymy of literacy acquisition with institutions that we call schools and with childhood is itself a fairly recent historical development. Other arrangements were once common. They included families, workplaces, and peer, religious, and political groups. We recognize that the environment in which one learns to read or write has a major influence on the level of ability to use and the likely use of those skills.

Social attributes (including ascribed characteristics like gender, race, ethnicity, and social class) and historical contexts, which are shaped by time and place, mediate literacy's impacts, for example, on chances for social or geographic mobility. Literacy seems to have a more direct influence on longer distance migration. When established widely, that relationship will carry major implications for the historical study of both sending and receiving societies and for immigrants. Literacy's links with economic development are both direct and indirect, multiple, and contradictory. For example, its value to skilled artisans may differ radically from its import for unskilled workers. Literacy levels sometimes rise as an effect rather than a cause of industrialization. Industrialization may depress literacy levels through its negative impact on schooling chances for the young, while over a longer term its contribution may be more positive.

Experiences of learning literacy include cognitive and noncognitive influences. This is not to suggest that literacy should be construed as any less important, but that its historical roles are complicated and historically variable. Today, it is difficult to generalize broadly about literacy as a historical factor. But that only makes it a more compelling subject, another theme of the chapters of this book. (See the sections Recent Emphases in Historical Literacy Studies, New Historical Literacy Studies, and Lessons from the History of Literacy, below.)

Literacy Studies has succeeded in establishing a new historical field where there was none. Statistical time series developed for many geographic areas and historical eras limit cavalier generalizations about literacy rates and their strong meanings, whether by demographers, economists, linguists, or literary historians. Three decades of scholarship have transformed how interdisciplinary historians and many other students conceptualize literacy. Both contemporary and historical theories that embrace literacy are undergoing major revision because of this body of research and recent studies that point in similar directions.

The view that literacy's importance and influences depend on specific social and historical context, which, in effect, give literacy its meanings—that literacy's impacts are mediated and restricted, that its effects are social and particular, that literacy must be understood as one among a number of communication media and technologies—replaces unquestioned certainty that literacy's powers were universal, independent, and determinative. (See Recent emphases in historical literacy studies, New historical literacy studies, below.)

Literacy's historians know how recently these ideas about literacy's transforming and developmental powers were central to theories that held sway in major areas of economics, demography, psychology, sociology, anthropology, history, and the humanities. The challenge to probe previous understandings with suitable historical data and test the strong theories of literacy attests to the contributions that interdisciplinary history can make. (See Lessons, below.)

The emergence of literacy as an interdisciplinary field for contemporary scholars opens the way for a richer exchange between historians and other researchers for the mutual reshaping of inquiry past, present, and future that is part of the promise of literacy's history.

Historical studies of literacy, finally, contribute to public discourse, debate, and policy talk internationally. The many crucial points of intersection include the demonstration that no golden age for literacy ever existed, that there are multiple paths to literacy for individuals and societies, that quantitative measures of literacy do not translate easily to qualitative assessments, that the environment in which literacy is learned affects the usefulness of the skills, that the connections between literacy and inequality are many, and that the constructs of literacy (its learning and its uses) are usually conceived far too narrowly.

Historians of literacy need to bring their criticisms and new conclusions to audiences throughout the academy and beyond. That ranks high among the aspirations of this book. Both historians and other students of literacy need to probe the nature of literacy as a historical subject and variable. In part, they can do this by bridging the present gap between the history of literacy and new research on printing, publishing, and readership, on the one hand, and new perspectives in the humanities, anthropology, and psychology, on the other hand. Literacy studies join other interdisciplinary histories in exploring new approaches to society and culture through narrative, feminist theories, literary theories, critical theory, and many other connections across the human sciences in the early twenty-first century.

Recent Emphases in Historical Literacy Studies

- Economic history—greater criticism, greater efforts at more precise specification
- Demography—to a lesser extent but more subtly
- Readers and their readings: Impacts, difference/differentiation
- Learning literacy(ies)/Using literacy(ies) including levels, limits, contexts, practice, performance
- Ethnographies of literacy in practice
- Deconstructions of literacy as promotion, expectation, ideology, theory

- Multiple literacies & multi-media contexts (including multi-lingual)
- Reading/textuality/criticism/reader response/literary theory
- Publishing & distribution/circulation/communications
- Religion: influences & impacts, consequences
- Cultures, high, middling, popular, etc.—intersections, interactions, separations
- Reading & writing: Creation, expression, performance
- History of emotions
- Political culture/political action
- Gender, social class, race, ethnicity, generation
- Connecting past, present, & future

New Historical Literacy Studies

1. Historical literacy studies must build upon their own past while also breaking away from it: sharper contextual grounding; time series; linkages, and interrelationships.
2. Comparative studies.
3. New conceptualizations of context for study and interpretation including material conditions, motivations, opportunities, needs and demands, traditions, transformations, historical "ethnographies," and micro-histories.
4. Critical examination of the conceptualization of literacy itself—beyond independent and dependent variables.
5. Literacy and the "creation of meaning"—linguistic and cultural turns, reading, and so on; for example, history of literacy and transformation of cultural and intellectual history; history of the book, and history of literacy.
6. Sharper theoretical awareness of the relevance of the history of literacy for many important aspects of social, economic, and psychological theory; history as grounds for testing theories.
7. Has the tradition of taking literacy as primary object of analysis—"the history of literacy"—approached its end point? From the history of literacy to "literacy in history"?
8. Policy issues: social problems, development paths, costs and consequences, alternatives and understandings.

Lessons from the History of Literacy

1. The historicity of literacy constitutes a first theme from which many other key imperatives and implications follow. Reading and writing take on their meaning and acquire their value only in concrete historical circumstances that mediate in specific terms whatever general or supposedly "universal" attributes or concomitant may be claimed for literacy.
2. That subjects such as literacy, learning, and schooling, and the uses of reading and writing are simple, unproblematic notions is a historical myth. Experience, historical and more recent, underscores their fundamental complexity—practically and theoretically, their enormously complicated conceptual and highly problematic nature.
3. Typical conceptions of literacy share not only assumptions about their unproblematic status, but also the presumption of the central value neutrality.

Historical literacy studies demonstrate that no means or modes or learning is neutral—all incorporate the assumptions and expectations, biases or emphasis of production, association, prior use, transmission, maintenance, and preservation.

4. Historical studies document the damages, human costs that follow from the domination of the practical and theoretical presumptions that elevate the literate, the written to the status of the dominant partner in what Jack Goody calls the "Great Dichotomy" and Ruth Finnegan the "Great Divide."

5. Hand in hand with simplicity and superiority have gone presumed ease of learning and expectation of individual along with societal progress. Historical studies reiterate the difficulties experienced in gaining, practicing, and mastering the elements of alphabetic literacy—seldom easy; learning literacy, and whatever lies beyond it, has always been hard work.

6. Multiple paths of learning literacy, employment of an extraordinary range of instructors, institutions, environments, and beginning texts, and diversity of conflicting or contradictory motivations pushing and pulling v. simple notions and images. Long transformation to twentieth-century notions that tie literacy acquisition to childhood.

7. Expectations and common practice of learning literacy as part of elementary education are themselves historical developments. The presumption holds that given the availability of written texts and elementary instruction, basic abilities of reading and writing are in themselves sufficient for further developing literacy and education. Failure reflects overwhelmingly on the individual.

8. Just as individuals followed different paths to literacy and learning, societies historically and more recently took different paths toward achieving rising levels of popular literacy: no one route to universal literacy and its associated "modern" concomitants.

These lists appear in Harvey J. Graff, "Assessing the History of Literacy in the 1990s: Themes and Questions," Chapter 5 in this book.

Note

* This introduction draws, in part, on my "Introduction," in *Literacy and Historical Development: A Reader* (Carbondale, IL: Southern Illinois University Press, 2007), 1-9 and "Introduction to Historical Studies of Literacy," *Understanding Literacy in Its Historical Contexts*, ed. Harvey J. Graff, Alison Mackinnon, Bengt Sandin, and Ian Winchester (Lund, Sweden: Nordic Academic Press, 2009), 14-22.

References

Barton, David (1994). *Literacy: An Introduction to the Ecology of Written Language.* Oxford: Blackwell.

Barton, David & Mary Hamilton (1998). *Local Literacies: Reading and Writing in One Community.* London: Routledge.

Gagnon, Paul, & Bradley Commission on History in the Schools (eds.) (1989). *Historical Literacy: The Case for History in American Education.* New York: Macmillan.

Graff, Harvey J. (1979). *The Literacy Myth: Literacy and Social Structure in the Nineteenth-Century City.* New York: Academic Press.

Graff, Harvey J. (1987). *The Legacies of Literacy: Continuities and Contradictions in Western Society and Culture*. Bloomington: Indiana University Press.

Graff, Harvey J. (1989). Critical Literacy versus Cultural Literacy: Reading Signs of the Times. Review of the book *Cultural Literacy*. *Interchange*, 20(1), 46-52.

Graff, Harvey J. (1993). Literacy, Myths, and Legacies: Lessons from the Past—Thoughts for the Future. *Interchange*, 24(3), 271–86.

Graff, Harvey J. (1995a). *The Labyrinths of Literacy: Reflections on Literacy Past and Present* (rev. ed.). Pittsburgh: University of Pittsburgh Press.

Graff, Harvey J. (1999a). Interdisciplinary Explorations in the History of Children, Adolescents, and Youth—For the Past, Present, and Future. *Journal of American History*, 85, 1538-1547.

Graff, Harvey J. (1999b). Teaching and Historical Understanding: Disciplining Historical Imagination with Historical Context. In B.A. Pescosolido & R. Aminzade (eds.), *The Social Worlds of Higher Education: Handbook for Teaching in a New Century* (pp. 280-293). Thousand Oaks, CA: Pine Forge Press.

Graff, Harvey J. (2001) The Shock of the "'New' (Histories): Social Science Histories and Historical Literacies," *Social Science History*, 25(4), 483-533.

Graff, Harvey J., Chad Gaffield, David Mitch, Anders Nilsson, and David Vincent (2005). Literacy as Social Science History: Its Past and Future—a Roundtable, in *Looking Backward and Looking Forward: Perspectives on Social Science History*, ed. Harvey J. Graff, Leslie Page Moch, and Philip McMichael (University of Wisconsin Press, 2005), 153-175.

Graff, Harvey J. (2007) (Ed.) *Literacy and Historical Development: A Reader* (Carbondale, IL: Southern Illinois University Press).

Hirsch, E.D., Jr. (1987). *Cultural Literacy: What Every American Needs to Know*. Boston: Houghton Mifflin.

Kaestle, Carl, Helen Damon-Moore, Lawrence C. Stedman, Katherine Tinsley, and W. Vance Trollinger, Jr. (1991). *Literacy in the United States: Readers and Reading since 1880*. New Haven, CT: Yale University Press.

Stearns, Peter (1991, April). The Challenge of "Historical Literacy." *Perspectives: American Historical Association Newsletter*, 29, 21-23.

Stearns, Peter (1993). *Meaning over Memory: Recasting the Teaching of Culture and History*. Chapel Hill: University of North Carolina Press.

Vincent, David (2003) "Literacy Literacy," *Interchange*, 34, 341-357.

2

Many Literacies: Reading Signs of the Times[1]

Legacies for the Future

Unlike my distinguished colleagues in the Fulton Endowed Symposium lecture series, I am a historian, a comparative social and cultural historian who has studied the history of literacy along with the history of children and youth, and urban places in North America and Europe. I have resided in departments and programs of history, although lately of English (as Ohio Eminent Scholar in Literacy Studies and Professor of English and History), not as a professor of education or a member of a College of Education.

In ways that I illustrate, *history is different*. It provides perspective. It allows us to reach out for new and different and even multiple understandings of ourselves and of others, often in their interrelationships. History—dare I say historical literacy (itself a contested quality)—mandates polishing, focusing, and refocusing the lens of time, place, and alternative spaces. It probes and prompts us to comprehend what has been, what might have been, and what might be: choice, agency, and possibility, in their fullness and their limits. Its values and virtues are rooted in the power of comparison and the power of criticism, taken together. An underutilized font of needed criticism, history can also be a source of liberation freedom from the fetters of the present as well as the past.

As an interdisciplinary field, as I am working to develop it (as the founding Ohio Eminent Scholar in Literacy Studies) at The Ohio State University, the history of literacy, the discourse of literacy, the expectations, and the practices of literacy—always challenging—can also be sources of humor, meeting the need to laugh at ourselves. Reading and writing are serious business but as crisis- and decline-mongers (for example, the recent NEA report on "reading at risk") remind us, they can be taken *too* seriously, especially when taken out of historical and cultural context, like much else about literacy. We must try to indulge that too.

Revisioning/reimagining myself and my contributions professional and academic-institutional provides an opportunity to foster, promote, and even "institutionalize" a different and fresh, historically grounded but also expansive, critical, and comparative approach to literacy and its study. From the Department of English to the humanities and social sciences and beyond, I attempt to bring critical-historical perspectives and modes of understanding to new relationships institutionally and intellectually. This might be construed in terms of simultaneously deconstructing and reconstructing literacy studies differently, from historical ground(ing) upward and outward.[2]

Slicing into Literacy's Past and Future

Every now and then, I look up and out from the past (where, as a historian, I live more or less comfortably much of the time) to ask if matters relating to literacy, its condition, relationships to lives and to its lessons, and our understandings, have improved or changed? Have we learned from our own experience over time long and short? And if so, what have we learned?

In asking such questions, I try to read *"signs of the times"*—which typically tell me that the answer(s) is not much, not enough, not as much as we need. Many implications follow, well beyond this lecture, that we might theorize or historicize, or both[3]

Among the many relevant questions, consider these and others closely related:

- What is the state of play between *practices* of literacy and *talk* about them? How do matters of discourse and ideology shape practices? What are the *limits* of current conceptualizations?
- What are the *new literacy myths*? What is their relationship to social, cultural, economic, and political change … and to historical change.[4]
- *Literacy or Literacies?* What's wrong with these terms and the conceptualizations on which they stand?

Among a long roster of critical questions and issues: consider two subthemes that we will follow:

- literacy myths: exaggerated expectations for and from literacy. The literacy myth refers to the belief, articulated in educational, civic, religious, and other settings, contemporary and historical, that the acquisition of literacy is a necessary precursor to and invariably results in economic development, democratic practice, cognitive enhancement, and upward social mobility;[5] and

- Literacy's *place(s)* in American culture and society—ambiguous and contradictory, sometimes surprisingly so.

In a recent article, British historian David Vincent helps to frame the problem when he observes with reference to the progress made by historical students of literacy:

> There remain, however, two reasons for retaining literacy as a historical problem in its own right. The first of these has to do with the present as with the past. Graff's *Literacy Myth* was engaged not just with the historiography of literacy but also with the educational politics of the late 1970s. He argued with every justification that the expectations invested in the contemporary school system required critical interrogation by historians as much as by other social scientists. But however great the impact of his work and that of other scholars, the effect on politicians and administrators appears negligible. The myths have proved remarkably resilient. Literacy lives in forms readily recognizable to the nineteenth-century pedagogues and administrators. [I]t is also a direct and immediate threat to the current generation of children, parents, and teachers."[6]

Examples from the recent past include new as well as old literacy myths, and questions about their relationships and connections, issues of change versus continuity, and their contradictory balance. Despite the foundationalism of literacy's coupling with change, the continuities may be at least as striking and at least as important. Their power is discursive and ideological as well as material[7] (see the figures).

"Signs of the time," to be "read," or epiphenomena of the long-term, *longue durée*, they are deeply routed in socio-cultural and political economic processes. However trivial or contradictory they may seem, a larger understanding, potential keys, ripples out from them individually and collectively. Consider, for example, Figures 2.1 and 2.2.[8]

Printing and Reading in Twenty-First Century American Market Culture

When I asked about the status of my prepaid order for several books in April 2003, the customer service representative from Russell Sage Foundation responded: "These books still have not been published. Unfortunately the printing of the new Harry Potter book has pushed back the printing of our publications, among many other presses."

Is all reading material created or constructed equal(ly)? How do we read this ambiguous sign—is it no more than the march of the market-

Figure 2.1

The Literacy Myth Past and Present

Reading is FUNdamental

Like Nike—just do it!

Literacy as fear, threat v. Illiteracy as fear, threat

Literacy as punishment

Literacy as ideology

False equality of opportunity, access, education, practice, technology

False equality in acquiring and using literacy

No child left behind, or many children left behind?

All it takes is books in the home

Knowledge economy, learning society

Many literacies—false equation, false equality

Responses to the Literacy Myth

Ignore it

Deny it

Claim that it's erroneous

Relegate it to the "past"

Reinvent it, knowingly or not

Literacy is a marketing problem

Figure 2.2

Slicing into Literacy's Past and Future ... Reading Signs of Our Times?

- Printing/literacy
- Depression literacy
- City literacy
- License plates for literacy
- Presidential literacy
- Subway literacy
- Punitive (including prison) literacy
- Rap against literacy
- UN or un-literacy
- "the good news on literacy"?

Figure 2.3

Lessons from the History of Literacy

1. The historicity of literacy constitutes a first theme from which many other key imperatives and implications follow. Reading and writing take on their meaning and acquire their value only in concrete historical circumstances that mediate in specific terms whatever general or supposedly "universal" attributes or concomitant may be claimed for literacy.

2. That subjects such as literacy, learning, and schooling, and the uses of reading and writing are simple, unproblematic notions is a historical myth. Experience, historical and more recent, underscores their fundamental complexity—practically and theoretically, their enormously complicated conceptual and highly problematic nature.

3. Typical conceptions of literacy share not only assumptions about their unproblematic status, but also the presumption of the central value neutrality. Historical literacy studies demonstrate that no means or modes or learning is neutral—all incorporate the assumptions and expectations, biases or emphasis of production, association, prior use, transmission, maintenance and preservation.

4. Historical studies document the damages, human costs that follow from the domination of the practical and theoretical presumptions that elevate the literate, the written to the status of the dominant partner in what Jack Goody calls the "Great Dichotomy" and Ruth Finnegan the "Great Divide."

5. Hand in hand with simplicity and superiority have gone presumed ease of learning and expectation of individual along with societal progress. Historical studies reiterate the difficulties experienced in gaining, practicing, and mastering the elements of alphabetic literacy—seldom easy; learning literacy and whatever lies beyond it, has always been hard work.

6. Multiple paths of learning literacy, employment of an extraordinary range of instructors, institutions, and environments and beginning texts, and diversity of conflicting or contradictory motivations pushing and pulling v. simple notions and images. Long transformation to 21st century notions that tie literacy acquisition to childhood.

7. Expectations and common practice of learning literacy as part of elementary education are themselves historical developments. The presumption holds that given the availability of written texts and elementary instruction, basic abilities of reading and writing are in themselves sufficient for further developing literacy and education. Failure reflects overwhelmingly on the individual.

8. Just as individuals followed different paths to literacy and learning, societies historically and more recently took different paths toward achieving rising levels of popular literacy: no one route to universal literacy and its associated "modern" concomitants.

place? Are at least some of our reactions little more than the ambivalence of academics, the peddlers of literacy (and now literacies)—certain privileged literacies, that is? Or something more?

Fears and fallacies rebounded with the predictably (repetitive) over-wrought and fearful rhetoric of and responses to the release in July 2004 of the National Endowment for the Arts' (NEA) "Reading at Risk." Specific diction follows from "A Nation at Risk," the prominent 1983 report on American education from the National Commission on Excellence in Education. But the fear and fallacy are long-standing. With no awareness that the terms or the data were neither novel nor unproblematic, the NEA's "literacy myth" soared higher than Minerva's owl. The shadow was the putative finding that reading literary-fiction (novels, poems, plays)—not reading per se or reading non-fiction—had declined. The myth of declining literacy came out of the shadows, with force.

Venturing beyond the study findings, NEA chair Dana Gioia ominously and hyperbolistically declared, "This report documents a national crisis. Reading develops a capacity for focused attention and imaginative growth that enriches both private and public life. The decline in reading among every segment of the adult population reflects a general collapse in advanced literacy. To lose this human capacity—and all the diverse benefits it fosters—impoverishes both cultural and civic life."

Other, creative or innovative readings of these results are possible; they need to be pursued. That all is not as we might (or might not) prefer, does not necessarily make for crisis. In an op-ed in the *New York Times*, one commentator, Andrew Solomon, decreed that a decline in reading literature is a "crisis in reading [that] is a crisis in national health"—depression, even Alzheimer's Disease follow, for him. Crises in politics and education along with health are "brought on by the decline in reading."[9]

But is "not reading" bad for health or reading per se always good? Or is that not quite the point? Asking "Is Reading Really at Risk?," Joseph Epstein mundanely concludes, "serious reading, always a minority interest, isn't at stake here. Nothing more is going on, really, than the *crise du jour*, soon to be replaced by the report on eating disorders, the harmfulness of aspirin, or the drop in high-school math scores." If correct, is that another sign of crisis or of reassurance?[10]

To return to Russell Sage books and Harry Potter, we surprise ourselves so frequently in noting that the number of books published continues to rise. That books are a presence. And that people continue to read—in one medium or another. The experts have long predicted the "death" of the book, along with those of "literature" and the "author" as well as the "reader." But books haven't vanished. In 2003, 175,000 books were published, an increase of 19 percent over 2002. Fiction books were published on an average of one every 30 minutes. "Books are the hot medium," at least books about politics, newspapers report.[11] Too many books? Enough—or not enough—readers? People continue to read and to purchase books, with significant numbers shifting to listening to recorded books and reading electronic books on Sony readers or Amazon's Kindle. That we know far too little about what they read, understand, and take with them, and with what effects, if any, marks another side of the literacy myth and collateral expectations of decline. Web surfers also read books; video gaming may be good for learning—for some at least.... My point is not to counsel contemporary comfort, but to exercise our own critical literacy in making diagnoses, prescribing treatments, and thinking flexibly about change. We should consider, for example:

- Asking if the issue is reading per se or what is (or should be) read?
- Locating different reading practices within the complex web of material and symbolic, experiential and proscribed reading in American culture, and its contradictions.

Depression Literacy: Literacy as Cure or Promise of Mental Health[12]

According to the *Medical Journal of Australia, depression literacy* is defined as community awareness and understanding of depression. In this formulation, it is presumed to underpin successful implementation of prevention, early intervention, and treatment programs. "Improving" depression literacy is a major goal of "beyondblue: the Australian national depression initiative." This is not, we underscore, practice in how to be depressed.

Scores, indeed hundreds of literacies—big and little—struggle to bloom and for recognition, often competing for attention and privilege in curricula, budgets, standards, tests, even law and policy—and for mention in print and other media. But is our gain of the "many" commensurate with the loss—distraction, dilution, and trivialization that accompanies it? What dangers inhere in the unceasing proliferation of many literacies (especially without an accompanying search for their points of connection or relationship)? Should we attend more to limits and boundaries—or are they no more than new hierarchies, built jointly on myths old and new? The notion of "many literacies" also mandates scrutiny of what we mean by reference to "literacy"—a task too often left unexplored.

"Many literacies"—a conception I have long supported—sits precariously between an essential, and a necessary recognition, and the dangers of trivialization and debasement of literacy. Overuse of the word "literacy" and the concept empties it of value and useful meanings. As in other important ways: there are limits to literacy and to literacies; just as there are abuses as well as uses.

The old adage, elevated by philosophy and psychology, remains, that literacy, especially when the *wrong audience* (read women, children, the poor, or deficient groups) *reads the wrong texts* (novels, especially romantic fiction, comic books, ideological texts from the radically political to the radically religious) threatens the social order and damages the reader. In that formulation, reading stimulates psychic dis-ease, rather than eradicating it. Need we ask: is there a relationship between uses or practices of literacy and depression (among other mental ailments)? There has long been at least a rhetorical relationship assigned to the connections presumed to link literary romanticism with mental imbalance.

Does "depression literacy" threaten to become an abuse of literacy, of "reading," as teachers and others are urged to "screen" for depression among their pupils from a frighteningly thin understanding and basis for observation and diagnosis? As elsewhere, there are dangers. Among them: more than reading and writing is at issue and at risk. From history, we take a mixed message.

City Literacy/City Defining Literacy[13]

Chicago did it. So did Seattle. Even Austin is getting into the act. Should Dallas follow the trend toward collective reading to build community and a civic conscience? Book clubs have long been favored by the erudite who enjoy sharing their insights and discovering new ones. Now city libraries and mayors are joining the effort by encouraging citywide reading of a selected book.

So the *Dallas Morning News* enthused editorially under the headline "Defining Dallas: Citywide efforts to forge ties." The movement to "forge ties" via reading in common across a city began in Seattle with underwriting from the Wallace-Reader's Digest Fund. Chicago chose *To Kill a Mockingbird*. But Dallas ought to stay away from controversial reading, counseled the *News*.

What is going on here? What expectations follow from a reinvented ritual of reading—noncontroversial reading—together? Is Bible reading an analog? Is this a matter of ability or of content—knowledge gained—or group performance and collective experience? Does it matter? Or, is this civic literacy, a new or an old literacy myth?

Recent students of reading, sociologist Wendy Griswold and her colleagues, observe: "Cities' and celebrities' sponsorship of the public's engagement with books reminds us of the extraordinary value that society attributes to reading. It is hard to imagine another medium being promoted so aggressively. The almost unquestioned assumption seems to be that reading and talking about reading is a social good," reiterating the conclusions of my own historical work. Making that connection clear, they continue, "Historian Harvey Graff has worked to debunk the 'literacy myth' that links literacy, schooling, modernization, democracy, and individual social mobility, but such critical voices have had little impact on the public or its institutions. Regardless of whether people are actually spending much time reading, they honor and encourage it to a remarkable extent."[14]

License Plates for Reading: Texas Literacy[15]

State Rep Helen Giddings, D-Dallas, wants to add yet another bold plate to the catalogue of designs. These plates would bear the motto "READ TO SUCCEED." They would cost $15 above license plates' normal price. The extra revenue would fund afterschool reading programs for Texas students in kindergarten through third grade. Texans couldn't ask for more painless way to raise money for a worthy statewide cause.

The *Dallas Morning News* editorialized in 1996, in support of a new literacy policy and funding system, albeit a limited one. Returning to the topic a year later, the newspaper opined that "license plates could drive up literacy rates"[16]: "you could point that motto out to the Nintendo-obsessed youngsters squirming in the back seat. You could ponder that statement instead of the salacious billboards for local topless bars. The plates may also help raise public awareness about the need to improve Texas literacy rates.[17]

Presidential Literacy/Illiteracy (a la President G. W. Bush),[18]
A Discourse of Crisis Associated with Literacy

On Mar. 28, 2000 in Manville, NJ, campaigning for the U.S. presidency, Gov. George W. Bush of Texas proposed a five-year, $5 billion program to address what he termed a national literacy crisis among children. He declared that every child should know how to read by third grade, and vowed that states that failed to improve student performance would lose federal aid, looking ahead to the damaging No Child Left Behind program.

"There is nothing more fundamental than teaching our children how to read," Mr. Bush said. "America must confront a national emergency.... Too many of our children cannot read. In the highest poverty schools ... in America, 68 percent of fourth graders could not read at a basic level in 1998.... We will not tolerate illiteracy amongst the disadvantaged students in the great country called America." He continued, "I know that this is something a little new. Others have proposed throwing money at the problem. But they have proposed resources without reform...."

In echo of language once used by the Kerner Commission to describe the country's racial chasm, Mr. Bush struck a tone all his own: "More and more we are divided into two nations: one that reads and one that can't, and therefore one that dreams and one that doesn't. Reading is the basis for all learning, and it must be the foundation for all other education reforms." Whether intentionally or not, Bush follows a long-standing semantic tradition in his use and abuse of the term "illiteracy" to label negatively, criticize, and condemn, explicitly and implicitly, by association, certain otherwise stereotyped groups who are associated with other negatively-charged characteristics. These include race, ethnicity, gender, class, geography. Illiteracy is a stigma; illiterates are stigmatized: Diseased, deficient, criminal, evil, excluded, marginalized, failing. "To be considered illiterate in contemporary America is not just to struggle with reading and writing—it is to be deemed unworthy, unproductive, a bad parent, and deserving of remarkably high levels of domestic intervention,"[19] St Clair and Sandlin observe.

Whether knowingly or not, Bush evokes Benjamin Disraeli's "two nations"—certainly more than Michael Harrington's "other America." He evokes and repeats many literacy myths. The conclusion and the clincher for public policy is simply and starkly this: "You teach a child to read, and he or she will be able to pass a literacy test."[20]

This new (if it is in fact new) presidential literacy suffers from the constraints and contradictions of the harmful No Child Left Behind program. But even more, turning the usual (and expected) relationships on their head, to the contrary, Bush's presidential literacy betokens an inverted stress on the power, the importance of illiteracy, a gendered masculine illiteracy, not literacy, which by implication may be associated with others in the population. Those of course are women and children for whom reading might be FUNdamental. But not for "real men," the leaders.

Even among recent presidents, Bush appears to read remarkably little and values the reading of others little more. AirAmericaRadio.com print ads state "Because he doesn't read." The self-proclaimed "education president" may not be a "reading president."[21]

Once more we are led to major questions about the ambiguous, ambivalent, conflicted, and contradictory place of literacy, and illiteracy, in American culture, today, yesterday, and tomorrow. They cry out for attention. I am struck by how little even the most acute of recent literacy studies probes this sphere, including the NEA and NAAL reading reports. Of course, this is treacherous territory. As Griswold observes, "Regardless of whether people are actually spending much time reading, they honor and encourage it to a remarkable extent...."

Subway Literacy,[22] Safe Literacy, and Civility? or How Would it Play in New York City?

"Subway passengers here snatched up free books, the first day of a program aimed at turning the capital's vast Metro into an underground library," reported the Mexico City press in January 2004. "The city started handing out 250,000 books during the morning rush hour; when commuters relax and read a little on a ride that can require some jockeying for space and a sharp eye for pickpockets.

"The first sprinkling of paper-backs is part of a plan to distribute 7 million books in two years, while trusting subway riders to return them." The idea emerged from discussions with Leoluca Orlando, former mayor of Palermo, Italy, and former New York City mayor Rudolph Giuliani's consulting firm on cutting crime. "We were convinced that when people read, people change," said the Metro's director.

Literacy would lead to safety, civility, and honesty. Clashing with American expectations, reading and subway riding connected in the cause of individual transformation. Not surprisingly, there were doubts about the program's value in preventing crime. "'Now we'll have an equal number of delinquents, but well educated,' said Omar Raul Martinez, director of a book and magazine publishing company."

Subway literacy raises countless problems of intuiting causes and consequences, among major complications of getting the causes and effects in correct order. What books? What kinds/levels/uses of reading? Such campaigns are clearly part of an attempt to influence at least in part what riders read. But what literacy myths are invoked? Who pays? Who benefits? Who reads? What are the uses of books and literacy? There are also questions about political culture. One thing is certain: this will never play in New York City.

Punitive Literacy/Literacy as Punishment[23] or the Return of Nineteenth-Century Criminology

"The province of Ontario is taking a tougher stance on welfare than has ever been tried before in Canada," reported the *New York Times* in August, 2001. "It plans to make passing a literacy test mandatory for receiving public assistance and it will screen recipients for drug or alcohol problems, cutting off benefits to those who refuse treatment...." The *Times* continued, "In a country where government compassion toward the disadvantaged is widely considered a national trait, the strict new measures to be imposed this fall have been characterized as mean-spirited, overly harsh and possibly in violation of Canada's human rights code."

One recipient, beginning a class on how to operate a cash register, found a literacy test for receiving public assistance to be unfair: she never finished high school. Others, born outside Canada, worried that they would be disadvantaged because they lacked a sufficient level of English. And others noted that their need for childcare was not met by classes or even a job.[24]

What is going on here? What are the critical relationships? Is literacy a punishment? A drug? A therapy or a cure? A toxin or a tonic? A not so subtle prod or rhythmic accompaniment? A sign of homogenizing and sanitizing assimilation, and its lack a marker for discrimination? Why *this* discourse?

There are more general challenges: Problems of causation? Expectations of and from literacy? Expansive literacy or limiting restricted literacy? Along with a return to criminologies of the past also a return to other "old ways": literacy tests and the battered hopes of literacy on the shoals of social class, race, gender, and ethnicity.[25]

Rap against Literacy/Rapping for Il- or Non-Literacy[26]

"A petulant rapper and producer named Kanye West has created 2004's first great hip-hop album. 'The College Dropout' ... is, among other things, a concept album about quitting school, a playful collection of party songs and a 76-minute orgy of nose-thumbing," reports the *New York Times*.

A high school teacher asks Mr. West to deliver a graduation speech, the album begins, "'something for the kids.' So he starts into a slightly unhinged (but totally addictive) singsong refrain: 'All my people that's drug dealing just to get by, stack your money till it gets sky-high/We wasn't supposed to make it past 25, joke's on you, we still alive.' He uses his casual voice to describe a world of dope and dyslexia, and when he raps, 'Hold up/hold fast/we make mo' cash/Now tell my mamma I belong in that slow class,' it is clear that he has been waiting for this moment for a long time."

Both literacy and illiteracy are inseparable from persisting, challenging, long-lasting, and contradictory currents in American (and worldwide) culture. What does the rapper represent? Is the rapper completely wrong? Is his approach to literacy—a hands-on, practical, streetwise literacy with some primacy on numbers, calculations, and strategies—apparently relevant to the lives and situations of real young persons? How does his advice or, even worse, his status and appeal as a model reach out and claim value and would-be successors? What are the places for literacy in American culture?

In sharp contrast is another rap: one with different promises—unmeetable promises, we must understand, dishonest promises, likely to create unmet, if not unmeetable expectations, from the National Center for Family Literacy. With Toyota the "proud sponsor" of a full page ad in *The Atlantic* (Dec., 2005):

> Because I can read,
> > I can understand, I can write a letter.
> > I can fill out a job application.
> > I can finally get off welfare,
> Because I can read,
> > I can learn. I can help my daughter
> > With her homework,
> > I can inspire her to be better,
> > I can be a role model.
> Because I can read,
> > I can succeed, I can
> contribute. I can live
> > my life without fear,
> > without shame.
> > I can be whatever
> > I want to be.
> Because I can read.

In the United States today, tragically, Kanye West speaks truer to life. The pretense that literacy by itself is transformative joins other political and cultural lies. It also thrusts responsibility on the individual.

UN or Un-Literacy: The Failure of a Rapprochement between Newer Literacy Research and Literacy as Ideology[27]

Toward the end of 2003, almost by accident, I discovered that the United Nations had proclaimed another world Literacy Decade for 2003-2012, trumpeting in the best spirit of the Literacy Myth: Literacy as Freedom. UNESCO created EFA—Education for All—Global Monitoring of its goals for a period of years. As if a mathematical equation, Education for All was joined with Literacy for Life. Its rhetoric is dazzling (just as the graphics of the reports are sparkling).[28]

Curiously, UNESCO failed to tell many of us about this initiative. I felt much as I did in the International Literacy Year 1990 when I learned that despite more than two decades of scholarly criticism and recommendations to abandon it, "functional literacy"—as a discourse at least, but also as an undefined human right—was alive, if not well. I missed the new World Literacy Decade, because, in the words of one UN official: "in reality not much is happening and there is no independent secretariat in UNESCO as we had for ILY."

Literacy as Freedom, UN Literacy Decade 2003-2012 declared:

> With over 860 million adults worldwide who cannot read or write—one in five adults—and more than 113 million children out of school, the United Nations has launched the Literacy Decade under the theme "Literacy as Freedom." Literacy efforts have so far failed to reach the poorest and most marginalized groups ... and priority attention will be given to the most disadvantaged groups, especially women and girls, ethnic and linguistic minorities, indigenous populations, migrants and refugees, disabled persons, and out-of-school children and youth....

The implementation of the Decade's plan of action comprises five two-year periods, that is, a decade, structured around gender, poverty, health, peace and freedom.

Listen to UNESCO's familiar word choices and reasoning: At the Literacy Decade launch ceremony at the UN in New York City, Deputy Secretary General Louise Frechette (13 Feb. 2003) stressed that "literacy remains part of the unfinished business of the 20th century. One of the success stories of the 21st century must be the extension of literacy to include all humankind." Emphasizing that two-thirds of all illiterate adults were women, Frechette stated that literacy was a prerequisite for a "healthy, just and prosperous world," noting that there is no tool for development more effective than the education of girls and women. For that reason, the focus of the first two years will be "Literacy and Gender." "When women are educated and empowered, the benefits can be seen immediately: families are healthier; they are better fed; their income, savings and reinvestments go up. And what is true of families is true of communities—ultimately, indeed, of whole countries." QED: Literacy by itself=the literacy myth in action.

Unselfconsciously elaborating the themes of the literacy myth, UNESCO Director-General Koichiro Matsuura noted that the downtrodden could find their voice through literacy, the poor could learn how to learn, and the powerless how to empower themselves. The drive for universal literacy was inseparably linked to the human rights agenda. Blending discourses, he equivocated but did not reconsider: Literacy was not a universal panacea for all development problems but as a tool of development, it was both versatile and proven. The initiative, with its special emphasis on literacy as freedom, was designed to "free people from ignorance, incapacity and exclusion" and empower them for action, choices, and participation. Noting that the growth rate of world literacy had slowed in recent years, Mr. Matsuura recognized the enormity of the challenge. Nevertheless, the Decade was launched under the banner *Literacy for all: voice for all, learning for all*.

The EFA Global Monitoring Report 2006, *Education for All: Literacy for Life* asserts without qualification that literacy is a right. "Literacy should be understood within a rights-based approach and among principles of inclusion for human development." The expected benefits of literacy—for life—include: human benefits—self-esteem, empowerment; political benefits—political participation, democracy, ethnic equality, post-conflict situations; cultural benefits—cultural change, preservation of cultural diversity; social benefits—health, reproductive behavior, education, gender equality; economic benefits—economic growth, returns to investment. That is a great deal for literacy—conceptually and materially—to carry.

Although I am not unsympathetic to this construction, I have reservations. This "right" is not conceptualized with respect to its necessary material underpinnings. Too often, it is more or less free floating, rather than integrated. Its powers are easily exaggerated. The dangers include disappointment. There is also the question of priorities. Literacy follows from sufficiencies of food, shelter, and security. It does not precede, replace, or directly cause them. The ability to read and write does not guarantee work, fair rewards, equality, or safety for self and family. These are hard-won lessons of social and economic development efforts in the second half of the twentieth century. As such, they must lead plans to complete "the unfinished business of the 20th century," to borrow and bend Louise Frechette's formulation.

The admirable great hopes for *Literacy as Freedom* and *Education for All: Literacy for Life* translate into a dream: locally sustainable literate environments that will give people opportunities to express their ideas and views, engage in effective learning, participate in the written communication which characterizes democratic societies, and exchange knowledge with others. This will include increasingly electronic media and information technologies, both for accessing and assessing the vast stores of knowledge available today.[29]

UNESCO claims that the latest schema for development will be different. This time policy, programs, capacity building, research, community participation; and monitoring and evaluation will all be different. "A key feature of the Decade will be the prominent role which learners take in the design of literacy strategies for their own situations." In sum, "Efforts to promote literacy are not new, but the persistent scandal of around 860 million people without access to literacy in today's world is both a chilling indictment and an urgent call for increased commitment." But we search in vain for political economy or political will.

Really how different? The Literacy Myth remains hegemonic despite all we know to the contrary. There has been marginal revision, but not a lot of learning from experience, including history. The twenty-first century falls into place, following the eighteenth, nineteenth, and twentieth centuries. The legacies of literacy and literacy myths, the latter narrow, causal, deceptive, remain ready for disappointment and damaged expectations.

"Will Anyone Accept the Good News on Literacy?"[30]

University of Illinois English professor Dennis Baron asks: Will anyone accept the good news on literacy? Specifically, he refers to the downward revision of the extent of total illiteracy in the U.S. in 2001 to about 5 percent compared with the much higher level of almost 50 percent in a 1992 national survey. "An actual upturn in American literacy might be news, but an attempt to correct an earlier misreading of our literacy, even one that brings illiteracy down from 47 percent to 5 percent, runs the risk of drawing a big yawn from the public. An illiteracy rate of 5 percent or less would not warrant a radical revamping of our schools or our tests, nor would it result in more dollars being pumped into our admittedly needy educational system." Nor great angst, talk of crisis and decline, and fear for the future.

Are we threatened by the possibility of "good news on literacy"? Would that be such a bad thing? Does literacy function ideologically as a great (if perhaps dull) cudgel with which to differentiate people from each other and also beat ourselves (some people harder than others) for perceived failures sometimes individually and sometimes collectively? What is the place of literacy in American and western and global culture? Where do the contradictions lie and the chips fall? And who holds those chips? The uses of literacy—and the abuses—are many.[31]

Fragmenting Knowledge and Fragmenting Literacy

Today's sometimes underappreciated good news has other dimensions. For example, despite the liberating and conceptually expanding powers of recent and current recognitions of "many" or "multiple literacies," there are contradictory qualities too.

Vartan Gregorian, president of the Carnegie Corporation, relates what he sees as the accelerating specialization and fragmentation of knowledge with a fragmenting of literacy(ies):

> Nowhere is this trend better reflected than in our evolving concept of literacy. According to the *Oxford English Dictionary*, "literacy" is the quality or state of being literate, or possessing education, especially the ability to read and write. Today, however, there is a profusion of required literacies; we have proponents of technological literacy, civic literacy, mathematical literacy, geographical literacy, scientific literacy, ethical literacy, artistic literacy, cultural literacy, analytical literacy, and so on. My favorite is "managerial literacy." That particular literacy includes 1,200 terms and concepts, according to the book *Managerial Literacy: What Today's Managers Must Know to Succeed.*[32]

For Gregorian, and for us, these literacies—and in a larger sense, these boundless conceptions of literacy, their cultures and ideologies, and their practices—are part of the problem, materially and metaphorically, not its resolution, as some say today. Mirroring the march of specialization and fragmentation, seeking to gain from their association with its advancement ("scientifically," for example), they exacerbate the very problems of learning and knowledge that—rhetorically, at least—they claim to confront. In doing that, the promise of both alphabetic literacy and its analogs, and of multiple literacies risks self-destruction with the loss of its own integrity and potential critical contribution.

To conclude, I return to a powerful statement by Johan Galtung that I first quoted in the 1970s: "What would happen if the whole world became literate? Answer: not so very much, for the world is by and large structured in such a way that it is capable of absorbing the impact. But if the whole world consisted of literate, autonomous, critical, constructive people, capable of translating ideas into action, individually or collectively—the world would change."[33]

Do we want the world to change?

Notes

1. Presented as the Mary Lou Fulton Endowed Symposium Series Distinguished Lecture, College of Education, Arizona State University Feb. 16, 2006. Different versions presented at Ohio State University 2004, CCCC 2004, and Western States Rhetoric and Literacy Conference, 2005. I thank the College of Education of Arizona State University; Dean of the College Eugene Garcia, the Fulton Endowment Advisory Committee, and, in particular, Terri McCarty for inviting me.

    See also Graff, "Literacy, Myths, and Legacies: Lessons from the History of Literacy," in *The Labyrinths of Literacy* (Pittsburgh: University of Pittsburgh Press, Composition, Literacy, and Culture Series, 1995), 318-349.
2. See also Graff, "Literacy Studies and Interdisciplinary Studies," in *The Scope of Interdisciplinarity*, forthcoming. See also chapter 7 below.
3. Major examples include "functional literacy" in the early 1990s, UNESCO Education for All: Literacy for Life initiative, and the National Endowment for the Arts reading surveys.
4. See Graff and John Duffy, "Literacy Myths," *Encyclopedia of Language and Education*, 2nd ed., Vol. 2 Literacy, ed. Brian V. Street and Nancy Hornberger (Berlin and New York: Springer, 2007), 41-52; chapter 3 below.
5. See Graff and Duffy, "Literacy Myths." See also Graff, *The Literacy Myth: Literacy and Social Structure in the Nineteenth-Century City* (New York: Academic Press, 1979; New Brunswick, NJ: Transaction Publications, 1991), Graff, "*The Literacy Myth* at 30," *Journal of Social History*, 43 (2010), 635-661, Chapter 4, below.
6. "The Progress of Literacy," *Victorian Studies*, 45, 3 (Spring 2003), 418-19. See also Wendy Griswold, Terry McDonnell, and Nathan Wright, "Reading and the Reading Class in the Twenty-First Century," *Annual Reviews in Sociology*, 31 (2005), 127-141.
7. See the figures of myths and lessons.
8. A note: Forgive my Texas-ocentricity—but it comes from years of living there. Texas is not so different from much of the United States with respect to literacy.
9. Solomon, "The Closing of the American Book," *New York Times*, July 10, 2004. For an argument similar to my own, see Leah Price, "You Are What You Read," *New York Times Book Review,* Dec. 23, 2007. In 2007, the NEA followed the 2004 "Reading at Risk" with "To Read or Not to Read."
10. Epstein, "Is Reading Really at Risk?" *The Weekly Standard*, Aug 16/23, 2004. See "Reading at Risk" report and comments in response. It has a re-run—to a lesser extent—in the release of the National Assessment of Adult Literacy 2003 results in late 2005 "A First Look at the Literacy of America's Adults in the 21st Century," a more mixed report, with gains for African and Asian Americans noted but not always emphasized in news reports. Few commentators seemed to connect the two surveys—a decline in literacy ability perhaps?
11. *New York Times*, Apr 25, 2004.
12. *Medical Journal of Australia,* 177 (7 Oct 2002), S117.
13. "Defining Dallas: Citywide efforts to forge ties," editorial, *Dallas Morning News*, Nov. 18, 2002.
14. Wendy Griswold, Terry McDonnell, and Nathan Wright, "Reading and the Reading Class in the Twenty-First Century," *Annual Reviews in Sociology* 31 (2005), 127-141. Question: is this really true or does it blur clear sight of ambiguity, ambivalence and contradiction? Does Griswold's own formulation implicitly endorse the notion of a "literacy myth"? But what is the place of books and of reading in American culture? Should the question be: reading or reading what? See also Price, "You Are What You Read"; Graff, *The Literacy Myth*.

15. *Dallas Morning News*, Aug 12, 1996. Note the dominance of the private over the public; the power presumed to ally with so little practice of literacy.

16. *Dallas Morning News,* Aug. 27, 1997.

17. There are other traditions having to do with license plates ... their making, that is. See below: for Ontario, Leah Price, "Read a Book, Get Out of Jail," *New York Time Book Reviews*, Mar. 2, 2009.

18. *New York Times*, Wed., 29 March 2000.

19. R. St Clair and J. Sandlin, "Incompetence and Intrusion: On the metaphoric use of illiteracy in US political discourse," *Adult Basic Education*, 14 (2004), 45-59.

20. George W. Bush, Townsend, Tenn., Feb. 21, 2001.

21. See Dennis Baron, "The President's Reading Lesson," *Education Week*, Sept. 8. 2004 for a critique of the outmoded reading pedagogy Bush is shown using in elementary school classrooms—"mindless drill that passes for reading instruction in too many American schools ... a class of children left behind." The image of Bush as a non-reader provoked a former presidential aide, Karl Rove, to publicize in the Wall Street Journal, an odd competition between Bush and Rove over who could read more books. Rove, "Bush is a Book Lover," *Wall Street Journal*. Nov. 26, 2008. Not surprisingly, a contrasting image of new president Barack Obama was promoted, including Obama "finding voice" in books. See Michiko Kakutani, "From Books, New President Found Voice," *New York Times*, Jan. 19, 2009.

22. "Mexico City subway now has riders and readers. But some have doubts about the program that aims to fight crime" *San Antonio Express News*, Jan. 24, 2004. The program was officially launched at a subway station named for Emiliano Zapata, hero of Mexico's 1910-1917 revolution.

    Mexico City was not the first major city that tried to launch a literary underground. Tokyo has dozens of tiny paperback borrowing libraries at subway stations. The newspaper report went on to state, unpersuasively to me, at least: "The administration of Mayor Andres Manuel Lopez Obrado, a potential presidential candidate in 2006, also may have voters in mind as it lends books to the city's poorer residents, who are more likely to use the Metro than wealthier Mexicans. The subway program comes amid a national push to increase literacy. President Vicente Fox is planning an expansion of the national library system and increased spending on textbooks." No much plan would be taken seriously in the United States, certainly not in New York City.

23. "Ontario's New Welfare Rule: Be Literate and Drug Free," *New York Times*, Aug. 9, 2001. For relevant observations, see Leah Price, "Read a Book, Get Out of Jail," *New York Times*, Mar. 1, 2009.

24. See also "Reading lessons added to sentence: Program tests teens in trouble and then helps them improve skills," *Dallas Morning News,* Sept 11, 2001; Price, "Read a Book, Get Out of Jail," *New York Times*, Mar. 1, 2009.

25. See Graff and Duffy, "Literacy Myths."

26. "No Reading And Writing, but Rapping Instead," *New York Times*, Feb. 9, 2004.

27. See also Nancy Hatch Dupree, "Rebuilding Afghanistan, One Book at a Time," op-ed, *New York Times*, July 19, 2008.

28. See *EFA Global Monitoring Report 2006. Education for All: Literacy for Life* (2005). It reads like a giant anachronism.

29. The report continues: Literacy is a plural concept, with diverse literacies shaped by their use in particular contexts. The Decade will work to promote literacies across the full range of purposes, contexts, languages, and modes of acquisition which communities of learners identify for themselves. Literacy is not only one of the six Education for All goals agreed at the World Education Forum held at Dakar, Senegal, in April 2000, but it is central to the other five goals.

30. Dennis Baron, "Will anyone accept the good news on literacy?" *Chronicle of Higher Education,* Feb. 1, 2002.
31. Not so different from Baron's point is the response—well within the terms of "the literacy myth"—to the NEA report "Reading at Risk." The results of that survey (with all the limits of that genre and trope) are no more surprising than the public response. That the results might prove not only less of a decline to be damned, but hint at more complicated relationships and changes was seldom admitted.

    Regarding fears, myths, and—more rare—facts: See and compare for example: Andrew Solomon, "The Closing of the American Book" op-ed, *New York Times*, July 10, 2004, with Charles McGrath, "What Johnny Won't Read," op-ed, *New York Times,* July 11, 2004. McGrath tries to get at what people are reading, if not literary books; reading in the context of other cultural activities and media, especially periodicals. He also expresses the fear that we are "slowly turning into a nation of 'creative writers,' more interested in what we have to say ourselves than in reading or thinking about what anyone else has to say."

    For another approach to and appropriation of literacy, see also Lani Guinier, "From Racial Liberalism to Racial Literacy: Brown v. Board of Education and the Interest-Divergence Dilemma," *Journal of American History*, 91 (2004), 92-118. See also her "Admissions Rituals as Political Acts: Guardians at the Gates of Our Democratic Values," *Harvard Law Review*, 117 (Nov 2003), 114.
32. (Dow Jones-Irwin, 1990) by Gary Shaw and Jack Weber. Gregorian continues, "We are told that if you are conversant with at least 80 percent of them you can confidently engage in 'meaningful conversations' with other experienced managers." Gregorian, "Colleges Must Reconstruct the Unity of Knowledge," *Chronicle of Higher Education,* June 4, 2004.

    I have a list of more than 500 "literacies" that I've seen mentioned in print. Although I support notions of "many literacies," I do not endorse the ceaseless, confusing, critically uncontrolled, and potentially dangerous proliferation of "literacies.
33. Johan Galtung, "Literacy, Education, and Schooling—For What?" (1976), reprinted in *Literacy and Social Development in the West*, ed. Graff (Cambridge: Cambridge University Press, 1981).

3

The Literacy Myth

co-authored with John Duffy

Introduction

The Literacy Myth refers to the belief, articulated in educational, civic, religious, and other settings, contemporary and historical, that the acquisition of literacy is a necessary precursor to and invariably results in economic development, democratic practice, cognitive enhancement, and upward social mobility (Graff, 1979, 1987). Despite many unsuccessful attempts to measure it (Inkeles & Smith, 1974), literacy in this formulation has been invested with immeasurable and indeed almost ineffable qualities, purportedly conferring upon practitioners a predilection toward social order, an elevated moral sense, and a metaphorical "state of grace" (Scribner, 1984). Such presumptions have a venerable historical lineage and have been expressed, in different forms, from antiquity through the Renaissance and Reformation, and again throughout the era of the Enlightenment, during which literacy was linked to progress, order, transformation, and control. Associated with these beliefs is the conviction that the benefits ascribed to literacy cannot be attained in other ways, nor can they be attributed to other factors, whether economic, political, cultural, or individual. Rather, literacy stands alone as the independent and critical variable. Taken together, these attitudes constitute what Graff (1979, 1987) has called "the Literacy Myth." Many researchers and commentators have adopted this usage.

Contemporary expressions of the Literacy Myth are evident in cities' sponsorship of book reading, celebrity appeals on behalf of reading campaigns, and promotions by various organizations linking the acquisition of literacy to self-esteem, parenting skills, and social mobility, among others. Individuals are seen to be "at risk," if they fail to master literacy skills presumed to be necessary, although functions and levels of requisite skills continue to shift (Resnick & Resnick, 1977; Brandt, 2001). In stark, indicting versions of the myth, failures to learn to read and write are individual failures. Those who learn to read and write well are considered successful, while those who do not develop these skills are seen as less intelligent, lazy, or in some other way deficient (St. Clair & Sandlin, 2004). These and other versions of the Literacy Myth shape public and expert opinions, including policy makers in elementary and adult education, and those working in development work internationally.

Such attitudes about literacy represent a "myth" because they exist apart from and beyond empirical evidence that might clarify the actual functions, meanings, and effects of reading and writing. Like all myths, the Literacy Myth is not so much a falsehood but an expression of the ideology of those who sanction it and are invested in its outcomes (see, for example, Goody, 1968, 1986, 1987; Goody & Watt 1968; Olson, 1977, 1994; Havelock 1963, 1976, 1986); for contrasting perspectives, see Akinasso, 1981; Graff, 1995a; Collins & Blot, 1995; Graff & Street, 1997). For this reason, the Literacy Myth is powerful and resistant to revision. This article examines the scope of the Literacy Myth, considering its varieties, its meanings, and its implications for policymakers in education and other fields who would use literacy in the service of large-scale social and economic transformations.

Definition and Measurement Issues

Problems inherent in the "literacy myth" begin with confusions over the meanings of the word "literacy" and efforts to measure it. Literacy has been defined in various ways, many offering imprecise and yet nonetheless progressively grander conceptions and expectations of what it means to read and write, and what might follow from that practice. For example, literacy has been defined as in terms of standardized test scores such as the Scholastic Aptitude Test or the Armed Forces Qualifying tests; the completion of specified grade-levels in school; and a generalized form of knowledge (Pattison, 1982) such as "computer literacy," "financial literacy," "civic literacy," neologisms as facile as they are inexact. In other contexts, literacy may be conflated with its desired ends, as when it is represented as "an agent of change," a formulation that confuses relationships of cause and effect.

The vagueness of such definitions allows for conceptions of literacy that go beyond what has been examined empirically, thus investing literacy with the status of myth. Since mythos is grounded in narrative, and since narratives are fundamentally expressions of values, literacy has been contrasted in its mythic form with a series of opposing values that have resulted in reductive dichotomies such as "oral-literate," "literate-pre-literate," "literate-illiterate," and other binaries that caricature major social changes. In such hierarchical structures, the "oral," "preliterate," and "illiterate" serve as the marked and subordinate terms, while "literate" and "literacy" assume the status of superior terms (Duffy, 2000). Such hierarchies reinforce the presumed benefits of literacy and so contribute to the power of the myth (for detailed examples, see Finnegan 1973; 1988; Ong 1967; 1977; 1982; Goody, 1986; 1987; Havelock, 1963, 1976, 1986).

We define literacy here not in terms of values, mentalities, generalized knowledge, or decontextualized quantitative measures. Rather, literacy is defined as basic or primary levels of reading and writing and their analogs across different media, activities made possible by a technology or set of techniques for decoding and reproducing printed materials, such as alphabets, syllabaries, pictographs, and other systems, which themselves are created and used in specific historical and material contexts (see Graff, 1987, 3-4). Only by grounding definitions of literacy in specific, qualified, and historical particulars can we avoid conferring upon it the status of myth.

Historical Perspectives

In contrast with its presumed transformative "consequences," literacy historically has been characterized by tensions, continuities, and contradictions. In classical Greece, where the addition of characters representing vowel sounds to Semitic syllabaries is seen by some as the origin of the first modern alphabet (Gelb, 1963), literacy contributed to the Greek development of philosophy, history, and democracy (Havelock, 1963, 1986; Harris, 1989). Yet literacy in classical Athens was a conservative technology, used to record the cultural memories of an oral civilization in a society based on slavery. Though achievements in the development of popular literacy in fifth-century Rome were substantial, they resulted neither in democratization nor the development of a popular intellectual tradition (Graff, 1987). Neither did the invention of the printing press in fifteenth century Europe lead to swift or universal changes in prevailing social, political, and economic relationships. These came more slowly.

By the eighteenth and nineteenth centuries in Europe and North America, literacy was seen as a potentially destabilizing force, threatening the established social order. Conservative elites feared that the widespread acquisition of reading and writing skills by the masses—workers, servants, and slaves—would make them unfit for manual labor and unwilling to accept their subordinate status. Education for the popular classes was often discouraged, in fear it might lead to discontent, strife, and rebellion. In some settings, reading and writing instruction was legally withheld, as was the case with slaves in the United States south. Implicit in these views was the suspicion that literacy was a precondition of intellectual, cultural, and social transformation, by which individuals might redefine themselves and challenge existing social conditions.

The reactionary view of literacy was largely trumped in the last decades of the eighteenth century and the first half of the nineteenth century by reformers. These reformers grasped the potential of schooling and literacy as means for maintaining social control. In their view, education—whether in public or private institutions was a means through which to instill discipline and prepare the working class for their places in an increasingly urban, industrial society. This meant that literacy lessons in the schools were offered not for their own sake, as a means for promoting intellectual and personal growth, but were instead taught as part of a larger project of instilling generally secular moral values and faith in commercial and industrial capitalism. The destabilizing potential of literacy remained, but it was moderated by education that emphasized discipline, good conduct, and deference to authority. In this way reformers seized upon literacy as a central strategy for maintaining social control.

The roots of this perspective are found in religious groups and secular reformers who competed to uplift and save the souls of the poor, and who also competed to influence expanding school systems. Religion, especially but not only Protestantism after the Reformation, was the impetus for learning to read. The bible served as both the repository of spiritual salvation and an important primer for new readers.

Building on the foundation of the Enlightenment, the second half of the nineteenth century witnessed the emergence of a synthesis of major influences on social thought—idealism, scientism, evolutionism, positivism, materialism, and progressivism—that encouraged belief in the eventual if not inevitable improvement of human beings and society.

Literacy was seen to be intrinsic to these advances, a technology through which faith in the progress of civilization and human improvement might be validated. The preferred venue for managing literacy was mass popular education.

This association of literacy with ideology, values, and a stable social order provides a historical basis of the literacy myth.

Major Elements of the Literacy Myth

The Myth of Decline

In contemporary popular discourse, literacy is represented as an unqualified good, a marker of progress, and a metaphorical light making clear the pathway to progress and happiness. The opposing value of "illiteracy," in contrast, is associated with ignorance, incompetence, and darkness. Advertisements run by the National Center for Family Literacy in the United States, for example, show an adult and a smiling child accompanied by text that reads in part: "Because I can read ... I can understand ... live my life without fear, without shame." Given such sentiments, it is hardly surprising that discussions of literacy would be characterized by persistent fears of its decline. Indeed, much of the contemporary discourse on literacy evokes what John Nerone (1988, Introduction, *Communication* 11, 1 qtd. in Graff, 1995a, xvii), has called "a sense of the apocalypse." In this discourse, the decline of literacy is taken as an omnipresent given and signifies generally the end of individual advancement, social progress, and the health of the democracy. Such associations represent a powerful variant of the Literacy Myth.

The narrative of decline extends beyond literacy to encompass the state of education generally, both higher and lower, as well as the state of society, morality, and economic productivity. In the United States, the decline of test scores in reading assessments is said to represent one "crisis"; the rise in reading "disabilities" another; the movement away from sound reading and writing pedagogy yet another (McQuillan, 1998; see also Graff, 1995a). Where the evidence does not support a decline in literacy rates among the general population, there is a perceived crisis over the kinds of literacy that are or are not practiced—for example, the crisis of declining numbers of people reading "good" literature, said to represent a threat to the ideals of participatory democracy (see, for example, NEA 2004).

That the myth of decline is largely unsupported by empirical evidence has done little to reduce its potency in contemporary discourse. Rather, the myth is argued by anecdote, often rooted in nostalgia for the past. Moreover, protestations over the decline of literacy are often a prologue for a more sustained argument for a "back to basics" movement in schools. If literacy has declined, it is because schools have strayed from teaching the fundamentals of reading, arithmetic, and other subjects defined, indistinctly, as "the basics." However, as Resnick & Resnick (1977) illustrate, expectations concerning literacy have changed sharply over time, as standards have been applied to large populations that were once applied only to a limited few. It may prove difficult to go back to basics, Resnick & Resnick have written, if "there is no simple path to which we can return" (385).

The myth of decline also neglects the changing modes of communication, and in particular the increasing importance of media that are not wholly reliant upon print. Developments in computer technology and the Internet have combined to change the experience of what it means to read, with print becoming but one element in a complex interplay of text, images, graphics, sound, and hyperlinks. The bias toward what Marcia Farr (1993) called "essayist literacy," or formal discursive writing characterized by strict conventions of form, style, and tone, both resists and fails to comprehend such changes. Such resistance and failures also have historical antecedents; changes in the technologies of communication have always been accompanied by apprehensions of loss. Plato's notorious distrust of writing was itself a rejection of a technology that threatened the primacy of dialectic in favor of a graphical mode of communication (see, for example, Havelock, 1963).

The myth of decline, then, is an expression of an ideology in which a particular form of literacy is seen to represent a world that is at once stable, ordered, and free of dramatic social change. More than nostalgia for a non-existent past, the myth of decline articulates a conception of the present and the future, one in which specific forms of literacy practice exemplify an ideological commitment to a status quo that may have already past.

The Myth of the Alphabet

Perhaps the strongest claims concerning literacy have been those attributed to the alphabet, whose invention in classical Greece was said to herald a great leap forward in the progress of human evolution. The "alphabetized word" was said to release human beings from the trance of tribalism and bring about the development of logic, philosophy, history, and democracy. To its proponents, the development of alphabetic literacy brought about profound changes in the very structure of human cognition, as the written word, liberated by its material nature from the "tyranny of the present" (Goody & Watt, 1968), could be objectified, manipulated, preserved, and transmitted across time and distances, leading to the development of abstract thought. Pictographs, hieroglyphs and other forms of representing speech were seen as prior and inferior to alphabetic literacy, which could more easily represent concepts—justice, law, individualism—and thus engendered the beginnings of philosophical thought.

The bias toward the alphabet resulted in what its proponents called a "great divide" (Goody & Watt, 1968; see also Havelock, 1963, 1976, 1986 and Olson, 1994, 1977), with rational, historical, individualistic literate peoples on one side, and "non-logical," mythical, communal oral peoples on the other. Among other things, such conceptions led to serious misunderstandings of non-Western writing systems, such as those of the Chinese and Japanese, which were erroneously thought to be inferior to the Western alphabet (Finnegan 1973, 1988; Street, 1984, 1995; Gough, 1968). In the most extreme versions of the myth, the alphabet was seen to represent the beginnings of civilized society.

In the nineteenth century, the myth of the alphabet was an element of the broader narrative of Western history and worked to ratify the educational, moral, and political experiences of colonial Western powers with the cultures of the colonized, especially those that did not practice literacy. To the extent that the alphabet was identified with civilization, its dissemination to non-literate, non-industrial, supposedly "primitive" cultures was intrinsic to the larger project and rhetoric of colonial expansion. These attitudes were not confined to colonial contexts but applied, as well, to minority populations in schools, workplaces, and communities, all of which might be "improved" by learning the literacy practices of the dominant group. In this way literacy, and alphabetic literacy in particular, has served as what Finnegan (1994) called the "mythical charter" of the dominant social and political order. The great debates of the past two centuries over reading pedagogy and instructional methods—for example, phonics, phonetics, "look-see" methods, and others—continue to reflect questions about the uses and powers of alphabets. In contemporary debates, they reflected divisions over order and morality as well as pedagogy (Graff, 1979).

Recent Work

Literacy and Economic Development

The assumed link between literacy and economic success is one of the cornerstones of Western modernization theories. Literacy or at least a minimal amount of education is presumed to be necessary and sufficient for overcoming poverty and surmounting limitations rooted in racial, ethnic, gender, and religious differences. Implicit in this formulation is the belief that individual achievement may reduce the effects of social and structural inequalities, and that economic success or failure corresponds at least in part to the quality of personal effort.

On a collective scale, literacy is thought to be a necessary precondition of modernization, a cause and correlate of economic growth, productivity, industrialization, per capita wealth, gross national product, and technological advances, among other advances (Graff, 1979, 1987; Levine, 1986). Literacy in this view becomes a commodity to be exported by the developed areas to so-called "developing nations," enabling individuals and nations to participate in the ongoing processes of globalization and partake of their presumed rewards.

Despite such expectations, there is little evidence that increasing or high levels of literacy result directly in major economic advances. Indeed, historical scholarship suggests that in the short run, at least, industrialization may be incidental to literacy development or vice versa, or even work to the detriment of opportunities for schooling. Literacy among the workforce was not a precondition to early industrialization in England and North America, for example. Schofield (1973) found that the literacy rates of textile, metal, and transport workers declined in the late eighteenth century, as these occupations did not require advanced reading and writing skills. Additionally, the demand for child labor disrupted education, as children in the factories had fewer opportunities to attend school. Industrial development may have depended on the inventiveness or innovativeness of a relative few, and thus stimulated their literacy development. It may equally have been disruptive to the lives of many other individuals, their families, their customary work and relationships, and their environments including arrangements for schooling (Furet & Ozouf, 1983; Graff, 1979; Levine, 1980).

It is possible that in nineteenth-century England and elsewhere to a significant extent, training in literacy was not so much for the purpose of developing skills to promote social, cultural, or economic advancement as it was "training in being trained" (Graff, 1979, 230, paraphrasing R. Dore, 1967, 292). Schooling and literacy education were the first steps in re-ordering the values and customs of rural populations entering the Industrial Age, instilling in them the industry, thrift, order, and punctuality required for the successful operation of the factory and a new social order beyond it. Literacy was not primarily or by itself a vehicle for economic advancement, but rather a means of inculcating values and behaviors in the general population that made large-scale economic development possible.

Recent scholarship does not support the assumption that literacy leads directly to economic advancement. Brandt (2001), for example, found that the value of literacy to individuals in the twentieth-century United States was influenced by more general social, political, and technological transformations that sometimes elevated the importance of literacy skills but at times undercut or undervalued them. Farmers, teachers, and others in Brandt's study, for example, found that literacy skills learned in the early part of the century were made less valuable or even obsolete by technological, institutional, and economic transformations of the latter part of the century. New forms of literacy training, specific to the needs to changing workplaces and communities, were required to advance or simply maintain one's former status. Literacy, in sum, did not change society. Rather, literacy itself was changed—its forms, uses, and meanings—in response to its environment. Such observations make clear that literacy's and schooling's contribution to economic development merit further detailed study, and that the presumptions of the Literacy Myth demand ever more careful qualification.

Problems and Difficulties

Democracy, Literacy, and the Social Order

One of the central tenets of the democratic state is that an educated, informed, and participatory voting public is necessary for the functioning of democracy. In this perspective, one must be able to read and write to understand the issues of the day and think critically about the choices required in a democracy. Whereas that formulation is undoubtedly true, it is also incomplete. It requires the further recognition that literacy and education are necessary but not sufficient conditions of a functioning democracy, which also relies upon participation, debate, and a diversity of viewpoints. While literacy and education can and have been used to stimulate democratic discourse and practices, it is equally true that literacy has been used to foster political repression and maintain inequitable social conditions.

History helps us to understand such tensions. Nineteenth century schoolbooks stressed the doctrines of order, harmony, and progress, while ignoring or justifying social conflicts and inequities (Graff, 1987, 326). Beyond the economic imperatives discussed previously, the purpose of literacy in these contexts was self-consciously conservative, a means for imposing morality, reducing criminality, lessening diversity, and encouraging deference to the established social order, especially in difficult times of change. Literacy was not a means for promoting democracy but rather an instrument for imposing social control. Yet literacy could be and was appropriated by groups and organizations promoting radical social change, for example among Chartists in nineteenth-century Great Britain and skilled labor organizers more widely. In the shop, meeting hall, and street, oral and written media came together. National literacy campaigns such as those in Cuba and Nicaragua also reflect the dialectical tensions of the literacy myth. Such movements propel literacy workers to action, raise literacy rates significantly, and allow for individual and group development. But literacy remains under the direction of political ideology and doctrine (Arnove and Graff, 1987). Only in the literacy myth does literacy operate as an independent variable,

The functioning of a mature democracy depends upon political structures and economic conditions that make participation possible for citizens. Literacy and education are important to the extent that they emphasize critical thinking, open debate, and tolerance for opposing views. Literacy by itself is not a cause for freedom and a guarantee of a working democracy. It is instead one of many important variables that influences the lives of citizens and their relationship to their governments.

Future Directions

Lessons of the Literacy Myth

Myths can be expressions of collective desires, of the many and the few, of their differential agency and power. Perhaps the Literacy Myth expresses a hope that literacy alone is enough to end poverty, elevate human dignity, and ensure a just and democratic world. A less benign reading is that the Literacy Myth is a means through which to obscure the causes of social and economic inequities in Western society at least by attributing them to the literacy or illiteracy of different peoples. In such a reading, literacy is a symptom and a symbol. Either way, the consequences of accepting uncritically the Literacy Myth are continuing to misunderstand the nature of literacy, its development, uses, and potentials to foster or inhibit social and economic development.

To argue that literacy has been accorded the status of myth is not to discount the importance of reading and writing, or to suggest that these are irrelevant in the contemporary world. That is clearly not the case. However, we may contrast the Literacy Myth, and its seamless connections of literacy and individual and collective advancement, with the more complex and often contradictory lessons that are consistent with historical and recent literacy development and practice.

One critical lesson is that literacy is not an independent variable, as in the Myth. It is instead historically founded and grounded, a product of the histories in which it is entangled and interwoven, and which give literacy its meanings. Ignorance of the historical record, in which crucial concepts, notions, arrangements, and expectations about literacy have been fashioned, severely limits understanding. Related to this, second, we must grasp the fundamental complexity of literacy, the extent to which it is a product of the intersection of multiple economic, political, cultural, and other factors. This realization mandates rejecting the simple binaries of "literate-illiterate," "oral-written," and others which have been used to postulate a "great divide." These constructs have been used to sort individuals and cultures in ways that are as damaging as they are conceptually inadequate. The legacies of literacy point instead to connections, relationships, and interactions.

In the Literacy Myth, reading and writing are a universal good and ideologically neutral. However, in a third lesson, the history of literacy and schooling demonstrates that no mode or means of learning is neutral. Literacy is a product of the specific circumstances of its acquisition, practice, and uses, and so will reflect the ideologies that guide these. School literacy, in particular, is neither unbiased nor the expression of universal norms of reading and writing; it reflects the structures of authority that govern schools and their societies.

Finally, despite the apparent simplicity of the literacy myth, the historical record points to a much richer and diverse record. It underscores the multiple paths to literacy learning, the extraordinary range of instructors, institutions, and other environments, of beginning "texts," and of the diversity of motivations for learning to read and write. While mass public schooling today presents the most common route for individuals learning to read and write, the diversity of learners, including adult learners, in Europe and North America demands flexible understandings and pedagogies for literacy development. There is no single road to developing literacy. Different societies and cultures have taken different paths toward rising levels of literacy. This suggests that the presumed "consequences" of literacy—individual, economic, and democratic—will always be conditioned by the particulars of time, situation, and the historical moment.

Such reflections offer a more complex narrative than that of the Literacy Myth. They may also point toward new and different ways of understanding, using, and benefiting from the broad and still developing potentials that literacy may offer individuals and societies (Graff, 1995 a, b).

References

Akinasso, F.N. 1981, "The consequences of literacy in pragmatic and theoretical perspectives," *Anthropology and Education Quarterly* 12, 163-200.

Arnove, R. and Graff, H. (eds.) 1987, *National Literacy Campaigns in Historical and Comparative Perspective*, Plenum, New York.

Brandt, D. 2001, *Literacy in American Lives*. Cambridge University Press, Cambridge.

Collins J., and Blot, R. 2003, *Literacy and Literacies: Texts, Power, and Identity*. Cambridge University Press, Cambridge.

Dore, R. 1967, *Education in Tokugawa Japan*, Routledge and Kegan Paul, London.

Duffy, J. 2000, "Never hold a pencil: Rhetoric and relations in the concept of 'preliteracy,'" *Written Communication*, 17.2, 224-257.

Farr, M. 1993, "Essayist literacy and other verbal performances," *Written Communication*, 10:1, 4-38.

Finnegan, R. 1973, "Literacy versus non-literacy: The great divide," in R. Horton and R. Finnegan (eds.), *Modes of Thought*, Faber and Faber, London.

Finnegan, R. 1988, *Literacy and Orality*, Blackwell, Oxford.

Finnegan, R. 1994, "Literacy as mythical charter," in D. Keller-Cohen (ed.), *Literacy: Interdisciplinary Conversations*, Hampton Press, Creskill, NJ.

Furet, F. and Ozouf, J. 1983, *Reading and Writing*, Cambridge University Press, Cambridge.

Gelb, I.J. 1963, *A Study of Writing*, University of Chicago Press, Chicago, IL.

Goody, J. 1986, *The Logic of Writing and the Organization of Society*, Cambridge University Press, Cambridge.

Goody, J. 1987, *The Interface Between The Written and the Oral*, Cambridge University Press, Cambridge.

Goody, J. and Watt, I. 1968, "The consequences of literacy," in J. Goody (ed.), *Literacy in Traditional Societies*, Cambridge University Press, Cambridge (originally published in 1963).

Gough, K. 1968, "Implications of literacy in traditional China and India," in J. Goody (ed.), *Literacy in Traditional Societies*, Cambridge University Press, Cambridge.

Graff, H. J. 1979, *The Literacy Myth: Literacy and Social Structure in the Nineteenth Century City*, Academic Press, New York and London (Reprinted with a new introduction, Transaction Press, New Brunswick, NJ, 1991.)

Graff, H. J. 1987, *The Legacies of Literacy: Continuities and Contradictions in Western Culture and Society*, Indiana University Press, Bloomington, IN.

Graff, H. J. 1995a, *The Labyrinths of Literacy: Reflections on Literacy Past and Present*, revised and expanded edition, University of Pittsburgh Press, Pittsburgh PA.

Graff, H. J. 1995b, "Assessing the history of literacy in the 1990s: Themes and Questions," in A. Petrucci and M. G. Blay (eds.), *Escribir y leer en Occidente*, Valencia, Universitat de Valencia, Spain.

Graff, H. J., and Street, B. 1997, "A response to Stan Jones, 'Ending the Myth of the 'Literacy Myth': A Response to Critiques,'" *Literacy Across the Curriculum*, Centre for Literacy, Montreal, 13, 1, 4-6.

Harris, W. V. 1989, *Ancient Literacy*, Harvard University Press, Cambridge, MA.

Havelock, E. 1963, *Preface to Plato*, Harvard University Press, Cambridge, MA.

Havelock, E. 1976, *Origins of Western Literacy*, Ontario Institute for Studies in Education, Toronto.

Havelock, E. 1986, *The Literate Revolution In Greece and its Cultural Consequences,* Princeton University Press, Princeton, NJ.

Inkeles, A. and Smith, D. 1974, *Becoming Modern: Individual Change in Six Developing Countries*, Harvard University Press, Cambridge, MA.

Levine, D. 1980, "Illiteracy and family life during the first Industrial Revolution," *Journal of Social History*, 14, 25-44.

Levine, K. 1986. *The Social Context of Literacy*, Routledge and Kegan Paul, London.

McQuillan, J. 1998, "Seven myths about literacy in the United States, Practical Assessment, Research and Evaluation," 6(1), retrieved January 9, 2006 from http://PAREonline.net/getvn.asp?v=6andn=1.

National Endowment for the Arts, 2004, *Reading at Risk: A Survey of Literary Reading in America*, Research Division Report #46, June.

Olson, D. R, 1977, "From utterance to text: The bias of language in speech and writing," *Harvard Educational Review*, 47, 3, 257-281.

Olson, D. R, 1994, *The World on Paper: The Conceptual and Cognitive Implications of Writing and Reading*, Cambridge University Press, Cambridge.

Ong, W. 1967, *The Presence of the Word*, Yale University Press, New Haven, CT.

Ong, W. 1977, *Interface of the Word*, Cornell University Press, Ithaca, NY.

Ong, W. 1982, *Orality and Literacy*, Methuen, London.

Pattison, R, 1984, *On Literacy*. Oxford University Press, Oxford.

Resnick, D. and Resnick, L. 1977, "The nature of literacy: A historical exploration," *Harvard Educational Review*, 47, 370-85.

Schofield, R.: 1973, "Dimensions of illiteracy," 1750-1850, *Explorations in Economic History* 10, 437-454.

Scribner. S. 1984, "Literacy in three metaphors," *American Journal of Education*, 93, 6-21.

St. Clair, R. and Sadlin, J. 2004, "Incompetence and intrusion: On the metaphorical use of illiteracy in U.S. political discourse," *Adult Basic Education*, 14, 45-59.

Street, B., 1984, *Literacy in Theory and Practice*, Cambridge University Press, Cambridge.

Street, B. 1995, *Social Literacies: Critical Approaches to Literacy in Development, Ethnography and Education*. Longman, London.

4

The Literacy Myth at Thirty[1]

The new *Encyclopedia of Language and Education* defines "literacy myth" thus:

> Literacy Myth refers to the belief, articulated in educational, civic, religious, and other settings, contemporary and historical, that the acquisition of literacy is a necessary precursor to and invariably results in economic development, democratic practice, cognitive enhancement, and upward social mobility. Despite many unsuccessful attempts to measure it, literacy in this formulation has been invested with immeasurable and indeed almost ineffable qualities, purportedly conferring on practitioners a predilection toward social order, an elevated moral sense, and a metaphorical "state of grace." Such presumptions have a venerable historical lineage and have been expressed, in different forms, from antiquity through the Renaissance and the Reformation, and again throughout the era of the Enlightenment, during which literacy was linked to progress, order, transformation, and control. Associated with these beliefs is the conviction that the benefits ascribed to literacy cannot be attained in other ways, nor can they be attributed to other factors, whether economic, political, cultural, or individual. Rather, literacy stands alone as the independent and critical variable. Taken together, these attitudes constitute what Graff has called "the Literacy Myth." Many researchers and commentators have adopted this usage.[2] (See Fig. 4.1. Note the range of "literacy myths.")

The inclusion of "literacy myths" in a state-of-the-art multi-volume reference work testifies to the import and power of the phrase descriptively, conceptually, analytically, and metaphorically or rhetorically—not necessarily with full endorsement or consistency—by scholars and commentators in many fields for many years. In much of the academy, this broad recognition of *The Literacy Myth*, the book, and its chief concept, interpretation, and way of understanding is part of the accepted wisdom and discourse—if not always in the ways I intended it. Joining a canon that I set out to challenge and change in the 1970s and 1980s admittedly is sometimes strange or strained. So, too, was the need especially in *The Literacy Myth*'s earlier years to reject charges that, as a critic of normative perspectives on literacy (in that discourse, a revisionist), to some persons, I was, somehow, anti-literate or a traitor to the educators' cause and investment in claims of the promises of schooling, as we see below. This continues to strike me as odd and unwarranted. After all, I make my way, and my living, through the manipulation of alphabetic symbols and the construction and criticism of texts.[3] (See Fig. 4.1. Fig. 4.1 also highlights "new" literacy myths. See Appendix for original arguments in *The Literacy Myth*.)

In this commentary, I reflect on *The Literacy Myth* and the "literacy myth" on the occasion of the book's thirtieth anniversary, a special and also a sobering moment. On the one hand, I speak to its broad influence in a number of fields of study; I also consider some of the criticisms encountered. On the other hand, I discuss what I think are its principal weaknesses and limits. The success of *The Literacy Myth* may be determined at least in part by the extent to which it stimulates new research and thinking that begin to supplant it. After considering the relevance and value of its general arguments for both persisting and newer questions and issues, I reframe my conclusions about social myths and in particular "the literacy myth."

The words "literacy myth" ring familiarly, signifying an uncommon level of recognition. In this, *The Literacy Myth*'s thirtieth year since first publication in 1979, I am humbled by its achievement, impressed by its continuing relevance, but also struck by the resilience and persisting power of "literacy myths" around us and by those who deny their presence and power (see Fig. 4.1). *The Literacy Myth*'s impact is clear, its influence wide.

Most rewarding is the still growing number of scholars and research students who express their gratitude in one form or another. Although many do not share my views entirely, some seek to revise or extend them, and some argue against them, they repeatedly say *The Literacy Myth* "made my work possible," "laid a foundation for me to build on," "gave me the confidence to test and argue against normative views and received wisdom," "legitimated my work," even "changed my life." I can think of no greater appreciation. The book's influence touched many disciplines across the humanities, social sciences, and education. *The Literacy Myth* was important in the making of New Literacy Studies, critical literacy studies, and literacy studies more broadly. It is not too much to claim that the book helped to shape that field. In addition, it is foundational to the field of historical literacy studies and the active pursuit of literacy's place in many other fields of study.

Figure 4.1

Recent Articulations of the Literacy Myth

1. Updating the longstanding Myth of Decline. "Computers are destroying literacy. The signs—students' declining reading scores, the drop in leisure to just minutes a week, that half the adult population is reading no books in a year—are all pointing to the day when literate American culture becomes a distant memory. By contrast, optimists foresee the Internet ushering in a new, vibrant participatory culture of words." Howard Gardner, "The End of Literacy? Don't Stop Reading," op-ed, *Washington Post*, Feb. 17, 2008.

    "But books haven't vanished. In 2003, 175,000 books were published, an increase of 19 per cent over 2002. Fiction books were published on an average of one every 30 minutes. "Books are the hot medium," at least about politics, newspapers report. *New York Times*, Apr 25, 2004.

    Too many books? Enough—or not enough—readers? People continue to read and to purchase books. That we know far too little about what they read, understand, and take with them, and with what effects, if any, marks another side of the literacy myth and collateral expectations of decline.

2. The United States faces a "perfect storm" owing to the simultaneous and interrelated powerful forces of "economic restructuring that has changed the workplace," "inadequate levels of literacy and numeracy skills among students and adults," and "sweeping demographic changes driven by immigration." "The combination of our relative (mediocre) position with respect to average performance and our leading position with respect to inequality in performance leads to concern about the growing danger to the wellbeing of our nation. This disparity in skills is related to the disparity we see in the educational attainment of our population and to the growing disparities in social and economic outcomes. Ignored, these differences may not only reduce our ability to compete internationally on a high-wage strategy, but also will surely threaten the cohesiveness of the nation." ETS, *America's Perfect Storm: Three Forces Changing Our Nation's Future* (2007), 15.

3. "Low intelligence is attributable to entire categories of work and the people who do that work—often poor people, people of color, and immigrants. Manual work requires little cognitive input. [Relatedly, p]oor academic preparation rules out sustained and serious involvement with core disciplinary topics and material of intellectual consequence." Ruling dichotomies: brain v. hand, mental v. manual, intellectual v. practical, pure v. applied. Mike Rose, "Intelligence, Knowledge, and the Hand/Brain Divide," *Phi Delta Kappan*, 89, 9 (2008), 632-639.

4. "Rebuilding Afghanistan, One Book at a Time": "[T]he international community has spent many billions of dollars toward the nation's reconstruction. Yet not much progress can be seen. Poor management and lack of coordination among aid agencies are the major reasons for this dismal record, but another very simple problem has been a failure to make sure that the Afghan people have access to books and other printed materials with the information they need to move forward. This is a serious flaw that affects health care, education, and government itself.... It is important that a high government body like the Ministry of

---

Figure 4.1 (cont.)

Education endorse the concept of distributing books to the population. Money is needed too, ideally from both foreign governments and the Afghan government. And experts are needed to write the simple, accurate texts that Afghans need—on subjects from health care and household management to science, culture, history and the environment." Nancy Hatch Dupree, "Rebuilding Afghanistan, One Book at a Time," op-ed, *New York Times,* July 19, 2008.

5. "Writing is a Basic Skill" that underlies and leads to other, higher skills. Mark Richardson, "Writing Is Not Just a Basic Skill," *Chronicle of Higher Education,* Nov. 7, 2008.

6. "Cities' and celebrities' sponsorship of the public's engagement with books reminds us of the extraordinary value that society attributes to reading. It is hard to imagine another medium being promoted so aggressively. The almost unquestioned assumption seems to be that reading and talking about reading is a social good." Wendy Griswold, Terry McDonnell, and Nathan Wright, "Reading and the Reading Class in the Twenty-First Century," *Annuals Reviews in Sociology* 31 (2005), 127-141.

7. "READ TO SUCCEED." The special license plates would cost $15 above license plates' normal price. The extra revenue would fund afterschool reading programs for Texas students in kindergarten through third grade. "READ TO SUCCEED," *Dallas Morning News,* Aug 12, 1996.

8. Dana Gioia, on NEA's *Reading at Risk* report: "This report documents a national crisis. Reading develops a capacity for focused attention and imaginative growth that enriches both private and public life. The decline in reading among every segment of the adult population reflects a general collapse in advanced literacy. To lose this human capacity—and all the diverse benefits it fosters— impoverishes both cultural and civic life."

9. City literacy/City defining literacy: "Chicago did it. So did Seattle. Even Austin is getting into the act. Should Dallas follow the trend toward collective reading to build community and a civic conscience? Book clubs have long been favored by the erudite who enjoy sharing their insights and discovering new ones. Now city libraries and mayors are joining the effort by encouraging citywide reading of a selected book." [Began in Seattle with underwriting from the Wallace-Reader's Digest Fund. Chicago chose *To Kill a Mockingbird.* Dallas seeks to stay away from controversial reading] "Defining Dallas: Citywide efforts to forge ties," editorial, *Dallas Morning News* Nov 18, 2002.

10. "Gov. George W. Bush of Texas today proposed a five-year, $5 billion program to address what he termed a national literacy crisis among children.... There is nothing more fundamental than teaching our children how to read," Mr. Bush said .in a speech.... America must confront a national emergency.... Too many of our children cannot read. In the highest poverty schools—I want you to hear this statistic—in the highest poverty schools in America, 68 percent of fourth graders could not read at a basic level in 1998.... We will not tolerate illiteracy amongst the disadvantaged students in the great country called America.... More and more we are divided into two nations: one that reads and one that

Figure 4.1 (cont.)

can't, and therefore one that dreams and one that doesn't. Reading is the basis for all learning, and it must be the foundation for all other education reforms." *New York Times,* March 29, 2000.

11. "To be considered illiterate in contemporary America is not just to struggle with reading and writing—it is to be deemed unworthy, unproductive, a bad parent, and deserving of remarkably high levels of domestic intervention." Ralf St. Clair and Jennifer A. Sandlin, "Incompetence and Intrusion: On the metaphoric use of illiteracy in US political discourse," *Adult Basic Education,* 14 (2004), 45-59.

12. With Toyota the "proud sponsor" of a full page ad in *The Atlantic* (Dec., 2005) for National Center for Family Literacy: adult woman and apparently African American or multi-racial child:

> Because I can read,
> > I can understand, I can write a letter.
> > I can fill out a job application.
> > I can finally get off welfare,
> Because I can read,
> > I can learn. I can help my daughter
> > With her homework,
> > I can inspire her to be better,
> > I can be a role model.
> Because I can read,
> > I can succeed,
> > I can contribute.
> > I can live
> > my life without fear,
> > without shame.
> > I can be whatever
> > I want to be.
> Because I can read.

13. Literacy as Freedom, UN Literacy Decade 2003-2012 The Decade was launched under the banner Literacy for all: voice for all, learning for all. The *EFA Global Monitoring Report 2006, Education for All: Literacy for Life* asserts without qualification that Literacy is a right. "Literacy should be understood within a rights-based approach and among principles of inclusion for human development." Benefits of literacy [for life] include: human benefits—self-esteem, empowerment; political benefits—political participation, democracy, ethnic equality, post-conflict situations; cultural benefits—cultural change, preservation of cultural diversity; social benefits—health, reproductive behavior, education, gender equality; economic benefits—economic growth, returns to investment.

14. "All it takes is books in the home.... Books had a huge effect even when wealth disparities were accounted for.... [I]f Canadians found it important enough to stock their homes with books, more of their children would soar in school, and

Figure 4.1 (cont.)

in life, too. If reading were cool, the sky would be the limit for Canadian 15-year olds, and eventually for the Canadian economy.

"Canada should try to become the world's most literate nation. The potential benefits are great. A country that is highly literate is more than just smart. It has high aspirations, and the means to achieve its ambitions. A wealth of ideas, rather than natural-resources wealth alone, is the foundation of a nation's prosperity in the new economy. Literacy is the greatest natural resource a country could have. It's renewable, too.

"A literate country is not a country of PhDs in English or French literature. It is a country whose young people are prepared for the one constant in their futures—change.... Only the literate can keep up in the learning economy.

"Canada will never be a manufacturing power ... a military power... But it can be a reading power.... Canada needs to become obsessed with reading [like it is with ice hockey.]" "Here's to a new goal: most literate nation," *The Globe and Mail*, Dec. 31, 2004.

15. You are What You Read. Leah Price, *New York Times Book Review*, Dec. 23, 2007.

16. "Historian Harvey Graff has worked to debunk the 'literacy myth' that links litcracy, schooling, modernization, democracy, and individual social mobility, but such critical voices have had little impact on the public or its institutions. Regardless of whether people are actually spending much time reading, they honor and encourage it to a remarkable extent." Wendy Griswold, Terry McDonnell, and Nathan Wright, "Reading and the Reading Class in the Twenty-First Century," *Annuals Reviews in Sociology* 31 (2005), 127-141.

The Literacy Myth also contributed to the unusually strong part that historical research has played in the making of literacy studies. It helped to legitimate, define, and shape critical approaches to the study and interpretation of literacy. It suggested frameworks, approaches, sources, and methods.[4]

Of course, not all agree.... Literacy myths continue to sprout like weeds. (See Fig. 4.1.) Consider a telling example. In an intemperate response to my own and Brian Street's criticisms of the International Adult Literacy Survey (IALS) international report, Literacy Economy and Society, Stan Jones, Center for the Study of Adult Literacy, Carleton University, "took grave exception" to our comments.[5] With the goal of "ending the myth of the 'Literacy Myth,'" Jones ironically announced: "one of the enduring myths of academic literacy research is that Graff laid to rest 'the literacy myth' once and for all. He did not." (I never claimed any such achievement. I do not believe that that, in fact, is possible.) Jones revealed a frequent misconception of myth and its workings.

Adopting a characteristic common to criticism of *The Literacy Myth*, Jones not only misunderstood social and cultural myth, he also exaggerated the terms and tenor of our criticism of the international quantitative survey. He ignored arguments raised against the intellectual, political, and social context, including the epistemology, of the social scientific research and interpretive traditions in which he worked and its implications for the study of literacy.

With others, Jones missed basic points. Never did Street or I claim that there was *no* relationship between, in Jones' words, literacy and economic success, income and literacy skill, labor force attainment and literacy, and occupational change and literacy. (See Appendix 1) To the contrary, we emphasized their complexity, variability, and contradictoriness in relationships among key factors, and in more general explanatory and interpretive terms that shape expectations, theory, and policy. Never did we allege that literacy was unimportant. Unwittingly, in the mode of his attack, Jones elevated the power of the "literacy myth."[6] He did nothing to "end the myth of the 'Literacy Myth.'" (See, for example, Fig. 4.1.)

The conception and power of the literacy myth depend, on the one hand, *on the understanding of myth*—including myth as a mode of understanding and communication—and, on the other hand, *on history*—the shaping power of the past. As he did with myth, Jones denied the relevance of historical understanding: "I have never understood why researchers such as Graff and Street who argue that literacy is narrowly specific to time and place should assume that relationships between literacy and anything that held over 100 years ago should necessarily hold today. Surely, any sensible understanding of how societies change must allow for changes in the relationship between personal characteristics and life chances."

Jones mocked arguments that Street and I, as anthropologist and historian, would not, and did not make. He also alluded to the reflexive linking of literacy with change, another literacy myth. The practice of arguing against what is not said is a common tactic of critics of *The Literacy Myth*. There are lessons about literacy—that is, reading and writing—here too.

To the contrary, I pointed to the lack of attention to history in the IALS study, including the historical context of its creation, application, and interpretation. As a faithful adherent of the literacy myth, Jones eschewed social, cultural, political, and economic contexts, including criticism of different conceptions of literacy and epistemologies of its research. Hostility to qualitative, ethnographic, and historical research or other alternatives to his own statistical, economistic data and methods also marks Jones' stance. Conviction in "strong" theories that link possession of literacy directly to major cognitive, economic, political, social, and cultural transformations is another element.[7]

Caught in his own contradictions, Jones cannot see this. There is no place for the benefits of history, especially an interdisciplinary history, in his view.[8] History's contributions include much needed perspective. They allow us to reach out for new, different, and even multiple understandings of ourselves and others, often in their interrelationships: History mandates focusing and refocusing the lenses of time, place, and alternative spaces. It probes and prompts us to comprehend what has been, what might have been, and what might be: choice, agency, and possibility, in their fullness and their limits. Its values and virtues are rooted in the powers of comparison and criticism, taken together. An underutilized font of needed criticism, history can also be a source of liberation: freedom from the fetters of the present as well as the past. Historical analysis and interpretation often have great power in stimulating fresh views, novel questions, and new understandings. This is the past alive in the present and shaping the future, not a dead hand hanging over us. It is a human science. This is the practice that I tried to develop in *The Literacy Myth* and subsequent research on the history of literacy. The power of the past in the historically-derivative literacy myth's hold on the present demands no less.

Myth as Mode of Analysis, Understanding, and Communication

For the literacy myth, history and myth inseparably intertwine. Myth itself becomes a mode of interpretation—explaining or narrating—and a means to communicate that understanding, not unlike reading and writing themselves (and their analogues). This includes recognizing literacy and the literacy myth as ideology and also as culture, and criticizing that ideology and culture. It also mandates critical exploration of the relationships between and among material reality, social relationships, institutions, policy, expectations, and social theory.

Yet the central, critical role of myth is often misunderstood: Such attitudes about literacy represent a "myth" because they exist apart from and beyond empirical evidence that might clarify the actual functions, meanings, and effects of reading and writing. Like all myths, the literacy myth is not so much a falsehood but an expression of the ideology of those who sanction it and are invested in its outcomes. For this reason, the literacy myth is powerful, resistant to revision, and longstanding.[9] Contradicting popular notions, myth is not synonymous with the fictive or the false. By both definition and means of cultural work, myths can *not* be wholly false. For a myth to gain acceptance, it must be grounded in at least some aspects of perceived reality and can not explicitly contradict all ways of thinking or expectations. Partial truths are not falsehoods. (See Fig. 4.1. We can observe the uses of myth in assertions of "literacy myth.")

Little did I think about these issues in 1971 when I wrote my first seminar paper on literacy. This was an exploration of the value of the 1861 Canadian Census for the study of literacy by historians of social structure and education. I began to think more about them by 1975 when I completed the dissertation that provided the basis for *The Literacy Myth* in 1979.[10] The semantic crystallization that stimulated the book's title followed the completion of the dissertation by about two years. I struggled to find the best title for both intellectual and marketing purposes. Initially, its power lay more with expressive rhetoric than influencing discourse. I had no inkling then of its appeal, power, persistence, or prominence.

I was more aware of the questions my foray into literacy data raised with respect to the social and political currents of the 1960s and 1970s, on the one hand, and the new social history and questions of social theory, on the other hand.[11] All historical works are at least in part products of their own times. For better *and* for worst, *The Literacy Myth* reflects and grew from the unprecedented interest and concern about education's relationships with social inequality, declining cities, race, discrimination, poverty, and the radical analysis and prescriptions that accompanied them. Influential critics ranged from Paul Goodman to Paulo Freire with John Holt, Herbert Kohl, Jonathan Kozol, George Dennison, and a number of others in between. With the Vietnam War overheating the social caldron, the plight of inner cities' protests and "riots" in the streets, radical politics pivoted around race, gender, and age. The contradictions of democracy's most-favored nation were very real. Those surrounding schooling had very sharp edges. It was no accident that the interests and the methods, sources, and conceptions of historians and historical social scientists were changing at the same time.[12] Researchers probed the roots of current relationships in new ways with renewed vigor. The seeds of contemporary arrangements and the value of social theory mandated new, critical studies. The roots of my own, and others' focus on literacy, lay here.[13]

The Literacy Myth and Literacy Myths

The Literacy Myth begins with contradictions: "A literacy myth surrounds us. Literacy is considered a basic human right and a tool for productive citizenship and fulfilling lives, yet world illiteracy continues at a high rate. Although literacy is closely associated with basic western values and key elements of our social thought, tests reveal that children are not learning to read."[14] Problems inherent in the "literacy myth" start with confusions over the meanings of the word "literacy" and efforts to measure it. Literacy has been defined in various ways, many offering imprecise, yet progressively grander conceptions and expectations of what it means to read and write, and what might follow from those practices, attitudinally and cognitively, individually and collectively.[15]

The vagueness of such definitions allows for conceptions of literacy that go beyond what has been examined empirically, thus investing literacy with the status of myth. Since mythos is grounded in narrative, and since narratives are fundamentally expressions of values, literacy has been contrasted in its mythic form with a series of opposing values that have resulted in reductive dichotomies such as "oral-literate," "literate-pre-literate," "literate-illiterate," and other binaries that caricature major social changes. In such hierarchical structures, the "oral," "preliterate," and "illiterate" serve as the marked and subordinate terms, whereas "literate" and "literacy" assume the status of superior terms. Such hierarchies reinforce the presumed benefits of literacy and thus contribute to the power of the myth. (See Fig. 4.1.)

Only by grounding definitions of literacy in specific, contextualized, and historical particulars can we avoid conferring on literacy the status of myth. In contrast with its presumed transformative "consequences," literacy historically has been characterized by tensions, continuities, and contradictions. In other words, when examined closely, literacy's history often contradicts the "literacy myth." Regardless, major elements of the literacy myth exert powerful influence, for example, the myth of literacy decline; the myth of the superiority of the Roman or Greek alphabet; the myth of literacy's link to economic development and social advancement; and the myth of literacy and democracy. In contemporary popular discourse, literacy is represented as an unqualified good, a marker of progress, and a metaphorical light making clear the pathway to progress and happiness. The opposing value of "illiteracy," in contrast, is associated with ignorance, incompetence, and darkness.

Given such sentiments, it is hardly surprising that discussions of literacy are characterized by persistent fears of decline. In this discourse, the decline of literacy is taken as an omnipresent given and signifies generally the end of individual advancement, social progress, and the health of the democracy. Such associations represent a powerful variant of the literacy myth. That the myth of decline is largely unsupported by empirical evidence has done little to reduce its potency in contemporary discourse.[16] Rather, the myth is argued by anecdote, often rooted in nostalgia for the past, and selective reading of evidence. The myth of decline neglects the changing modes of communication, and in particular the increasing importance of media that do not depend completely on print. Literacy myths are also rooted in culture and ideology, institutions and policies, and expectations.

The bias toward the alphabet resulted in what its proponents (and their critics) called a "great divide," with rational, historical, individualistic literate peoples on one side, and "non-logical," mythical, communal, oral peoples on the other.[17] The assumed link between literacy and economic success is one of the cornerstones of Western modernization theories. Literacy or at least a minimal amount of education is presumed to be necessary and sufficient for overcoming poverty and surmounting limitations rooted in racial, ethnic, gender, and religious differences. Implicit in this formulation is the belief that individual achievement may reduce the effects of ascribed social and structural inequalities. Despite such expectations, there is little evidence that increasing or high levels of literacy result directly in major economic advances. (In fact, they may well follow from, and depend upon such advances.) Although literacy and education can and have been used to stimulate democratic discourse and practices, literacy has been used to foster political repression and maintain inequitable social conditions.[18] (See Fig. 4.1.)

Revising Literacy

As a recognizable field of literacy studies emerged, literacy's significance as an important variable for many subjects across the realms of social science and other interdisciplinary histories was accepted. Its relevance expanded just as expectations of its universal powers were qualified and contextualized. Earlier expectations (and theories) that literacy's contribution to shaping or changing nations, and the men and women within them, was universal, unmediated, independent, and powerful have been quashed, in theory and in history (if not in all practice). Literacy—that is, literacy by itself—is now seldom conceptualized as independently transformative. To the contrary, we now anticipate and recognize its impact to be shaped by specific historical circumstances, complicated rather than simple, incomplete or uneven, interactive rather than determinative, and mediated by a host of other intervening factors of a personal, structural, or cultural historical nature, rather than universal. In other words, literacy is a historical variable, and it is historically variable.

Social attributes (including ascribed characteristics like gender, race, ethnicity, and class) and historical contexts, shaped in turn by time and place, mediate literacy's impacts, for example, on chances for social or geographic mobility. Literacy seems to have a more direct influence on longer distance migration than on shorter moves. That relationship, for example, carries major implications for the historical study of both sending and receiving societies and for immigrants among other migrants. Literacy's links with economic development are both direct and indirect, multiple, and contradictory. For example, its value to skilled artisans may differ radically from its import for unskilled workers. Literacy levels sometimes rise as an effect rather than a cause of industrialization. Industrialization may depress literacy levels through its negative impact on schooling chances for the young, while over a longer term its contribution may be more positive.

This is the story that *The Literacy Myth* began to tell in 1979.[19] It is a story of past, present, and future that we are still writing (indeed, still living). In three nineteenth-century Canadian cities and elsewhere in North America and Western Europe, illiteracy undoubtedly hindered people's advancement culturally, materially, and occupationally (in normative sociological terms). But the level of literacy demanded for survival did not block all progress or adjustment. Class and ethnicity primarily determined social position—not literacy or education by themselves. Literacy exerted an influence which worked cumulatively. Entry into skilled work was more difficult, and some of the limited demands placed upon literacy skills could not be met by illiterate individuals in their circumstances. The responses and techniques useful to work, institutional contacts, and other activities were more often difficult for them to acquire. Nevertheless, demands made on individual illiterates who persisted in the cities seldom precluded occupational stability, economic and property mobility, or the transactions that homeownership entailed. Nor did illiteracy prevent successful adaptation to new urban environments, access to channels of communication, or opportunities for intergenerational mobility. Demands made on literacy for practical uses in this society were insufficient to deter some success, limited as it was, by these illiterate adults. Illiteracy was restrictive, but its limits were surmountable.

Class, ethnicity, race, and gender were the major barriers of social inequality. The majority of Irish Catholic adults, for example, were literate—and selected migrants—but they stood lowest in wealth and occupation, as did laborers and servants. Women and blacks fared little better, regardless of literacy. Possession of literacy was not in itself an achievement that brought material rewards to individuals. It guaranteed neither success nor a rise from poverty. In practice the meaning of literacy was more limited, mediated by the social structure and narrowly circumscribed for many individuals. Social realities contradicted the promoted promises of literacy. The potential uses of literacy were many, but in common activities potential literacy alone carried few concrete benefits while an imperfect literacy was sufficient for many needs. Literacy's uses were often non-instrumental ones. Yet, the higher uses of literacy and the corresponding benefits and status were often limited.[20] On the larger, societal level, literacy even if imperfect was especially important. This related directly to the moral bases of literacy and the reestablishment and maintenance of social and cultural hegemony. Literacy was more central to the training, discipline, morality, and habits it accompanied and advanced than to the specific skills it represented.

Historical research and interpretation challenge nineteenth and twentieth century images and understandings of the importance of literacy and, conversely, the negative consequences of its absence. Our notions about the relationships of literacy to such major processes as schooling, long-distance migrations, adaptation and assimilation to new urban environments, and chances for advancement are changing. Social class, ethnicity, race, gender, and geography emerge as key factors, but usually in more complicated and contradictory ways than we long presumed. Literacy's power and influence were seldom independent of other determining and mediating factors. Literacy was not a lynchpin in nineteenth-century society, especially in terms of the achievement of literacy erasing disadvantages stemming from social ascription. Nor did illiterates lack human resources or were they imprisoned in cultures of poverty. (See Appendix *The Literacy Myth*: Précis, Fig. 4.1.)

Experiences of learning literacy include cognitive and non-cognitive influences. This is not to suggest that literacy should be construed as any less important, but that its historical roles are complicated and historically variable. Today, it is difficult to generalize broadly about literacy as a historical factor. But that only makes it a more compelling subject, with implications for today and tomorrow. The views that literacy's importance and influences depend on specific social and historical contexts, which, in effect, give literacy its meanings; that literacy's impacts are mediated and restricted; that its effects are social and particular; that literacy must be understood as one among a number of communication media and technologies replace an unquestioned certainty that literacy's powers were universal, independent, and determinative.

How Literacy Myths Live On and Do Their Work

Nonetheless, literacy myths live on: among the public, policy-makers, and a number of academics. (See Fig. 4.1) Highlighting the issue, British historian David Vincent speaks to the historical foundations of literacy myths and their continuing impact: "Graff's *Literacy Myth* was engaged not just with the historiography of literacy but also with the educational politics of the late 1970s. He argued with every justification that the expectations invested in the contemporary school system required critical interrogation by historians as much as by other social scientists. But however great the impact of his work and that of other scholars ..., the effect on politicians and administrators appears negligible. The myths have proved remarkably resilient. Literacy lives in forms readily recognizable to the nineteenth-century pedagogues and administrators...." The consequences of the past in the present are enormous: "it is also a direct and immediate threat to the current generation of children, parents, and teachers," continues Vincent.[21] Criticism has its limits, another lesson relating to literacy (among other matters). Contrary to Stan Jones and others, the need for critical historical work remains compelling. The past and the present are inseparable.

The literacy myth is powerful, resilient, flexible, complex, and historically-rooted.[22] Characterized by its contradictoriness, it is marked by the long duration of its hegemony. It is also marked by its potential to work constructively and progressively but at the same time with limiting or negative force, for both individuals and groups. For some persons—perhaps most impressively for African Americans, denied literacy by slave codes—their history and faith joined with the literacy myth's promise of the benefits of reading and writing to both push and pull many people to literacy. They were not alone. For others, the contradictions were too great, the opportunities to gain and practice reading and writing too limited, the payoffs neither frequent nor clear. For many blacks today and recently, the power of the literacy myth has waned, in part owing to contradictory outcomes. For others with initial social and cultural advantages, the power of the promise seemed true. Their success was not always incumbent on the tenets of the literacy myth, but their experience stood in support of ideologies rooted in access to and achievement of literacy and schooling. This contrasted starkly with those who appeared to fail.

The power of the literacy myth lies in the first place in its resiliency, durability, and persistence. It serves to organize, simultaneously focus but obscure, and offer an explanation for an impressive array of social, economic, and political assumptions, expectations, observations, and theories, on the one hand, and institutions, policies, and their workings, on the other hand. Powerful contradictions lie at its core and in its consequences. As noted, socio-cultural myths, like the literacy myth, are never wholly false. Otherwise they would not gain acceptance or hegemony. Part of the literacy myth's resiliency also stems from the slipperiness of its linguistic or discursive condition. "Myth" is often misunderstood.

In the case of the United States, but elsewhere too, the partial "truths" of the literacy myth functioned within the context of the political and moral economies, political and social ideology, and the dominant culture, as they developed historically. Elemental struggles took place between ideologies of progress (or success) and those of decline (or failure) in the specific contexts of transformations to commercial and then industrial capitalism in an avowedly democratic republic. In the conflicts between the promise of progress and the threat of decline lay many of the ideological and practical contradictions of literacy: from literacy as "liberating" to literacy as restricted and socially and culturally controlling. In other words, the vexed question of "success" v. "failure," and their social and cultural correlates, lay at the core of the development of mass compulsory schooling and its contradictions.

A larger understanding follows from the historical development of school systems in relationship with changing social hierarchies. This pivoted on schools' ability to create a common denominator of a relatively low level of mass literacy. This level of literacy often contributed more to social order, cultural cohesion, and political stability than other possible ends. Although none of this was unique, the achievement of a peculiarly "American synthesis" relating to literacy—what I call "the moral bases" of literacy—took hold with some telling conflicts (including exclusion of literacy to slaves at a time when literacy was linked with individual religious and political salvation) and the dominance of a single standard of language, heritage, history, values, and personal characteristics. This transpired in the face of the diversity of a society divided by class, race, ethnicity, national origins, and gender. In their own historical timing, these connections were associated with a massive shift in consensus that illiteracy was becoming a greater danger than literacy, especially if literacy was not acquired independently of supervision and instruction. Mass literacy required social and individual controls, proper texts for beginning and practice, proper tutelage, proper environments for acquiring literacy: the "common" school and its desired ends. Here were the engines and the hallmarks of the literacy myth.

Within the synthesis that gave rise to, promoted, and long maintained the hegemony of the literacy myth were dreams of mobility—making it in America—but also the facts of mobility; an evangelical Protestantism rooted in salvation for the individual and safe progress for the nation; a class structure inseparable from capitalism, its needs, and its costs; meritocratic and stratified notions of egalitarianism; radical individualism rooted in processes of social inequalities and conflict, including race, class, gender, ethnic and national origins, age, and region among other distinctions; and limits to collective action. In this constellation of factors, literacy represented an achievement, but for many people one with limits to its usefulness and its rewards. In other words, there were limits to social mobility with the assistance of literacy. Failure, however, had at least as powerful an impact as success. The consequences were the responsibility of individuals and families, not of society or schools.

In its American setting, the literacy myth also held out the promise of (but never quite promised) achievement replacing social ascription on the steps up the social ladder. In these and related ways, schools were central to the diffusion of democratic culture and ideals, but they also mediated the contradictions between democratic ideals and continuing social inequality. "Achievement," its concomitants and failures, cut deeply into this cultural process. Literacy as symbol and as fact did not always work well together, whether for order, jobs, or citizenship. Regardless, the literacy myth lives on.

Lessons of the Literacy Myth

Myths can be expressions of collective desires, of the many and the few, of their differential agency and power.[23] Perhaps the literacy myth expresses a hope that literacy alone is enough to end poverty, elevate human dignity, and promote a just and democratic world. A less benign reading is that the literacy myth is a means through which to obscure the causes of social and economic inequities in Western society at least by attributing them to the literacy or illiteracy of different peoples. In such a reading, literacy is a symptom and a symbol. Either way, the consequences of accepting uncritically the literacy myth are continuing to misunderstand the nature of literacy, its development, uses, and potentials to foster or inhibit social and economic development.

To argue that literacy has been accorded the status of myth is not to discount the importance or reading and writing, or to suggest that these are irrelevant in the contemporary world. That is clearly not the case. However, we may contrast the literacy myth, and its seamless connections of literacy to individual and collective advancement, with more complex and often contradictory lessons that are consistent with historical and recent literacy development and practice.

A first critical lesson is that literacy is not an independent variable, as in the myth. It is instead historically founded and grounded, a product of the histories in which it is entangled and interwoven, and which give literacy its meanings. Ignorance of the historical record, in which crucial concepts, arrangements, and expectations about literacy have been fashioned, severely limits understanding. Related to this, second, we must grasp the fundamental complexity of literacy, the extent to which it is a product of the intersection of multiple economic, political, cultural, and other factors. This realization mandates our rejecting the simple binaries of "literate–illiterate," "oral–written," and others that have been used to postulate a "great divide." These constructs have been used to sort individuals and cultures in ways that are as damaging as they are conceptually inadequate. The legacies of literacy point instead to connections, relationships, and interactions.

In the literacy myth, reading and writing are a universal good and ideologically neutral. However, in a third lesson, the history of literacy and schooling demonstrates that no mode or means of learning is neutral. Literacy is a product of the specific circumstances of its acquisition, practice, and uses, and so reflects the ideologies that guide them. School literacy, in particular, is neither unbiased nor the expression of universal norms of reading and writing. It reflects the structures of authority that govern schools and their societies.

Finally, despite the apparent simplicity of the literacy myth, the historical record points to a much richer and diverse record. It underscores the multiple paths to literacy learning; the extraordinary range of instructors, institutions, and other environments; beginning "texts;" and the diversity of motivations for learning to read and write. While mass public schooling today presents the most common route for individuals learning to read and write, the diversity of learners, including adult learners, in Europe and North America demands flexible understandings and pedagogies for literacy development. There is no single road to developing literacy. Different societies and cultures have taken different paths toward rising levels of literacy. This suggests that the presumed "consequences" of literacy—individual, economic, and democratic—will always be conditioned by the particularities of time, situation, and the historical moment. (For examples, see Fig. 4.1.)

Such reflections offer a more complex narrative than that of the literacy myth. They may also point toward new and different ways of understanding, using, and benefiting from the broad and still developing potentials that literacy may offer individuals and societies.

Re-viewing *The Literacy Myth* after thirty years

What would I do differently if crafting *The Literacy Myth* today? An impossible question to answer fully or with assurance, I can identity certain key elements.

The quantitative analysis is the most problematic aspect of the book. While I must admit that the presence of numbers in such a quantity of tables and graphs by itself sufficed to persuade more than a few readers, the statistically-minded were not always swayed. The numerical data are cross-tabulations and percentages. They have the advantage of accessibility, but they do not constitute sophisticated statistical tests of arguments and relationships. To put it squarely: for statistical purposes, the numerical data are weak, albeit suggestive. Moreover, the argument presented, especially in Part I, is multivariate, whereas the data are generally bivariate. As footnote 30 on page 76 explains, at the moment when I began to replicate the analysis with more powerful statistical techniques, computer centers at two universities lost my data tapes. As I wrote in that 1979 footnote, "Multivariate replication, to my great regret, proved impossible."

Writing today, I would also be more sensitive to the limits of the analysis and the need for more direct temporal and geographic comparisons. I would also make more, interpretively and rhetorically, of the major contradictions that the analysis discovered. I believe that that strategy might provide more ballast to the kind of social historical discourse I was attempting to fashion and deploy—and its continuing relevance and power. In the process, the connections and disconnections of the analysis to issues of social theory, social policy, and social institutions could also be strengthened. In other words, literacy, both as practice and as symbol, and the literacy myth are contradictory and work dialectically. They can only be understood in those terms.

The Literacy Myth pioneered in its quantitative analysis and in its effort to explore and build arguments from both quantitative and qualitative historical materials. I recognized the insufficiency of either approach or method in and of itself. Today, I would attempt to probe more consistently both when and how the qualitative and the quantitative complement each other and when and how they conflict or contradict. Quantity and quality carry special burdens with respect to the understanding of literacy and its contexts.

Similarly, *The Literacy Myth* innovated with its attention, especially in Chapter 7, to variations in individuals' levels of literacy and the quality of abilities held popularly. Historically, that remains an understudied dimension of literacy. Today, with care and controls, it may be explored further, partly in relationship with the history of the book and the history of reading/readership, two important fields that were barely on the horizon of most historians in the mid- to late-1970s.[24] These approaches to research are seldom brought to bear on common questions or problems. They have the potential to break new ground with respect to popular literacy skills and the vexed questions surrounding the actual uses of literacy. They may also be suggestive for questions about literacy's relationships to cognition and economics.

In my view, perhaps the basic limitation of *The Literacy Myth* is the imbalance in the assessment of literacy's advantages or benefits, *and* literacy's limits—their inseparable, dialectical and contradictory relationships. In 1979, my emphasis fell more fundamentally on the latter. Achieving a greater balance and appreciation of complicated connections proved to be more than I could muster intellectually and discursively in the 1970s. That should be—and is, I believe—becoming an important goal for new research. Laying the foundation and beginning to erect the structure of the literacy myth remain a very satisfying and significant achievement.[25]

The Literacy Myth: Old and New Directions

Before closing, I comment briefly on a handful of the many matters arising from *The Literacy Myth*. All of these themes merit more critical and comparative historical attention.

First: history of the book and reading. As suggested above, historians of reading, writing, publishing—of "the book," as their enterprise is typically termed—need to cooperate and collaborate more with historians of literacy and *vice versa*. Literacy levels are often the missing link in studies of the circulation of print media and the foundations of readership. In the least, literacy rates help to set parameters for closer attention to reading of different kinds. These fields have much to teach each other.[26]

Second: multiliteracies. Among contemporary scholars of literacy, multiple literacies—dimensions beyond traditional alphabetic or "textual" literacy—the domain of the many proclaimed "new literacies"—from digital and visual to "scientific" and spatial, and beyond—compete for attention and a place on both research agendas and, increasingly, school and university curricula.[27] Claims about both "many" and "new" literacies raise fundamental questions in themselves. Partly owing to an apparent lack of sources but perhaps as much to matters of conceptualization and method, in general historians of literacy have not pursued these lines.

Medieval and early modern scholars, however, reveal their promise. Leading examples include Michael Clanchy's *From Memory to Written Record: England, 1066-1307* and Stuart Clark's *Varieties of the Eye: Vision in Early Modern European Culture*. Increasingly, they are joined by historians of science, technology, and the arts high and everyday who demonstrate, sometimes brilliantly, the centrality of visual and experimental modes of reading, writing, and thinking in creativity, discovery, invention, and other forms of innovation.[28] They point toward the need to criticize and possibly rethink the roles we assign to literacy in historical development.

Numeracy, to take one key example, is among the multiple modes of literacy. In *The Literacy Myth*, I offered anecdotal evidence that workers unable to read alphabetic texts were able to count and that colors were sometimes substituted for alphabetic markers. In exciting new research, Jorg Baten and his colleagues argue that numeracy may have been more broadly based than literacy in Western Europe than in the east, even by 1600. They conceptualize it as a form of human capital. Its contribution to economic growth and development may have exceeded popular literacy's, especially in advance of both mass schooling and industrialization.[29]

Third: economic growth past. In *The Literacy Myth*, I joined Roger Schofield and others in questioning a direct connection between popular literacy levels, as evidence of skill and/or cognition, and rates of literacy's spread, and the main lines of historical economic growth and development. That connection lay at the heart of the literacy myth. We argued for a lesser and a less direct connection between literacy and, in particular, industrialization, compared with, for example, literacy's more direct relationships with commercial capitalism. I urged greater attention to the importance of workplace experience and learning on the job, on the one hand, and, on the other hand, schooling's impact on attitudinal, behavioral, and other noncognitive attributes. No one denied the importance of literacy and education. But they were configured as less direct and independent relationships. For formulations with human capital at their core, and for proponents of the literacy myth, such skepticism verged on sacrilege.

For the past and the present, debate continues about literacy and other levels of education as forms of or direct contributions to human capital. In various formulations, versions of the literacy myth may be located and assessed differently, yet they remain present and influential. In a careful review of education and economic growth, David Mitch points to the variety of relationships examined by scholars. "[C]orrelation is not causation.... Thus, the contribution of rising schooling [or literacy] to economic growth should be examined more directly." With respect to the British industrial revolution, Mitch concludes, "other factors contributed to economic growth other than schooling or human capital more generally.... The British industrial revolution does remain as a prominent instance in which human capital conventionally defined as schooling stagnated in the presence of a notable upsurge in economic growth," despite expectations to the contrary. Such historical instances "call into question the common assumption that education is a necessary prerequisite for economic growth."[30] Of course, this does not deny that it is significant.

Fourth: economic growth recent and present. But what of the fate of the literacy myth in more recent decades and the present? Has post-industrialism's dependence on advanced technology and the knowledge economy's dependency on advanced education proved it correct or made it obsolete? Mitch offers a mixed verdict, finding that increases in mass schooling seem to explain growth in relatively short periods of time, "with a more modest impact over longer time.... [S]chooling should not be seen as either a necessary or sufficient condition for generating economic growth." There are many other possible influences.[31]

Others disagree.[32] In their new book *The Race Between Education and Technology*, economists Claudia Goldin and Lawrence F. Katz offer the fullest brief for the United States' economic (and political) dependence on human capital whose foundation is rooted in education. In their view, technologies stimulate advances in productivity when they are they are used by workers prepared to operate new machines. Rising levels of education constitute that preparation and account for what they proclaim "the human capital century." Goldin and Katz believe that today's economy requires an even higher level of education and fear that may not be developing.

The argument is powerful but not completely persuasive. It shares much with the beliefs regarding both education and technology that underlay the literacy myth (sometimes adjusted for inflation over time). In a trenchant review, political scientist Andrew Hacker responds, "I'll grant that their correlations show that education and economic growth have risen in tandem. But it just might be that the causation runs the other way. As the production of goods and services becomes more efficient, not only does national wealth increase, but there is less need for teenage labor. So society finds itself able to underwrite more schools and colleges, and keep more young people in them longer."[33]

Hacker and others point to complications in the relationships among education, high technology, and jobs. While the income gap between college graduates and others has widened, the "outsized sums accruing to the very top tiers" account for a great deal of the difference, not the earnings of graduates as a whole. The intellectual emphasis in much of the college curriculum and the job skills mandated for the workforce do not match well. Even more important is the fact that an enlarging chasm exists between the rising numbers of graduates in technological fields and the more limited number of jobs expected to be available for them. For example, the estimated number of engineers graduating by 2016 is four times greater than the expected number of new jobs.

Cutting across these relationships is another pattern that raises even more questions for the literacy myth. Hacker notes that the *Occupational Outlook Handbook* "lists hundreds of jobs involved with high-tech instruments, including installing, repairing, and debugging them. These workers outnumber college-trained scientists, and even engineers." These technicians are most often high school graduates who meet the demands of their jobs primarily with the knowledge gained at work. High-tech employers do not always seek workers with degrees.[34] Yet these technicians are central to the needs of a post-industrial knowledge economy as we know it, despite their uncomfortable connection with the expectations derived from the literacy myth.

That is not all. There is good reason to envision today's economy in different terms. Connecting the present with the past, in *One Nation*

Divisible, Katz and Stern write: "Much like early twentieth-century America…, abrupt economic change—the introduction of new technologies and modes of organizing work—led in two quite different directions, toward a high and a low road to increased productivity…." The resulting bifurcation of work creates a great divide between a high path to raising productivity through high-performance workplaces, worker training and participation, wage incentives, and job security. The low road reduces labor costs by outsourcing labor, employing fixed-term and part-time contracts, and lobbying government to reduce real minimum wages and the power of unions.[35] It owes little to literacy and education.

Many of the fastest growing jobs cluster on the low road. In one analysis, jobs in the lowest quartile of earnings will account for about 40 percent of growth in the top thirty occupations. These include many food and service workers, clerks, guards, nurses, and computer software engineers. Katz and Stern summarize: "Less than 25 percent of the top thirty jobs will require a bachelor's degree or higher; 54 percent will require short on-the-job training. Outside the top thirty, 25 percent of new jobs will require a bachelor's degree or more—but almost 50 percent will require no more than short-to-medium-term on-the-job training." Seventy-five percent will require less than an associate's degree.[36] Poorly paid, dead-end jobs that lack benefits also appear within the most technologically sophisticated industries. Contrary to many predictions, models, and expectations, the literacy myth remains very much with us in the early twenty-first century, often contradictorily as the post-industrial economy takes this bifurcated form.

Fifth: developing nations past and present. The last century and a half witnessed what we may call the globalization of the literacy myth.[37] Literacy—usually in one or another form of the literacy myth—takes pride of place, at least symbolically, in many designs for rapid economic and social development. In some cases, the inspiration lies in an image, not a clear and accurate vision, of an earlier developing west. In others, it may be an elaborate blueprint. In some cases, the imperative or stimulus is internal to the target state, in Tokugawa Japan, Russia and the Soviet Union, or China, among prominent cases. In others, especially after World War II, impetus, "aid," or detailed plan was exported from the west by development specialists in universities, NGOs, government agencies, or the United Nations. Both could be embedded in national literacy campaigns.[38] Both derived to some extent from myths about the place of literacy in modernization. Ironically, a number of efforts included alphabetic or linguistic reform and simplification based on erroneous assumptions about indigenous alphabets or characters that followed from the literacy myth's canonization of the classical Greek alphabet.

Thus the adoption of the literacy myth could derive from a limited understanding, or a better comprehension of efforts at making societies, economies, or polities more literate, and their limits; in effect acts of imitation or mimesis. At stake was the effort to compete or catch-up with, or surpass other nations, sometimes from a foundation in a different or opposing political ideology or organization. We know too little about the actual operation of these attempts at mass literacy and their impacts. There is reason to believe that they may be more effective at raising literacy rates and beginning accelerated development in the short- than in the long-run. In the longer-term, both literacy and other stimuli for growth may stall or decline. Further growth depends on internal developments aimed at supporting it, greater resources to commit, institutional articulation, and social and cultural changes, at home and abroad, that sometimes precede but at other times follow economic development.

With its decidedly mixed record of assisting literacy and development, UNESCO remains one of the last bastions of unqualified literacy myths. Its most recent World Literacy Decade, 2003-2012, proclaimed under the banner of *Literacy as Freedom: Education for All* (EFA), *Literacy for Life*. At the launch in February, 2003, Deputy Secretary General Louise Frechette stressed, "literacy remains part of the unfinished business of the 20th century. One of the success stories of the 21st century must be the extension of literacy to include all humankind."

Emphasizing that two-thirds of all illiterate adults were women, Ms. Frechette declared literacy a prerequisite for a "healthy, just and prosperous world": "When women are educated and empowered, the benefits can be seen immediately: families are healthier; they are better fed; their income, savings and reinvestments go up. And what is true of families is true of communities—ultimately, indeed, of whole countries." "Literacy and Gender" constituted the focus of the first two years. With its emphasis on literacy as freedom, the initiative was designed to "free people from ignorance, incapacity and exclusion" and empower them for action, choices and participation."[39] Here is the literacy myth in action. Ironically, UNESCO lacked the funds to tell the world about its latest campaign for Literacy for Life.

The Future of the Literacy Myth: Increasing Its Legibility and Transparency

The final sentences of *The Literacy Myth* comprise one important element that I would change, and several that I would not:

The underlying assumptions of the importance of literacy … have been maintained to the present, uncritically accepted, for the most part, and constantly promulgated. These assumptions, tied to modern social thought and theories of society, of social change, and of social development, form the basis of the "literacy myth." The paradigms of progressive, evolutionary social thought have outlived their usefulness and are in a state of crisis, as more and more critics and commentators illustrate. This does not mean of course that literacy … has not been important or can not be potentially more important.

If we are to understand the meanings of literacy and its different values, past and present, these assumptions must be criticized, the needs reexamined, the demands reevaluated. The variable and differential contributions of literacy to different levels of society and different individuals must be confronted. Demands, abilities, and uses must be matched in more flexible and realistic ways, and the uses of literacy seen for their worth, historically and at present. Literacy, finally, can no longer be seen as a universalistic quantity or quality to be possessed however unequally by all in theory. Needs, aspirations, and expectations must be best met for all members of society.[40]

The Literacy Myth ends with these words: "literacy must be accorded a new understanding—in historical context. If its social meanings are to be understood and its value best utilized, the 'myth of literacy' must be exploded."

Is it possible to lose or overcome, transcend, or explode the literacy myth? Or is our critical task a *different* one: to understand and mold it for individual and collective well-being and progress? Do we in fact *need to retain* literacy myths? Can the literacy myth be transformed and redirected?

Our task is *not* to disprove or "explode" the literacy myth, but to understand it, and reinterpret it to serve more equitable, progressive humane goals. The most useful future for the literacy myth depends on increasing its legibility and transparency. In an age of multiple literacies and economic decline, we have no choice. The costs of waiting are too great.

Appendix

What *The Literacy Myth* (1979) Actually Stated: A Précis

The Literacy Myth begins "A literacy myth surrounds us. Literacy is considered a basic human right and a tool for productive citizenship and fulfilling lives, yet world illiteracy continues at a high rate. Although literacy is closely associated with basic western values and key elements of our social thought, tests reveal that children are not learning to read" (2).

"[I]lliterates clearly seized a variety of approaches to adaptation and adjustment, in confronting their urban environments and in attempting to reduce the social structural forces they met. Family formation, family structure, patterns of home and property ownership, residential patterns—these were all drawn on by the illiterates, as they sought to survive and sometimes succeed in an unequal society. These were not the actions of marginal, disorganized, or isolated men and women, whose illiteracy was paralytic..." (113).

"Three themes unify this analysis of literacy and illiteracy.... Each holds significance for revision and re-interpretation. These threads...converged in the thought (113) and assumptions about the uneducated, the immigrant, and the poor, contributing to arguments and social theories that have dominated discussions of the importance of literacy to both the nineteenth and the twentieth century... (114).

"The first theme concerns the nineteenth-century views of immigrants, especially the Irish and Catholics, as the illiterate, disorderly, dissolute, and unwashed dregs of their society who brought their problems to North America with themselves. Despite this long-accepted conclusion, the great majority of migrants to these cities, regardless of origins, religion, age, or sex, were literate, confirming other research which directly relates distance of migration to literacy. North America received a select group of immigrants, including the Irish, who, nevertheless, often remained poor despite their education. The illiterate, moreover, were selected as well—negatively—by the disadvantage of their ascriptive characteristics, especially in ethnicity, but also in race, sex, and age" (114).

"Second theme: Social thought and social ideals have, for the past two centuries, stressed the preemption of ascription by achievement as the basis of success and mobility, and the importance of education and literacy in overcoming disadvantages deriving from social origins. In the three cities, in 1861, however, ascription remained dominant. Only rarely was the achievement of literacy sufficient to counteract the depressing effects of inherited characteristics, of ethnicity, race, and sex. The process of stratification, with its basis in rigid social inequality ordered the illiterates as it did those who were educated. Only at the level of skilled work and its rewards did literacy carry a meaningful influence. Literacy, overall, did not have an independent impact on the social structure: ethnicity, primarily, mediated its role, while literacy largely reinforced that of ethnicity. Literacy's very distribution, along with its economic value, followed this pattern of ethnic differentiation.... Illiteracy (114) of course was a depressing factor; the converse, however, did not hold true." [illiteracy a greater disadvantage than literacy an advantage] (115).

"Within these basic limits, literacy could be important, of course, to individual men and women as well as to their society. Though most of the differences remain revealingly small, literacy did result in occupational and economic advantages. Skilled work may not always have required literacy, but literacy facilitated opportunities for entry to it, and consequently, commensurate remuneration. Literacy, to be sure, carried little independent influence and its absence precluded few kinds of work; yet the acquisition of literacy brought to some individuals potential advantages in social and cultural areas as in material ones. Access to a rapidly expanding print culture (not, though, altogether distinct or isolated from oral and community patterns), literature, additional news and information, and some channels of communication were open to those able to read and write" (115).

"Third theme. A "culture-of-poverty" interpretation has predominated in discussions of the poor, the immigrants, and the uneducated. Generally assumed to be disorganized, unstable, irrational, and threatening to social order, without schooling their plight was assured. Illiterates in the three cities, contrary to stereotypical expectations, proved themselves to be far more adaptive, integrated, and resourceful in confronting the urban environment with its unequal society. Using their traditions and human material resources effectively and impressively, they strove to protect themselves and their families against the ravages of the marketplace and poverty" [purchased homes, regulated family size] (115).

"The place of the illiterate in this society ... broadens our perspective. Illiteracy undoubtedly hindered people's advancement culturally, materially, and occupationally (in normative sociological terms), but the level of literacy demanded for survival was not one to block all progress or adjustment. Class and ethnicity primarily determined social position—not literacy or education by themselves. Literacy exerted an influence which worked cumulatively; entry into skilled work was more difficult, and even some of the limited demands placed upon literacy skills could not be met by such disadvantaged individuals. The responses and techniques useful to work, institutional contacts, and other activities were more difficult for them to acquire. Nevertheless, demands made on individual illiterates who persisted in the cities seldom precluded occupational stability, economic and property mobility, or the transactions that homeownership entailed. Nor did illiteracy prevent successful adaptation to new urban environments, access to channels of communication or opportunities for intergenerational mobility. Demands made on literacy for practical uses in this society were insufficient to deter some success, limited as it was, by these illiterate adults. Illiteracy was restrictive, but its limits were surmountable. Class, ethnicity, and sex were the major barriers of social inequality. The majority of Irish Catholic adults, for example, were literate—and selected migrants—but they stood lowest in wealth and occupation, as did laborers and servants. Women and blacks fared little better, regardless of literacy. Possession of literacy was not in itself an achievement that brought material rewards to individuals; it guaranteed neither success nor a rise from poverty. In practice the meaning of literacy was more limited, mediated by the social structure and narrowly circumscribed for many individuals; social realities contradicted the promoted promises of literacy. The potential uses of literacy were many, but in common activities potential literacy alone carried few concrete benefits while an imperfect literacy was sufficient for many needs. Literacy's uses were often noninstrumental ones. Yet, the higher uses of literacy and the corresponding benefits and status were often precluded" (320-321).

"On the larger, societal level, literacy even if imperfect was especially important. This related directly to the moral bases of literacy and the reestablishment and maintenance of social and cultural hegemony. Literacy was more central to the training, discipline, morality, and habits it accompanied and advanced than to the specific skills it represented. In this way, we can understand the significance of literacy's perceived contribution to attitudinal and value preparation and socialization, relatively unchanging from the mid-nineteenth to the late twentieth century. Here as well, we may locate the full meaning of the contradictions between the perceived and promoted influences of literacy and schooling and the existential reality. Literacy, it seems certain, was not the benefit to individuals that it was promised to be; nevertheless, it had sufficient impact at the level of skilled work and in its consensual acceptance for its larger limitations and other purposes to the blurred and largely ignored. Consequently, on the basic level of social and economic progress and those who determined it, literacy was more valuable to the society's goals and needs than to those of most individuals within it. Conceptually, as should be clear, the meaning, needs, and assessment of literacy shift as the focus moves from one level of society to another. The needs for literacy, and the demands made, differed not only from the larger unit to the individual, but also from individual to individual, much as the ideals for literacy's role and the practical needs and uses of literacy were not always synonymous. Individual employment of reading and writing and the uses that reformers promoted for popular literacy were not the same, as we have seen, and, in fact, they could be contradictory, as nineteenth-century reading habits indicate. These contradiction or conflicts, however, did not interfere with the everyday employment of literacy or its social purposes" (321).

Notes

1. For important assistance of various kinds, I thank Peter N. Stearns and David Mitch; the graduate students who spoke about *The Literacy Myth* at a keynote panel at the Expanding Literacy Studies interdisciplinary international conference for graduate students, The Ohio State University, April, 2009—Maria Bibb, University of Wisconsin, Madison; Patrick Berry, University of Illinois, Champaign-Urbana; and David Olafsson, St. Andrews University and Reykjavík Academy; the audience at my lecture at Kent State University; and OSU Literacy Studies student Shawn Casey for his help with bibliographic research.

2. Harvey J. Graff and John Duffy "Literacy Myths," *Encyclopedia of Language and Education*, 2nd ed., Vol. 2 Literacy, ed. Brian V. Street and Nancy Hornberger (Berlin and New York: Springer, 2007), 41, chapter 3 above. In what follows, I draw on that article. In general, see Graff, *The Literacy Myth: Literacy and Social Structure in the Nineteenth-Century City*, Studies in Social Discontinuity (New York: Academic Press, 1979; new edition with new introduction, New Brunswick, N.J.: Transaction Publications, 1991); *The Legacies of Literacy: Continuities and Contradictions in Western Society and Culture* (Bloomington: Indiana University Press, 1987); *The Labyrinths of Literacy* Composition, Literacy, and Culture Series (Pittsburgh: University of Pittsburgh Press, 1995).

    For different but related views of literacy myths, see Ruth Finnegan, "Literacy versus non-literacy: The great divide," in *Modes of Thought*, ed. R. Horton and R. Finnegan. (London: Faber and Faber, 1973); J. McQuillan, "Seven myths about literacy in the United States," *Practical Assessment, Research and Evaluation*, 6(1), (1998), retrieved January 9, 2006 from http://PAREonline.net/getvn. asp?v=6andn=1; Elspeth Stuckey, *The Violence of Literacy* (Portsmouth, N.H.: Boyton Cook, 1990).

    For the field of historical studies of literacy in general, see "Bibliography of the History of Literacy in Western Europe and North America," in *Literacy and*

Historical Development: A Reader, ed. Harvey J. Graff (Carbondale: Southern Illinois University Press, 2007.), 417-439; chapter 9 below.

Recently, I returned to the more active pursuit of literacy and literacy studies as the Ohio Eminent Scholar in Literacy Studies, director of LiteracyStudies@OSU, a university-wide interdisciplinary initiative, and Professor of English and History at The Ohio State University, beginning in 2004.

See Figure 4.1 for outline and highlights of literacy myths, past and present. It presents recent articulations of the literacy myth, mostly from nonacademic, more popular sources. Note the range and conceptions of the myths.

3. Beginning in the 1970s, my work developed explicitly against the grain and against the canon. I comment later on the period in which the research and writing took place. That is important in reading *The Literacy Myth* after 30 years. Although this may seem the stuff of bad jokes, in the late 1970s and 1980s, accusations that I was somehow anti-literate and a traitor to the beliefs of the academy, rooted in myth of individual advancement through educational achievement, were not so funny. In the United States, the predominant association in such responses was with the impact of schooling of the children of immigrants.

    Fig. 4.1 highlights "new" literacy myths. See also Appendix on original arguments in *The Literacy Myth*.

4. Among many signs of influence is the foundational dependence of such classic works as Brian Street's *Literacy in Theory and Practice* (Cambridge University Press, 1984). See also Colin Lankshear with Moira Lawler, *Literacy, Schooling and Revolution* (London: Falmer Press, 1987), among many other examples. In addition, there are translations, reprints and anthologizations, keynote addresses, and the like. *The Literacy Myth*'s role in the development of LiteracyStudies@ OSU is another testament. More recently, see the studies of John Duffy, *Writing from these Roots: The Historical Development of Literacy in a Hmong-American Community* (Honolulu: University of Hawaii Press 2007) and Lesley Bartlett, *The Word and the World: The Cultural Politics of Literacy in Brazil* (Cresskill, NJ: Hampton Press, 2010); "Literacy's Verb: Exploring What Literacy Is and What Literacy Does," *International Journal of Educational Development*, 28, (2008), 737-753; "Human Capital or Human Connections? The Cultural Meanings of Education in Brazil," *Teachers College Record* 109 (2007): 1613-1636; "To Seem and to Feel: Situated Identities and Literacy Practices," *Teachers College Record*, 10 (2007), 51-69.

5. See Harvey J. Graff "The Persisting Power and Costs of the Literacy Myth: A Comment on *Literacy, Economy and Society: Results of the First International Adult Literacy Survey (IALS)*, Organisation for Economic Co-Operation and Development and Statistics Canada (1995)," *Literacy Across the Curriculum*, Centre for Literacy, Montreal, 12, 2 (1996), 4–5; and Brian V Street, "*Literacy, Economy and Society*: A Review, *Literacy Across the Curriculum*, Centre for Literacy, Montreal, 12, 3 (1995), 8-15 [both reprinted in *Working Papers on Literacy*, Centre for Literacy, No. 1, 1997], Graff's and Street's comments were invited by the Centre for Literacy, Montreal.

    Stan Jones replied, "Ending the Myth of the 'Literacy Myth': A response to critiques of the International Adult Literacy Survey," *Literacy Across the Curriculum*, Centre for Literacy, Montreal, 12, 4 (1996), 10-17 [reprinted in Working Papers on Literacy, 1997]. Jones is author of the data analysis chapters in that landmark report and also the Canadian report, Reading the Future: A Portrait of Literacy in Canada.

    Graff and Street responded, "A Response to Stan Jones, 'Ending the Myth of the "Literacy Myth": A Response to Critiques…,'" *Literacy Across the Curriculum*,

Centre for Literacy, Montreal, 13, 1 (1997), 4–6. [reprinted in Working Papers on Literacy, 1997].

See also Street's *Literacy in Theory and Practice*, with its dependence on *The Literacy Myth*. Similarly, among many examples of *The Literacy Myth*'s influence, see Colin Lankshear, *Literacy, Schooling and Revolution* or Rab Houston, "The Literacy Myth? Illiteracy in Scotland, 1630-1760," *Past and Present*, 96 (1982), 81-102.

6. An example of Jones's exaggerations: "Harvey Graff (1996) and Brian Street (1996) have both claimed in recent issues of this newsletter that the International Adult Literacy Survey (IALS) misrepresents what literacy is and makes false claims about the relationship between literacy and other characteristics of individuals and societies."

7. See Graff and Street comments; Street, *Literacy in Theory and Practice*; Graff, "Assessing the History of Literacy in the 1990s: Themes and Questions," in *Escribir y leer en Occidente*, ed. Armando Petrucci and M. Gimeno Blay (Valencia, Spain: Universitat de Valencia, 1995), 5-46, chapter 5 below; Graff, "Literacy Studies and Interdisciplinary Studies: Reflections on History and Theory," in *The Scope of Interdisciplinarity*, ed. Raphael Foshay, forthcoming, chapter 7, below; Graff and Duffy, "Literacy Myths," chapter 3 below.

8. On interdisciplinarity in literacy studies, see Graff. "Literacy, Myths, and Legacies: Lessons from the History of Literacy," in *The Labyrinths of Literacy*. Composition, Literacy, and Culture Series (Pittsburgh: University of Pittsburgh Press, 1995), 318-349; and Graff. "Literacy Studies and Interdisciplinary Studies." More generally, see Graff, "The Shock of the '"New" Histories': Social Science Histories and Historical Literacies," Presidential Address, Social Science History Association, 2000, *Social Science History*, 25, 4 (Winter 2001), 483-533; Graff, "Literacy as Social Science History: Its Past and Future," in *Looking Backward and Looking Forward: Perspectives in Social Science History*, ed. Harvey J. Graff, Leslie Page Moch, and Philip McMichael (Madison: University of Wisconsin Press, 2005), 153-154; Graff, "General Introduction" and "Introduction to Historical Studies of Literacy," special double issue, *Interchange*, 34, 2-3 (2003), "Understanding Literacy in its Historical Contexts: Past Approaches and Work in Progress," co-editor with Alison Mackinnon, Bengt Sandin, and Ian Winchester, 117-122, 123-131.

9. Graff and Duffy, "Literacy Myths," 42.

10. More explicit in my mind were the recent ground-breaking articles by Lawrence Stone and Roger Schofield: Stone, "Literacy and Education in England, 1640-1900," *Past & Present* 42 (1969), 69-139, and Schofield, "The Measurement of Literacy in Pre-industrial England," in *Literacy in Traditional Societies,* ed. Jack Goody, (Cambridge: Cambridge University Press, 1968), 311-325.

11. I have written about the latter in "The Shock of the '"New" Histories': Social Science Histories and Historical Literacies," Presidential Address, Social Science History Association, 2000, *Social Science History*, 25 (2001), 483-533.

12. See Graff, "The Shock of the '"New" Histories'"; Graff, "Assessing the History of Literacy," and with respect to the history of education, see Michael B. Katz, *The Irony of Early School Reform: Educational Innovation in Mid-Nineteenth-Century Massachusetts* (Cambridge, Mass.: Harvard University Press, 1968), Katz, "The Origins of Public Education," *History of Education Quarterly,* 16 (1976). 381-408, Katz, *Reconstructing American Education* (Cambridge, Mass.: Harvard University Press, 1989).

13. See Fig. 4.1. Note the play of past and present in the figure.

14. *The Literacy Myth*, 2. This and the following paragraphs draw on Graff and Duffy, "Literacy Myths," especially 42-43.

15. In my historical work, I begin with basic levels of alphabetic literacy: reading and writing.
16. See for example, J. McQuillan, "Seven myths about literacy in the United States," *Practical Assessment, Research and Evaluation*, 6(1), (1998), retrieved January 9, 2006 from http://PAREonline.net/getvn.asp?v=6andn=1; R. St. Clair and J. Sadlin, "Incompetence and Intrusion: On the Metaphorical Use of Illiteracy in U.S. Political Discourse," *Adult Basic Education*, 14 (2004), 45-59. See also Carl Kaestle, Helen Damon-Moore, Lawrence C. Stedman, Katherine Tinsley, and William Vance Trollinger, Jr., *Literacy in the United States: Readers and Reading Since 1880* (New Haven: Yale University Press, 1991).
17. See, for example, Jack Goody, and Ian Watt, "The Consequences of Literacy," in *Literacy in Traditional Societies*, ed. Jack Goody (Cambridge: Cambridge University Press, 1968) (originally published in 1963), 27-68; and compare with Ruth Finnegan, "Literacy versus Non-literacy: The Great Divide," in *Modes of Thought*, ed. R. Horton and R. Finnegan (London: Faber and Faber, 1973), 112-144; Kathleen Gough, "Implications of Literacy in Traditional China and India," in *Literacy in Traditional Societies*, ed. Goody, 69-84; John Duffy, *Writing from these Roots*.
18. See Fig. 4.1. Again note the play of past and present in the figure. For further discussion, see below.
19. See also Graff, *Legacies* and *Labyrinths*; Lee Soltow and Edward Stevens, *The Rise of Literacy and the Common School in the United States* (Chicago: University of Chicago Press, 1981); Rab Houston, *Literacy in Early Modern Europe,* 2nd ed. (London: Longman, 2002); David Vincent, *The Rise of Mass Literacy: Reading and Writing in Modern Europe* (Cambridge: Polity. 2000).
20. This draws on *The Literacy Myth*, 320-321.
21. David Vincent, "The Progress of Literacy," *Victorian Studies* 45 (Spring 2003), 418-419. See also Wendy Griswold, Terry McDonnell, and Nathan Wright, "Reading and the Reading Class in the Twenty-First Century," *Annual Reviews in Sociology* 31 (2005), 127-141; and R. St. Clair, and J. Sadlin, "Incompetence and Intrusion."
22. This brief discussion draws on my joint keynote presentation with Deborah Brandt, "Continuing the Conversation on Literacy Past, Present and Future," for the NCTE Assembly of Research, The Ohio State University, February, 2005.
23. Discussion of lessons draws on Graff and Duffy, "Literacy Myths," 49-51.
24. SHARP, the Society for the History of Authorship, Readers, and Publishing, is one organization with which to begin. See also, for example, Guglielmo Cavallo and Roger Chartier, eds. *A History of Reading in the West* (Amherst: University of Massachusetts, 1999); David Finkelstein and Alistair McCleery, eds., *Book History Reader*. 2nd ed. (London: Routledge, 2006) and *An Introduction to Book History* (London: Routledge, 2005).
25. Of course, much needs to be done. For discussions of that, see Graff, "Assessing the History" and "Literacies, Myths, and Legacies."
26. See above; for example, for some of the possibilities, see Scott E. Casper, Jeffery D. Groves, Stephen W. Nissenbaum, and Michael Winship, eds., *The Industrial Book, 1840-1880*, Vol. 3 of *A History of the Book in America*, (Chapel Hill: University of North Carolina Press, 2007); Graff, *The Literacy Myth*, ch. 7.
27. See, for example, New London Group, "A Pedagogy of Multiliteracies designing Social Futures," in *Multiliteracies: Literacy Learning and the Design of Social Futures*, ed. Bill Cope and Mary Kalantzis (London: Routledge, 2000), 9-37.
28. See Michael T Clanchy, *From Memory to Written Record: England, 1066-1307*. 2nd ed. (Oxford: Blackwell. 1993); Stuart Clark, *Varieties of the Eye: Vision in Early Modern European Culture*. (Oxford: Oxford University Press, 2007. For science and technology, see for example, Eugene Ferguson, "The Mind's Eye:

Nonverbal Thought in Technology," *Science*, 197 (1977), 827-836; Ellen J. Esrock, *The Reader's Eye: Visual Imaging as Reader Response* (Baltimore: Johns Hopkins University Press, 1994); Arthur I. Miller, *Insights of Genius: Imagery and Creativity in Science and Art* (Cambridge, Mass.: MIT Press, 2000 (1996)); Luc Pauwels, ed., *Visual Cultures of Science* (Hanover, NH: University Press of New England, 2006).

29. Graff, *The Literacy Myth*, ch. 5; Brian A'Hearn, Jorg Baten, and Dorothee Crayen, "Quantifying Quantitative Literacy: Age Heaping and the History of Human Capital," *Journal of Economic History*, 69 (2009), 783-808. Thanks to David Mitch for telling me about this work and to Baten for sharing this article in advance of publication.

30. Mitch, "Education and Economic Growth in Historical Perspective," *EH.Net Encyclopedia*, ed. Robert Whaples, July 26, 2005. http://eh.net/encyclopedia/article/mitch.education; Mitch, "The Role of Education and Skill in the British Industrial Revolution," in *The British Industrial Revolution: An Economic Perspective*, ed. Joel Mokyr (Boulder: Westview, 1999), 241-279. See also, David Vincent, *The Rise of Mass Literacy: Reading and Writing in Modern Europe*. (Oxford: Polity, 2000). Note that literacy and schooling are not perfectly synonymous or interchangeable. Nor are specific job skills and more general cognitive advances.

31. Mitch, "Education and Economic Growth."

32. See Claudia Goldin and Lawrence F. Katz, *The Race Between Education and Technology* (Cambridge: Harvard University Press, 2008); Sascha O. Becker and Ludger Woessmann, "Was Weber Wrong: A Human Capital Theory of Protestant Economic History," *Quarterly Journal of Economics*, forthcoming; online at http://epub.ub.uni-muenchen.de. For a very different economic analysis, see Lant Pritchett, "Does Learning to Add up Add up? The Returns to Schooling in Aggregate Data," in *Handbook of the Economics of Education*, Vol. 1, ed. Eric A. Hanushek and Finis Welch (Amsterdam: North-Holland, 2006), 635-695.

For a very interesting argument for an increasing value of literacy, specifically of writing, as a development of the so-called knowledge economy or society, see Deborah Brandt, "Writing for a Living: Literacy and the Knowledge Economy," *Written Communication*, 22 (2005), 166-197, "Drafting U.S. Literacy," *College English*, 66 (May 2004) 485-502, "Changing Literacy," *Teachers College Record*, 105 (2003), 245-260. She writes, for example, "Some analysts estimate that knowledge, most of it codified in writing, now composes about three fourths of the value added in the production of goods and services.... Writers put knowledge in tangible, and thereby transactional, form," "Writing for a Living," 166, 167. Writing itself is productive and a force of productivity, in this view.

33. Andrew Hacker, "Can We Make America Smarter?" *New York Review of Books*, April 30, 2009. Hacker notes that the United States can not expect to repeat the doubling of degrees in the 1960s.

34. Hacker, "Can We Make America."

35. Michael B. Katz and Mark J. Stern, *One Nation Divisible: What American Was and What It Is Becoming* (New York: Russell Sage Foundation, 2006), 180. See also Doug Henwood, *After the New Economy* (New York: The New Press, 2003); Jeff Madrick, "Goodbye, Horatio Alger," *The Nation*, Feb. 5, 2007.

36. Katz and Stern, *One Nation Divisible*, 181. See also Henwood, *After the New Economy*.

37. Of course, the process began much earlier in the history of the expansion of the West.

38. See Robert F. Arnove and Harvey J. Graff, ed., *National Literacy Campaigns in Historical and Comparative Perspective* (Plenum, 1987, 2nd ed. New Brunswick, N.J.: Transaction, 2008).

39. *Literacy for Life. Education For All Global Monitoring Report, 2006* (Paris: UNESCO, 2005); *United Nations Literacy Decade: Education for All.* Second Progress Report to the General Assembly for the period 2005-2006; *Education for All by 2015. Will We Make It? EFA Global Monitoring Report 2008* (Paris: UNESCO/Oxford: Oxford University Press, 2007); Joseph P. Farrell, "Literacy and International Development: Education and Literacy as Basic Human Rights," in *The Cambridge Handbook of Literacy*, ed. David R. Olson and Nancy Torrance (Cambridge: Cambridge University Press, 2009), 518-534; Arnove and Graff, ed., *National Literacy Campaigns.*

40. *The Literacy Myth*, 323-324.

5

Assessing the History of Literacy: Themes and Questions

Histories of Literacy

The history of literacy is well established as a regular, formal, significant, and sometimes central concern of historians of a wide range of topical, chronological, and methodological inclinations. This is a far cry from the intellectual landscape I confronted with my first literacy studies in 1971. The pioneering 1969 essays of Carlo Cipolla and Lawrence Stone both dominated and largely occupied the then short shelf to which few historians or other scholars turned.[1] The active thrust and exceptional growth in historical literacy studies over the past two decades have propelled the subject to new prominence. Highlighting increasingly the spheres of reading and of writing, stimulating searches for interdisciplinary approaches (methods and interpretive frames), and probing relations of past to present stand out among the impacts.

The maturation of the historical study of literacy has been enormously beneficial, inside the academy and on occasion beyond its walls. Nevertheless, this significant body of scholarship demands attention more broadly, both in terms of what it may contribute to other researchers, planners, and thinkers, and in terms of its own growing needs for inter- and intra-disciplinary cooperation and constructive criticism. For example, historical literary studies were long marked by their attention to the exploitation of quantitative data and to issues of quantity, series, and measurement. As important as that has been to intellectual advances, that emphasis has also become a limitation on new conceptualizations and interpretations.

My principal concern in this chapter is the present state of historical literacy studies and their implications. For literacy's historians and others interested in that history, the present stands as an "awkward age" or stage of development. That I sense this aspect of the moment is perhaps not surprising, for historical studies in general after almost two decades of proliferating "new histories" are themselves in something of an awkward age. The seemingly ceaseless appearance of books and articles surveying the discipline, searching for trends, and sometimes proposing new emphases and directions underscore this condition.[2] As the history of literacy joins the historiographical mainstream, it suffers from similar challenges and questions. Literacy studies, though, may be an exceptional case. For example, the distinctions between quantities and qualities, or those between individuals and collectivities, to take two of the many central dichotomies, complicate all questions of interpretation and meaning, as well as source criticism and research design.

In reflecting on the "awkward age" of historical studies of literacy, I am tempted to conceive the field's development in terms of life courses or cycles, at least metaphorically, and to posit the present situation as one of late adolescence or even youth.[3] A generational perspective is perhaps more accurate and resonate than a life course one. For the purposes of discussion and assessment, we might conceive of three modern generations of historical literacy studies.

The first generation includes principally the late-1960s work of Stone (1969), Cipolla (1969), and Schofield (1968), and was foreshadowed by the 1950s studies by Fleury and Valmary (1957) in France and Webb (1955) in England. Their contributions were several: to advance a "strong" case for the historical study of literacy—its direct study, that is, and for its import and significance as a historical factor; to review the general course of literacy's chronological trends and principal transitions and passages; to identify sources for fuller, systematic exploitation—primarily but not exclusively, numerical sources; to advance the case(s) for the utility of routinely-generated, systematic, and sometimes comparable and "direct" measures; and to posit, sometimes speculatively, the factors most closely tied to and responsible for changes in the course of literacy over time, its dynamics, distributions, impacts, and consequences.[4]

A second generation grew directly from and was clearly stimulated by the first, more sweeping and speculative students. Major studies of the second generation include Schofield's (1973) later work, Egil Johansson's studies (1977, 1981), and book-length reports by Lockridge (1974), Furet and Ozouf (1977, 1983), Cressy (1980), Stevens and

Soltow (1981), Rab Houston (1985), and myself (Graff, 1979, 1981). In addition, there were numerous articles, monographs, local and regional studies, and theses and dissertations, mostly unpublished, especially in Great Britain and France.[5]

The emphases became a larger, more detailed erection and exploitation of the quantitative record, usually but not always from signatory or census sources; greater concern for a more evidentially and sometimes also more contextually grounded historical interpretation of changing patterns, especially of distributions and differentiations in levels of literacy; relating literacy's trends to social and economic developments, institutional interventions, and state activities (especially factors like the availability of formal schooling and public school systems, political transformations and events like the French Revolution) and the ideological aspects of the subject; concern with class formation; attention to the uses of literacy in terms both of patterns of reading/writing and individual and group attitudinal and psychological changes; and an increased awareness of the contradictory nature of the subject and recognition of the difficulties in building historical interpretations upon a quantitative analysis of secular trendlines and patterns of distribution and differentiation. The value of comparative frameworks was also recognized, though comparative studies remained rare.

As a result of this rich second generation of work, we know much more about literacy's social patterns over time and the fairly systematic and patterned variations in its distributions over time and place. We are perhaps also more hesitant and cautious in explanation and attribution of meaning.

At the same time as this "second generation" matured, the subject of literacy was "discovered" by an increasing number of historians and historical social scientists, especially those employing quantitative methods and numerical sources which included some information on literacy (either on an aggregate, an ecological, or an individual level) or which were fairly easily linked to information sources on literacy. Thus, literacy increasing featured in studies of economic change, demographic behavior, cultural development and conflict, class formation and stratification, collective actions of all kinds, family formation and structures, and the like. The literature on these and related subjects now reflects this. Revealingly, in this sphere of studies, literacy tended to be conceptualized most often as an independent variable, presumably useful in the explanation of another, dependent variable which was itself the object of more direct and sustained study.[6]

In the growing numbers of studies that took literacy itself as the central object of study and discussion, literacy could be and was conceptualized as either or both dependent or independent variable. At once a source of analytic and conceptual flexibility, this could also be a problem and a source of interpretive confusion and weakness. Whether surprising or not, the nature of literacy as a (historical) variable is rarely examined critically.

Importantly, another group of historians, especially interested in cultural, printing and publishing, or literary questions, also tended increasingly to consider literacy within their purview. Although in early research they rarely studied directly or seriously took into account literacy's levels and patterns, they presumed it a central factor or parameter for their own work. Here one thinks of press and newspaper histories, *l'histoire du livre*, studies of popular culture which include new interest in oral culture and its interactions with the written and printed, and histories of print and publishing. Exemplary of intellectual trends with their mixed success is the work of Robert Darnton (1982, 1983, 1984), Elizabeth Eisenstein (1979), and Roger Chartier (1987, 1989). We have learned much from such work, too much and too complex to summarize. A great deal of it, unfortunately, remains relatively unconnected to work focused directly on literacy itself. (For interesting efforts, see Gilmore, 1989; in general, Martin, 1968-70; Allen, 1991; Burke, 1978; Carpenter, 1981; Chartier, 1987, 1989; Darnton, 1982, 1983, 1984; Davidson, 1986, 1989; Eisenstein, 1979; Engelsing, 1973, 1974; Feather, 1985; Febvre and Martin, 1958; Ginzburg, 1980; Hall, 1979, 1983; Hall and Hench, 1983; Joyce, et al, 1983; Kaestle, et al, 1991; Kaplan, 1984; Spufford, 1981; and Stock, 1983, 1990. See also the journals *Revue francais d'histoire du livre*, *Publishing History*, and critiques by Davis, 1975; Darnton, 1972.)

Virtually all this scholarly work, it should be underscored, has labored under the specter and shadows of modernization theories with their strong assumptions of literacy's role, powers, and provenance: an issue that must be confronted critically. Some students have chosen to challenge the assumptions of modernization's links to and impacts upon literacy (or vice versa). Others have assimilated their work within the traditions of modernization theories, suffering conceptual and interpretive difficulties (which the empirical record alone seldom meets squarely and many of which remain to be examined critically). In some cases, the latter assumption actually substitutes for empirical, as well as critical research. Problems also include the persisting presence of such obstructive dichotomies such as literate versus illiterate, print versus oral, quantity versus quality, cognitive versus noncognitive impacts, and the like, none of which are interpretively rich or complex enough to advance our understanding.[7]

Themes and Lessons in the History of Literacy[8]

Whatever their limits (further discussed below), two "generations'" historiography of literacy, harvested carefully, yields a rich crop of emphases, themes, and lessons. Regardless of the terms of my offering—the menu is selective—they are fruits of hard, rigorous labors of historical research and interpretation. As that kind of product, they are contested terrain with much to argue. For me at least, the import of the cultivation only heightens the stakes.

Not only is the historiography of literacy sometimes an interpretive battlefield, but so too are large questions about the nature of the relationships tying literacy, on the one hand, to learning, schooling, and education, and, on the other hand, to developmental consequences for groups and individuals. Still common assumptions of simplicity, directness, and linearity fall quickly to the quagmire that obstructs the progress of the harvester. In the themes and lessons considered, we also find important parallels between historical foundations and developments and contemporary configurations and their "crises" (see also Graff, 1992).

The historicity of literacy constitutes a first theme, from which many other key imperatives and implications follow. Several decades of serious, often revisionary, scholarship and criticism join in the conclusion that reading and writing, whatever their requirements or consequences— they are hotly debated—take on their meaning and acquire their value only in concrete historical circumstances that mediate in specific terms whatever general or supposedly "universal" attributes or concomitants may be claimed for literacy. Ranging from "ancient literacy" to proclaimed "post-modern" literacies, this holds true for literacy's "uses" both practical and symbolic, as studies of the past three millennia show. Awareness of this historicity, which gains support from contemporary research in anthropology, psychology, and literary criticism, is perhaps the single most significant contribution of recent historical scholarship, even if the point requires wider broadcast.[9] Indeed, the conceptualization, assumptions, and expectations one brings to considerations of reading and writing are revised radically when literacy is revisioned historically.

Conversely, although seldom appreciated, present-day conceptions, arrangements, and practices of literacy as well as schooling and learning are historically founded and grounded. They are also strong and powerfully resistant to change. Ignorance of the circumstances in which crucial concepts, arrangements, and expectations were fashioned, the means by which they have been maintained, and their consequences together limit severely if not contradict directly contemporary analysis, diagnosis, prescription. (Use of the medical metaphor is itself part of this history.)

That subjects such as literacy, learning, and schooling, and the uses of reading and writing are simple, unproblematic notions is a historical myth, our studies reveal. Experience, historical and more recent, to the contrary underscores their fundamental complexity, practically and theoretically; their enormously complicated conceptual and highly problematic nature. The results of two "generations" of literacy's historical researchers almost unanimously undergird this conclusion, whose acceptance opens or reopens a lengthy list of questions.

Long-persisting problems gain new import in this revision. Among them are the many "great debates," for example, surrounding human language acquisition and usage; literate as opposed to oral, among other communicative modes—and their presumed "consequences"; relations of literacy to hierarchies of power and wealth as opposed to egalitarian democracy; literacy's contributions to development economic, political, social; and the status of "texts." Even elementary literacy as learned and practiced is quite complex physiologically, neurologically, and cognitively. Its social and cultural dimensions add on numerous layers of complex meanings—among them "continuities and contradictions," as I term them (Graff, 1981, 1987a). How little we know about learning—and about teaching, too, especially respecting the level of literacy.

Especially prominent among the central complications of our traditions or legacies of literacy are a) the extraordinary frailty and fragility of conceptions and conceptualizations of literacy, and b) the contradiction of consequences expected from its acquisition. With respect to the first, presumption of literacy's unproblematic simplicity accompanies "naturally" or "essentially" assumptions that emphasize its strong, uniform, universal, unitary, unwavering nature and impact. With respect to the second, "strong" notions or theories of literacy directly and linearly associate rising levels (in some versions, when a specified "threshold" is achieved) with large-scale impacts, especially the advancement of both individuals and societies. Termed in various formulations the "consequences," "correlates," or "implications" of literacy, the number and variety of imputed effects on individuals or societies are dizzying.

Literacy, it has been claimed, correlates with economic growth and industrialization, wealth and productivity, political stability and participatory democracy, urbanization, consumption, and contraception.[10]

These wholesale claims rarely stand up to either empirical or conceptual probing historically or contemporarily. The "strong theory" of literacy—despite its hold on popular and policy opinions—turns out to be much weaker, with literacy's impacts seldom so direct, unmediated, abstract, or universalistic. Constituting much of what I call literacy's central contradictions (discussed in detail in my books *The Literacy Myth* and *The Legacies of Literacy*), these legacies taken together constitute "the literacy myth," a powerful force despite its massive criticism and rejection in some circles. The contradictions nevertheless give the lie not only to "strong" theories but also to proclamations of a "Grand Dichotomy" or "Great Divide" rhetorically erected between literate and nonliterate persons, societies, and civilizations. Such formulations or notions rest far more on expectations and faith than they do on ambiguous evidence of complex, usually context-dependent relations and more complicated, oblique connections, with which the newer historical literature is filled.[11] What is at issue, of course, is seldom admitted: it is the purpose of literacy, and other learning. Those issues are inseparable from their historical course.

Typical conceptions of literacy share not only assumptions about their unproblematical status, but also the presumption of their central value neutrality (which is itself often represented as beneficial, a "good"). To the contrary, historical studies repeatedly demonstrate that no mode or means of learning is neutral. Not only does all "knowledge," however elementary, incorporate the assumptions and expectations, the biases or emphases of its production, association, prior use, maintenance and preservation. So too do the so-called "tools" or skills.[12] With them, there are biases with respect to their transmission—the circumstances of learning and practice—and quite likely fundamental biases in their very nature, for example, the newly appreciated textual biases of formal schooling—"school" literacy—and most reading and writing shaped by such formative encounters, tutelage, and generally restricted or regulated practice.

Studies of the "media" of literacy, from script to print and beyond, only begin to suggest the intricately interacting relationships; contemporary confusion about the "future of print" compared to the visuality and aurality of electronic media have an impressively lengthy set of precedents.[13] The history, only partially studied and understood, challenges all presumptions of unmediated, linear relations and impacts.

Recent studies in cognitive psychology and anthropology demonstrate the consequences for literacy of the specific contexts or circumstances of acquisition, practice, and uses—and of its place in the culture (Scribner and Cole, 1981). Raising more questions than they answer and challenging the received wisdom, such research joins other cognitive, linguistic, and historical studies in pointing toward more refined conceptions of skills, abilities, competencies, and knowledge in relatively precise but flexible learning, social, cultural, and communicative contexts.

That alphabetic literacy is one, albeit exceptionally valuable, set of abilities and competencies, among others, with which it interacts, slowly influences thinking about schooling and learning, and much else. Here, for example, confusions between long-standing and theoretically touted all but boundless potentials of literacy when contrasted with more common levels of ability and everyday practices can be excessive. Here, too, we find contradictions in literacy's history, in part from traditions of overvaluing alphabetic literacy by itself and slighting (or worse) other "literacies." We neglect the extent to which "school" literacy is a very special use of literacy and language. Words are not only taken out of "the context for action," but they are also removed from other, nonschool uses, including much of oral language usage and writing (Olson, 1977). Historically, we locate the long- lasting structures of authority erected on these bases, as certain forms of literacy and language abilities support social differentiation, social stigmatization, reinforcement of inequality—and school failure among the young, and not so young—among these "literate biases."

Enormous implications for teaching and learning, for developing more effective literacies (conceived, that is, in the plural), follow from placing "traditional alphabetic" literacy within appropriate communicative contexts along with, say, numeracy and scientific literacy, oral and aural abilities, spatial literacy or graphicacy as some geographers put it, visual and aesthetic literacies, and so on. Historians of science suggest that invention and discovery may owe more to visual than alphabetic literacy. It may be difficult to formulate satisfactory notions of "functional" literacy(ies) without expanding our understanding of communicative contexts and channels. For such study, history provides a rich laboratory only partly used. The challenges of precise comparison across space as well as time loom large.

Historical studies amply document the damages, the human costs in domains developed and undeveloped, that follow from the long domination of practical and theoretical presumptions that elevate the literate, the written—as opposed to the nonliterate—to the status of the dominant partner in what Jack Goody calls the "Great Dichotomy" and Ruth Finnegan the "Great Divide." In part the arrogance of the imperial West but more the triumph of Goody's "technology of the intellect" over the intellect and the human spirit themselves, traditions of narrowly construed intellectualism and rationalism rationalized their reification of light over darkness, civilization over barbarity, developed over primitive, formally schooled over natural, written over spoken, literate over oral.

Hand in hand with simplicity and superiority have gone presumed ease of learning and expectation of individual, along with societal, progress. Despite our tardiness in recognizing its implications, historical studies repeatedly reiterate the difficulties regularly, perhaps normally experienced in gaining, practicing, and mastering the elements of alphabetic literacy. Acquiring even basic elements of abilities that may—or may not—prove necessary and useful in acquiring further skills, information, knowledge, or mentalities is seldom easy—for reasons both obvious and devious. Learning literacy, and whatever lies beyond it, has always been hard work.

Only in part a matter of instructional media, technology, pedagogy, institutional setting, age, or social circumstances, motivation—the widest range of perceptions of need, sometimes defensively or fearfully, sometimes with great pleasure and satisfaction—our studies agree, is a great stimulus toward at least the effort to learn one's letters. Sometimes this is a matter of individuals; sometimes it is collective. Unfortunately, scholars, like ourselves, who live by and depend upon our manipulation of the tools of traditional learning are not well placed to appreciate common experiences past or present.

Recent research also helps to replace the complicated historical and richly human images missing from our common operational and legitimizing myths: of multiple paths of learning literacy and much more, the employment of an extraordinary range of instructors, institutions and other environments, and beginning "texts"—and the diversity of sometimes conflicting or contradictory motivations pushing and pulling. We rediscover the informality and possibility of elementary learning without the lockstep enforced march of age-grading and wholesale psychologies of human cognition and learning based on simplistic presumptions of human aging. In this respect, both the early modern "discovery" of children and a "special" stage of "childhood," and the last two centuries' efforts to institutionalize them constitute more complicated relationships than usually accorded them.

In contrast to the variety of historical paths, the great reforming dream was formal, compulsory, mass public schools as expected sites for virtually universal transmission of a minimal level of literacy reciprocally disseminated with the tenets of secular morality. This was a literacy presumed nonetheless useful and also socially secure, as opposed to literacy gained without the proper leavening agents of carefully crafted learning environments with methods and materials created expressly for their employment. The first dreamers long predated the massive nineteenth-century efforts to construct school systems, which in turn awaited the present century for many areas. Distrust, even fear, of the unwashed masses united them, although for centuries the fear of schooled masses dominated over fear of the ignorant or those who learned outside the bounds of formal educational institutions. Before that reversal and the subsequent achievement of mass schooling, and long accompanying its development in many places, looser arrangements continued whose poor press was written by reformers who sought to destroy them. Those arrangements have much to tell us.[14]

While underscoring the relative recency and historical constructedness of the means of mass literacy provision and most of other education—as opposed to notions of their inevitability or destiny—caution and hindsight also demand that we not succumb to understandable and attractive reasons to romanticize nostalgically the "premodern" past. Mass public school systems, despite their failings, have undoubtedly increased opportunities and elevated educational achievement. The price paid has included culturally and individually restricted literacy, and other learning—in circumstances that led many pupils to disdain or undervalue literacy and other learning, their practice and use. It also included persistent inequalities of opportunity and outcomes, greater rewards for the well-off than for the poor, among much else. Limits of dependence on literacy, itself restricted and often poorly disseminated, set rigid constraints on the contribution from schools to polity and culture as well as economy. And of course, nearly universal elementary schooling never halted popular cultural practices that include "improper" use of literacy to read scorned or censured writing!

Among the prices paid and among those we now seek to redevelop with adult literacy programs has been the long standing condemnation, then obscuring and forgetting that for a great many persons, traditional alphabetic literacy of reading and sometimes writing was acquired in the widest variety of informal, as well as formal circumstances, and at a wide range of chronological ages. This included self-teaching and learning some level of ability in homes, dame schools, work places, fields, class and political domains, cultural settings, carceral institutions, and chance occurrences, sometimes at ages younger but far more often older than the limited span of childhood and early adolescence that came to be defined as the "critical period." Modernization of schooling into mass systems rested in part on the denial of previously common courses or paths. Simultaneously, approved practices respecting institution and age hardened into expectations, policies, and theories, all with their authoritative guardians. Until recently, in the wake of these legacies, tutelage of adults attracted relatively little effort. Ironically, there are long traditions of adult education seldom called into play (Levine, 1985).

Expectations and common practice of learning literacy as part of elementary education—all the formal schooling that most common scholars experienced until the late nineteenth and early twentieth centuries—are themselves historical developments, research shows. This presumption holds that given the availability of written texts and elementary instruction, beginning basic abilities of reading and writing are in themselves sufficient for further developing an individual's literacy and subsequent education and their advancement. No serious obstacle to achieving a desired degree of literacy or additional learning need trouble those hungry for more. Learning and using literacy, the "foundation," were easy. (No matter that the cognitive and psychological place of reading and writing as foundations is not well understood, or that reading has so long been poorly taught, or that debates over reading methodologies persist over centuries with much heat and little light.) Among the corollaries is that failure reflected overwhelmingly on the individuals—and their race, ethnicity, class, gender, etc.—not on schools, society, culture, polity. "Blaming the victim," this pattern is called.

Just as individuals followed different paths to literacy and learning, societies historically and more recently took different paths toward achieving rising levels of popular literacy. Despite massive expectations of one sure road to progress, inscribed in "strong" theories and "standard versions," historical research emphasizes that there is no one route destined to culminate in universal literacy and its associated "modern" concomitants. Similarly, with respect to the contributions of literacy and education, there has been no one route to economic development, industrialization, political democracy, or other parcels of the "modernization" complex. In some cases, at some times, literacy worked as causal agent indirectly or directly. In others, it did not. In some circumstances, literacy was influenced by development, an effect rather than a contribution. And in others, the impact on literacy and education was negative—in European early industrialization, for example. Sequencing and timing—chronologically and causally—are very important, say, in contrasting the nature and degree of social unrest during industrialization, or the adaptation of large numbers of immigrants. Still, those relationships vary widely. Literacy often has served noncognitively, attitudinally, behaviorally, and symbolically in furthering social and economic development. That is no small contribution; it is not, however, the one typically touted (Graff, 1979, 1991, 1981, 1987a; "Education," 1981; Winchester, 1978, 1980, 1990).

The great danger today is one that twentieth-century education on all levels shares with literacy models: the simple presumption that economic growth and development depends simply and directly on investment in and high rates of productivity from systems of formal education. Quantity and quality are confused; educational purpose is distorted. The consequent fears of "crisis" and "decline" rigidly narrow the frame of education—including literacy—and all but guarantee disappointment and repetition of the cycle. The legacies of literacy stand close at hand.

A Future for the History of Literacy?

A "third generation" of historians of literacy awaits us. In part, I believe, discussion must now focus upon its "needs and opportunities": questions, sources, methods. Recent studies begin to point the way. Not coincidentally, groundbreaking work in contemporary studies usefully demonstrates basic areas and aspects of interdisciplinary collaboration.

Two recent and original directions in the social scientific study of literacy offer novel leads. In particular, I think of the social-psychological work—sometimes brilliant and path-breaking in its implications—of the experimental, ethnographic and comparative cognitive psychologists, Sylvia Scribner and Michael Cole, especially in their *The Psychology of Literacy* (1981) and in Scribner's further studies of the skills, including reading and writing, required and utilized in different kinds of work settings and demands. I also think of the community-based ethnographies of literacy and education exemplified by anthropologist and linguist Shirley Heath in *Ways with Words: Language, Life and Work in Communities and Classrooms* (1983). Together, this research underscores the import for literacy of context of learning and use, nature of acquisition, culture and traditions, and the like. Especially striking are the focus, in theory and in practice, on reading and writing in communicative and cultural context, and on ethnography. By example and analogy and conceptualization, they contribute to an agenda for the "third generation."

Several other recent studies underscore these directions as they also lead us into different and wider terrains. Jan Radway's *Reading the Romance: Women, Patriarchy, and Popular Literature* (1984; see also Radway, 1986) proposes, and with a group of contemporary romance readers illustrates, that reading can be usefully and critically (and as her work in particularly evidences, sympathetically) studied in contexts social, cultural, and political economic. Her imaginative practice is informed by anthropological, feminist, and literary critical perspectives. Radway also hints at the possibilities for historical efforts at this direction. Creative research by David Vincent (1981) and Sally Mitchell (1981) shows potential for historical applications via autobiographical and literary sources, for working-class and middle-class women, respectively. The pioneering and idiosyncratic, if not always persuasive, writings of Carlo Ginzburg (1980) and Robert Darnton (1984), and more recently Roger Chartier and his associates (1987, 1989), suggest the depths and insights that close study of reading practices set into socioculturally informed communicative contexts may yield. In these examples, I add, the limits of the work are as rich as are the real achievements. (See also Scribner, 1981, 1984; Burke, 1978, 1987; Isaac, 1976a, 1976b, 1982; Stout, 1977; Kaplan, 1984; Goody, 1986, 1987; Thomas, 1986; Muchembled, 1986; Allen, 1991; Davidson, 1986, 1989; Gross, 1988; Gilmore, 1989; and Kaestle, 1991, for additional examples.)

The occasion for these reflections, happily, coincides with a significant moment for historical studies of literacy. If my surmises are at least partially accurate, the field of inquiry is today at a crossroads. We ask, not at all frivolously or lightly, "Whither historians of literacy?" If the second generation—having firmly established the field of the history of literacy—is winding down, and if my sensing a diminishing of new researchers and research projects focused directly on literacy is also an accurate reading, and if we presume that literacy deserves and demands further study, we then recognize that 1) many gaps in the record remain to be completed; 2) many questions—some only relatively recently posed—remain to be answered; and 3) key problems in conceptualization, interpretation, and explanation mark these efforts.[15] Consideration of the outline and agenda of a hypothetical "third generation" may be of more than academic interest.

In part, we need to shift our dialogue from quantitative methods to critical questions asked of both quantitative and qualitative findings and their relationships. We need to ponder further the links in terms of both continuities and changes between the second generation and my proposed "third generation." We need not only to take stock and assess, but also to undertake those activities with an aim toward future studies conceived and designed in novel ways. These discursive reflections aim to stimulate that discussion.

The achievements of historical literacy studies are many and clear, we see. Persisting patterns of limitations also mark the field. We recognize limits of quantitative analysis alone, and of aggregative and ecological methods and research designs. In some ways, I aver, we are only now coming to the most important questions and issues. In addition to time series and patterns of variation, that perhaps will be deemed one of the major contributions of generations one and especially two. There indeed has been a shattering of "received wisdom" (as in "literacy myths," to use my lexicon), expectations, assumptions—and that is no small accomplishment. The obverse, however, is the question of what will replace them—in part a theoretical issue. The "great debates" about literacy's relationships all reflect this: from literacy's relationships to economic (i.e., commercial and/or industrial) and social development, to political mobilization, religion, social mobility, social class formation, work and leisure life patterns, and social change more generally. Questions about method, such as those of dependent versus independent variables, levels of aggregation, problems of correlational analysis, follow. The demand for critical reflection now falls upon conceptualization, method, and interpretation.[16]

In one way, the path lies in moving beyond literacy as a dichotomous variable, perceived as either conservative and controlling or as liberating, as useful or not. This might constitute moving toward a historical cultural politics and a historical political economy of literacy. There are a number of possible avenues. Synoptically, I suggest some, with an eye toward setting an agenda for the "third generation."

First and most generally, historical literacy studies must build upon their own past while also breaking away from it. The work of the "second generation," such as that of Furet and Ozouf (1977), Cressy (1980), or Soltow and Stevens (1981), delineates parameters, baselines, and key interrelationships. Those relationships in turn offer opportunities to investigate more precisely the linkages and to seek refinements in specifying factors and their interactions. These range from literacy's relations with class, gender, age, and culture to overarching themes of economic development, social order, mobility and stratification, education and schooling, actual uses of literacy, language and culture, and so on.

One demand falls upon much sharper contextual grounding, often in clearly delineated localities. Others encompass the completion of time series, among other quantitative analyses. Major opportunities for close, critical contextualization and connective interpretation exist in contemporary research into Kaestle's (1985, 1991) "history of readers and reading," *l'histoire du livre*, Chartier's (1987, 1989) history of "texts, printing, readings" (see also Gilmore, 1989; Allen, 1991). Despite sometimes brilliant openings, the potential of these scholarly practices is unfulfilled; their integration into histories social, cultural, economic, or political remains a major challenge.

Second is the advancement of comparative study. This requires a greater appreciation and emphasis on source criticism and recognition of the different meanings of different measures of literacy (as well as literacy's uses) among different populations as evidenced from varying sources. Contextualization here is also critical for comparisons, as Johansson's (1977, 1981, 1985) and Houston's (1985) work in particular illustrates. Also critical is the search for indicators of the levels and the quality of literacy, permitting us to advance beyond the constraining dichotomy of literate versus illiterate (compare, for example, Graff, 1979, with Kaestle, 1991). Novel approaches to combining records and to record linkage stand out on this agenda.

Third is the major need for new conceptualizations of context in the historical study of literacy. Recognizing that literacy only acquires meaning and significance within specified historical contexts does not in itself reduce the risks of abstracted analysis. Novel work in anthropology and psychology, like that of Heath (1983) and Scribner and Cole (1981), mentioned above, provides important suggestions and guidelines for historians. The tasks lie not only in defining and specifying contexts for study and interpretation but also in delineating the varying levels of context—vertically or horizontally, for example—and in experimenting with ways to operationalize them. Stevens' (1985, 1988) focus on illiterates in judicial settings and Johansson's (1977, 1981, 1985) perspective on church and community indicate two opportunities to probe more intensively. Carlo Ginzburg's (1980) study may provide another; so too may those of Radway (1984), Darnton (1972, 1982, 1983, 1984), Vincent (1981, 1989), and Mitchell (1981). Gilmore's (1989) localized case study reiterates the richness of records. For the recent past, oral histories, library use records, and participant observation, or ethnographies of communications, offer other possibilities.[17]

Contexts for analysis are many and diverse. They range from those of acquisition, use, and action, to those of individual, family, group, or community, gender, or social class. The scope for defined study is itself variable, but should include material conditions, motivations, opportunities, needs and demands, traditions, and transformations. In this way, linguistic forms, dialects, communication channels and networks, "pushes" and "pulls" from religion, culture, politics, the economy, and so forth, may be incorporated. Literacy's relationship to personal and/or collective efficacy and activism or agency—a source of much debate—may also be explored further, in part in analysis of specific events and processes and in part in terms of patterns of communications and mobilization within defined contexts. Class formation and vital behavior are just two of the many key topics calling for examination.

Are "historical ethnographies"—conceptualized fully in terms of literacy among the many modes and relations of communications—of literacy possible? Recent work, such as that noted here, contains fascinating hints in that direction that merit fuller examination. A number of recent studies in popular culture—for example, those of Ginzburg (1980), Burke (1978, 1987), LeRoy Ladurie (1978), Scribner (1981, 1984), Wrightson and Levine (1979), Davidson (1986), Vincent (1989), Stout (1977), and Isaac (1976a, 1976b, 1982)—may prove stimulating beginning models. Clearly, the subject and its significance stimulate a fair test. The current interests (within anthropology and elsewhere) in an anthropology of communications in ethnographies of reading and writing at varying levels of context and generality are guides to follow. (See, for example, Heath, 1983; Tannen, 1982; Whiteman, 1981.)

On one hand, literacy may be viewed as one among other "media" and its roles and impacts evaluated. On the other hand, ethnographic and communicative approaches have the potential to expand perspectives while simultaneously grounding them more precisely for meaningful interpretation. Novel contextualization can also be a boost to the renewal and refinement of quantitative studies. Attention to context, in sum, offers both new and better cases for study, opportunities for explanation, and approaches to literacy's changing and variable historical meanings and contributions.

A fourth consideration follows. This is the difficult but necessary demand for critical examination of the conceptualization of literacy itself. The "second generation" has taught us about the contradictions central to literacy's history. It has also revealed the problems in treating literacy as an independent variable and the confusions that inhere in treating literacy as either or both dependent and independent. Questions of contextualization may well limit analysis of literacy as independent; they will also, I think, stimulate new formulations of the nature of literacy as a dependent factor. In the process, new considerations about levels and quality of literacy must transcend the related limits of the tradition of conceptualizing literacy as a dichotomous variable. Psychological and anthropological studies promise to contribute here too. The body of work of the "second generation" collectively underscores the special complications whose resolution ranks high on any agenda. To transcend it requires excavation of other relevant aspects of cultural communications—including the oral and visual, along with the written or printed, and today the electronic—among which literacy, in shifting degrees and mediations, takes its place.

Fifth is the question of literacy and what might well be termed the "creation of meaning." Historical studies of literacy have been little influenced by recent debates in intellectual and cultural history, literary criticism and philosophy, cognitive psychology, cultural anthropology and ethnography, or critical theories of communication. To some extent, the origins of these current emphases stem from dissatisfaction with traditional approaches to "texts," their reading, understanding, and communication. More recently, the entire enterprise of grasping the "creation," maintenance, and communication of "meaning" has changed in major ways related to issues central to literacy. The parallels with literacy studies have not mandated a parallel course. (Chartier, 1987, 1989, and Hall, 1979, 1983, are the exceptions.)

Cultural and intellectual history are themselves, along with many areas of the humanities and the social sciences—the human sciences—in a significant time of ferment and exploration; so too are literary criticism, cognitive and cultural psychology, and some areas of philosophy. Concerns about interactions between readers and texts, reader responses to writing and print, shaping of individual and collective processes of cognition, and the ways in which "meaning" is created, influenced, transmitted, and changed are common, if not always clarified.[18] Chartier (1989), for example, raises questions and advances hypotheses about modes and practices of early modern French reading, reading as active and creative, reception aesthetics and horizons, appropriation, interpretive communities, textuality and orality, printing and circulation. Kaestle (1991) confronts readers, readership, and readability in twentieth-century American society.

At least partly to its detriment, the history of literacy largely stands in isolation from interdisciplinary rapprochement. Questions about literacy's contribution to individual, class, and collective awareness, patterns of cognitive (and also noncognitive) attitudinal formation, and cultural behavior more generally all underscore this need. The nagging issue of the uses of literacy, and their consequences, demands further new exploration.

The need for a sharper theoretical awareness of the relevance of the history of literacy for many important aspects of social, economic, and psychological theory, constitutes a sixth point. This is implied in the foregoing, and too frequently implied (rather than argued directly) in the literature. Historical studies of literacy provide significant opportunities for testing theories. In so far as their results continue to raise criticisms of "normative" theoretical expectations and assumptions, there may also be prospects for essaying new formulations. Both historical practice and historians' contributions to other interested parties can only benefit from this.

A seventh consideration, raised as a question of methodology, indeed of epistemology, links all of the above. Has the tradition, from two generations of studies, of taking literacy as primary object of analysis—"the history of literacy" per se—approached an end point? Should a "third generation" rooted at least in part in the foregoing refocus itself in terms of literacy as a significant—indeed a necessary—component of other relevant investigations? The question, simply put, is that of shifting from "historical studies of literacy" to "histories that encompass literacy within their context and conceptualization," from "the history of literacy" to "literacy in history."[19] There is reason to argue, I think, that the limits of the second generation's conceptualization encourage the exploration of what that transformation would entail. To move in this direction is no simple task: I call for the reconceptualization not only of the history of literacy and the histories of reading and writing/printing within it but also the histories of culture and society.

Eighth, and finally, I call attention to the relevance of the history of literacy for a number of policy issues in societies developed and under-developed today, and to the contributions that reconceptualization might bring to them. Historical analysis can contribute to understanding and fashioning responses to deal with those problems that are sometimes deemed "literacy crises." In grasping that there are many paths to literacy, that literacy's relations to social and economic development are complex, that the quantity and the quality of literacy (and literacy's possession and its use) are not linearly related, that the consequences of literacy are neither direct nor simple, and that literacy is never neutral, historians have much to share with their fellow students and to offer those who formulate social policies. That is no small contribution.[20]

Consider for example the concept of multiple paths to the making of literate societies and states. The historical study of literacy shows clearly that there is no one route to universal literacy, and that there is no one path destined to succeed in the achievement of mass literacy. In the history of the Western world, we may distinguish the roles of private and public schooling in various configurations in the attainment of high rates of popular literacy, as well as the operation of informal and formal, voluntary and compulsory schooling. Mass literacy was achieved in Sweden, for example, *without* formal schooling or instruction in writing (Johansson, 1977, 1981; Graff, 1987, 1988). High rates of literacy have followed from all of these approaches in different cases and contexts. The developmental consequences are equally varied. This stands in stark contrast to dominant assumptions among policy-makers, planners, and social scientists.

The past provides a different set of experiences than those that might sustain these common expectations. Although neither all the research nor the balance sheet of historical interpretation is in, we may argue that historical experiences provide a better guide to such crucial questions as how and to what extent basic literacy contributes to the economic and individual well being of persons in different socioeconomic and cultural contexts, and under what circumstances universal literacy can be achieved. The costs and benefits of alternative paths can be discerned, and estimated, too. Thus, the connections and disconnections between literacy and commercial development, a generally positive relationship, and literacy and industrial development, often an unfavorable linkage at least in the short run of decades and half-centuries, offer important case studies and analogs for analysis. The data of the past strongly suggest that a simple, linear, modernization model of literacy as prerequisite for development and development as stimulant to increased levels of schooling will not suffice. Too many periods of lags, backward linkages, setbacks, and contradictions exist to permit such cavalier theorizing to continue without serious challenge and criticism.

Literacy's relationships with paths to economic development, mentioned above, present other cases in point. So, too, do the connections of literacy with social development. There too, we discover a history of continuities and contradictions, and of variable paths to societal change and development. From the classical era forward, leaders of polities and churches, reformers as well as conservers, have recognized the uses of literacy and schooling. Often they have perceived unbridled, untempered literacy as potentially dangerous, a threat to social order, political integration, economic productivity, and patterns of authority. Increasingly, however, they came to conclude that literacy, if provided in carefully controlled, structured, formal institutions created expressly for the purposes of education and transmission of literacy and supervised closely, could be a powerful and useful force in achieving a variety of important ends. Predecents long predated the first systematic mass efforts to put this conception of literacy into practice, in Rome, for example, and in the visionary proposals of the fifteenth- and sixteenth-century Christian humanists. For our purposes, the Reformations of the sixteenth century represented the first great literacy campaigns. They were hardly homogeneous efforts, as Sweden reminds us, in either design or degree of success. Nonetheless, they were precedent-setting and epochal in their significance for the future of social and educational development throughout the world.

With the Enlightenment and its heritage came the final ideological underpinnings for the "modern" and "liberal" reforms of popular schooling and institutional building that established the network of educational, social, political, cultural, and economic relationships central to the dominant ideologies and their theoretical and practical expressions for the past two centuries. Prussia took the lead, and provided a laboratory that United States, Canadian, English, French, and Scandinavian school promoters and reformers regularly came to study. North Americans and Swedes followed in Prussia's wake, and, in time and in their own ways, so did the English, French, Italians—and more recently vast areas of the underdeveloping world.

Of course, other important uses of literacy—for personal advancement, entertainment, study, collective action, and the like—must not be slighted. The significance and potential of literacy to individuals and to groups throughout history, even if sometimes taken out of context and exaggerated, are undoubted. The role of social class and group-specific demands for literacy's skills, the impact of motivation, and the growing perceptions of its value and benefits are among the major factors that explain the historical contours of changing rates of popular literacy. In other words, "demand" must be appreciated, as well as "supply," stimuli from "below" as well as force and compulsion from "above:" in intricately reciprocal and dialectical relationships. Literacy's limits, history emphasizes, and its roles in promoting and maintaining hegemony, merit emphasis too. Their deeper exploration and understanding may depend on the new approaches suggested above.

Especially with the transitions from preindustrial social orders based in rank and deference to the class societies of commercial and then factory capitalism, the integrating and hegemony-creating purposes of literacy provision through formal schooling only increased. Schooling, with its transmission of morally leavened and often qualitatively low levels of skills, became more and more a vital aspect of the maintenance of social stability, particularly during times of massive if confusing social and economic transformations—and a regular feature of the young's life course. Many people, most prominently social and economic leaders and social reformers, grasped the uses of schooling and the vehicle of literacy for promoting the values, attitudes, and habits deemed essential to order, integration, cohesion, and certain forms of progress. The people's acceptance of literacy's import—not a simple process—forms the other dimension of this historical equation.

Recognizing the emergence of the history of literacy's "third generation" and its relevance to nonhistorians is at once a first step and a paradigmatic one. We may then speak of the future of the past, and that of the present, too.

Notes

1. While not attempting definitiveness or exhaustiveness, the reference list for this text offers an overview of the major works in the field, older and more recent. For complete references, see chapter 9 Bibliography.
2. For example, Stone's call for retreats from social scientific and quantitative studies and hopes for "new narratives," the attacks on social history, among many others. See, for example, Abrams (1980); Darnton (1972); Higham and Conkin (1979); Hobsbawm (1980); Kammen (1980); LaCapra and Kaplan (1982); Rabb and Rotberg (1982); Stone (1979), among a large bibliography.
3. Readers, I hope, will agree that this frame of reference has some merit and usefulness despite the fact that it also reflects my present research and writing on the history of growing up! The overlaps with literacy's history in fact are many and instructive. See my *Conflicting Paths: Growing Up in America* (Harvard University Press, 1995).
4. See for example the works of Jack Goody, Eric Havelock, Walter Ong, and also Marshall McLuhan.
5. For bibliography, see Graff (1981a, 1987a); Houston (1983); Bartoli Langeli and Petrucci (1978); Bartoli Langeli and Toscani (1991); Furet and Ozouf (1977); Pelizzari (1989); Vinao Frago (1989). See also chapter 9 below.
6. Examples of this enormous literature appear in Graff (1981a, 1987a). Graff (1987a) and Houston (1988) offered stock-taking summaries.
7. Compare for example Cipolla (1969) or Stone (1969), with Lockridge (1974), Graff (1979, 1981c, 1987a, 1988, 1992); Soltow and Stevens (1981), Houston (1983, 1985). See also Finnegan (1988), Heath (1983), Scribner and Cole (1981), Street (1984), Levine (1982, 1985), Bloch (1989). See also below.
8. In this section, I shall make no effort to provide extensive citations for the generalizations proffered. Readers may refer to the References as constituting one large segment of the body of research and interpretation on which I draw. See also Graff (1992).

9. Consider for example the range of revision in anthropologist Jack Goody's (1968, 1986, 1987, and with Ian Watt, 1968) stance on literacy's "consequences", in part from his familiarity with historical and related research. Walter Ong reflects the influence albeit to a lesser extent as does psychologist David Olson. Nevertheless, much contemporary thinking, even by some historians who should now know better, goes on as if a quarter-century's learning and debates had not occurred. Wider communication both inside and beyond the academy merits a higher place on our agenda.

10. The best-known "strong case" is Jack Goody and Ian Watt, 1968, originally published in 1963. By 1968, Goody withdrew from the language of causal consequences to looser formulations. For a critical discussion and bibliography, see Graff, 1987a, esp. Epilogue. Anthropologist Ruth Finnegan's (1988) writings are very important among this literature.

11. For some of the human "costs" from such dominant notions, see for example Botstein and more generally "Literacy in America" (1990); K. Levine (1985); Kozol (1985); Katz (1988); Aronowitz and Giroux (1988). For historical and international comparisons, see Arnove and Graff (1987). For seemingly unselfconscious but very influential sway of these presumptions, see Hirsch (1987, 1988).

12. The almost cyclical "debate" over "skills" versus "content," which spans the entire educational realm from literacy learning to graduate training is another version of this. Today's war over undergraduate "core curricula" in such terms is especially silly and wasteful of time and energy. Ian Winchester (1990) relates this issue to the philosophy of science and its revision. There is a large literature on vocational schooling, among the functional and/or utilitarian literacies. For recent years, see Levine, 1985; Katz, 1988, among others.

13. The works of Walter Ong, Marshall McLuhan, and Elizabeth Eisenstein provide starting points on these typically misunderstood and much debated issues. More generally, the research and interpretations of historians of classical and medieval literacy has been richer and more instructive than that of modernists.

14. Suggestive here, for example, are the studies of Galenson (1981), Laqueur, (1976a); Spufford (1979). The story of early modern Sweden where exceptionally high levels of reading but not writing literacy and of female literacy were achieved largely without mass institutional schooling is told by Egil Johansson (1977, 1981, 1985).

15. That the perception is not mine alone is confirmed by my correspondence with Armando Petrucci about this conference and my presentation.

16. Analogies with studies of printing and reading may be drawn in similar terms. The promise of both *l'histoire du livre* and the history of reading remains to be achieved despite some of the grander claims proffered. See relevant entries in the Reference list below.

17. On the possibilities from oral history, see the continuing work and the database developed by Paul Thompson (1974, 1978) at the University of Essex in England. See also Radway (1984), Cook-Gumperz (1986), Heath (1983), Tannen (1982), Whiteman (1981). See most recently Kaestle (1991).

18. This literature, actually several different bodies of it, is much too vast to cite here. See for introductions, LaCapra and Kaplan (1982); Higham and Conkin (1979); Rabb and Rotberg (1982); Allen (1991); Bauml (1980); Chartier (1987, 1989); Davidson (1986); Hebrard (1980), Kaplan (1984), among the References. See also such journals as *Critical Inquiry*, *New Literary History*, *Representations*.

19. As this presentation suggests, what I envision certainly includes but also goes beyond the usual lines of *l'histoire du livre* or the history of reading.

20. For a more sustained discussion, see Graff, 1992. See also Arnove and Graff, 1987.

6

National Literacy Campaigns and Movements: Historical and Comparative Perspectives

Introduction to the Transaction edition
co-authored with Robert F. Arnove

Reflecting on the publication of the first edition of *National Literacy Campaigns: Historical and Comparative Perspectives,* we find that the lessons learned from surveying comparatively four centuries of literacy movements are as important today as two decades ago. The UNESCO Institute for Lifelong Learning announced on September 6, 2007 that "International Literacy Day provides an occasion to put the spotlight on the neglected goal of literacy which is crucial not only for achieving education for all but, more broadly, for attaining the overarching goal of reducing human poverty." Despite major international initiatives spanning over five decades to reduce illiteracy and provide basic education to all, current data indicate that more than 860 million adults lack minimal capacities to read, write, and calculate. Two-thirds of this number are women. Within regions, such as sub-Saharan Africa, over 50 percent of the population is illiterate.[1]

What Have We Learned?

In examining large-scale societal mobilizations to achieve universal levels of literacy since the Protestant Reformation, we found these enduring lessons:

- Literacy must be conceptualized in relationship to other critical factors (such as economic realities, social and political structures, and cultural patterns), not viewed in and of itself;
- Literacy efforts need to last long enough to be effective;
- Local initiative should be mobilized in conjunction with national will;
- There will be a significant minority who will oppose or not be reached by literacy efforts of centralized authorities;
- Eventually emphasis will have to be placed on schooling for youth (in order to limit future illiteracy); and
- Literacy must be viewed and understood in its various contexts.

A Focus on Campaigns and Movements

Although we focused on centrally organized literacy mobilizations by secular and religious authorities, several of our case studies looked at largely decentralized, non-school-based literacy movements in countries such as Sweden (seventeenth to nineteenth centuries) and the United States (nineteenth century). In recent years, initiatives at both the international and local levels strongly advocate the need for comprehensive, life-long education that galvanizes all agencies of a society in the long-term task of providing "critical literacy." By this, educators mean a full range of abilities to decode and encode various symbols systems that equip individuals to live fuller lives, contribute to their societies, and relate successfully to an expanding circle of communities. For many scholars as well as policy-makers, the perspective of literacy campaigns as social and political movements is very useful.

In fact, as our lessons indicate, a campaign is only the initiation of decades-long efforts to spread and reinforce literacy. Among twentieth-century campaigns, we find that the 1961 Cuban campaign was followed by the "battle for third grade," followed by battles for sixth- and ninth-grade levels of literacy skills. In China, initial estimates of the number of characters to be considered literate have increased as the evolving context required more sophisticated reading and writing skills. In Nicaragua, the 1980 campaign was followed by years of war and a struggle for national survival, leading, in 2007, to massive new literacy efforts.

Refocusing Literacy Efforts

In the North and West, as well as in the South, the task has shifted from "functional" to "critical literacy." This literacy seeks to enable people to understand and cope with the multiple forces, both local and global, that impinge on their lives.

As we noted in the first edition of *National Literacy Campaigns*, the world map of illiteracy is also the map of poverty, a fact recognized by activists within the field of literacy. If, as we also have noted, the meaning of literacy is context-based, then the evolving global economy and national development policies implemented around the world, has led, in many cases, to increasing impoverishment of billions of people. Moreover, an economic and social agenda advocated by major international financial and technical assistance agencies, such as the World Bank, the International Monetary Fund, and various binational technical assistance agencies (North American and European) has led to the decentralization and privatization of public school systems, the principal agency for reaching and teaching the youth of a country. This agenda, we believe, may seriously lessen the role of the state in committing the resources necessary to meet the challenge of achieving universal literacy.

There is a need for a complementarity of efforts between formal school systems and out-of-school programs for adults as well for the young between governmental and non-governmental organizations, between international and national and local agencies in providing an infrastructure of opportunities to acquire and practice literacy skills. Further, education sector initiatives need to be complemented by economic policies that reduce poverty and increase meaningful employment prospects. Literacy must be tied to roles that engage acquired skills.

Unfortunately, literacy initiatives following the international conference on "Education for All" held in Jomtien, Thailand, in 1990, have tended to concentrate primarily on providing universal basic schooling for children in grades one to four. Efficiency guidelines provided by international donors like the World Bank have recommended that literacy efforts be focused on adults under thirty-five years of age. For the 2000 "World Education Forum," in Dakar, Senegal, networks of educators across the globe pointed out these shortcomings concerning the conceptualization and implementation of literacy programs.[2] Their critique of most governmental literacy efforts, or lack thereof, underscores many of the issues posed by Graff in his writings on "the literacy myth."[3]

"Literacy Myths"

Too often, literacy campaigns and movements rest on what one of us has designated "the literacy myth," a powerful and enduring force, and often a misleading or disappointing one. As Graff and Duffy write, the "literacy myth" refers to the belief, articulated in educational, civic, religious, and other settings, contemporary and historical, that the acquisition of literacy is a necessary precursor to and invariably results in economic development, democratic practice, cognitive enhancement, and upward social mobility. Despite many unsuccessful attempts to measure it, literacy in this formulation has been invested with immeasurable and indeed almost ineffable qualities, purportedly conferring upon practitioners a predilection toward social order, an elevated moral sense, and a metaphorical "state of grace" As essays in this book show, such presumptions have a venerable historical lineage and have been expressed, in different forms, from antiquity through the Renaissance and Reformation, and again throughout the era of the Enlightenment, during which literacy was linked to progress, order, transformation, and control. Associated with these beliefs is the conviction that the benefits ascribed to literacy cannot be attained in other ways, nor can they be attributed to other factors, whether economic, political, cultural, or individual. Rather, literacy stands alone as the independent and critical variable.[4]

Among the myths is that illiteracy is largely a problem of developing countries of the "South," despite significant pockets of adults unable to read and write in Europe and North America. Equally deceptive is the fact that literacy is defined and measured with regard to a population's ability to read and write in colonial languages; this is particularly the case with regard to Africa. The persistence of colonial languages in the upper levels of African school systems fails to take into account lingua franca, such as Kiswahili, that enable individuals to interact effectively with another and communicate across national borders.[5] The emphasis on English as a universal language leads to its use as the medium of instruction in higher education to the detriment even of well-established national languages.

A Call to Action

A more realistic and holistic view of literacy builds upon the knowledge, skills, and experiences of individuals within their specific circumstances. It takes into account basic learning needs and emphasizes learning, not only top-down instruction.[6] It appreciates the power of national campaigns but also their limits. A humanistic and democratic appreciation of literacy inextricably involves enabling people to not only understand their rapidly changing contexts, but also to take action to achieve more equitable and open societies.

As Cairns has observed, literacy is fundamentally a political issue involving these questions: "What sort of society do we want? Are we seriously improving the skills and training of the poorly educated? Will we make this a priority, and commit funds and expertise in age of dwindling resources?" He goes on to note that these questions lead to others which "starkly clarify the values we put on people and their ability to realize their full potential."[7]

Similarly, at the Literacy Decade launch ceremony at the United Nations, in February, 2003, Deputy Secretary General Louise Frechette stressed "literacy remains part of the unfinished business of the twentieth century. One of the success stories of the twenty-first century must be the extension of literacy to include all humankind."[8]

Notes

1. UNESCO Institute for Lifelong Learning, "Announcement, 6 September 2007: International Literacy Day 2007: Springboard to the African Regional Conference in Support of Global Literacy," 1.
2. See, for example, EFA Global Monitoring Report, *Literacy for Life* (Paris: UNESCO. 2005); Rosa-María Torres, "Lifelong Learning: A New Momentum and a New Opportunity for Adult Basic Learning and Education (ABLE) in the South," Instituto Fronesis (Quito-Buenos Aires), available on the Internet at [www.fronesis.org]; last accessed 9/16/2007; and "Día Internacional de la Alfabetización"; Foro Latinoamericano de Políticas Educativas (FLAPE). *Info-novedades*, No. 37, September 7, 2007, available on the Internet at [www.foro-latino.org], last accessed on September 10, 2007. Also see, September 8, 2007, International Literacy Day memo to the United Nations Literacy Decade (UNLD) Section to Mr. Mark Richmond (director of the Division for the Coordination of UN Priorities in Education) and Ms. Margarete Sachs-Israel (head of the UNLD) from Members of the Latin American Group of Specialists in Literacy and Written Culture (GLEACE) and the Latin American Council for Adult Education (CREAAL), both available on the Internet respectively at [http://www.crefal.edu.mx/], and [http://www.creal.org/]; last accessed September 10, 2007.
3. Harvey J. Graff, *The Literacy Myth: Literacy and Cultural Integration in the Nineteenth-Century City* (New Brunswick: Transaction, 1991 ed.).
4. Harvey J. Graff and John Duffy, "The Literacy Myth," in *Encyclopedia of Language and Literacy*, Vol. 2 Literacy, ed. Nancy Hornberger and Brian Street (Berlin and New York: Springer 2007-, 41-52, chapter 3 in this volume.
5. Birgit Brock-Utne, *Whose Education for All?: The Recolonization of the African Mind* (Boulder, Co.: NetLibrary, Inc., 2000); and her "Education for All—In Whose Language?" *Oxford Review of Education*, 27 (March 2001): 115–134.
6. See, for example, Torres, "Lifelong Learning."
7. John C. Cairns, in "Introduction" to Audrey Thomas, "Adult Illiteracy in Canada – A Challenge," Occasional Paper 42 (Ottawa, Ontario: Canadian Commission for UNESCO, 1983), 8.
8. Frechette as quoted in "Literacy as Freedom"—United Nations Launches Literacy Decade (2003-2012) by Horst Rutsch for the *United Nations Chronicle Online Edition*. Available on the Internet at [http://www.un.org/Pubs/chronicle/2003/webArticles/022103_literacy.html]; last accessed on September 17, 2007.

7

Literacy Studies and Interdisciplinary Studies: Reflections on History and Theory[1]

One of the slights of hand of interdisciplinarity is that it deludes us into the belief that we've escaped our disciplinary boundaries. But that delusion also allows us freedom from interdisciplinary longing. Such freedom and our now more comfortable habitation in disciplinary mobility are well suited to the spatial and geographic paradigms we currently inhabit. We think of ourselves as global: rather than defy boundaries, we leap over them, less disciplined, perhaps, but also less frustrated by imaginary constraints. Worrying less about how to find something real on the other side of the interdisciplinary divide, we have more room to think about the consequences of interdisciplinary tourism, to ponder the new terms we've erected as touchstone of our common project, and to offer richer readings of those real (and sometimes hyperreal) objects of our study (Peters, 2005, p. 451).

Literacy Studies

Claims about literacies, and their lack, surround us, multiplying like metaphorical insects. Different observers see either an abundance of literacies forming foundations for flowing multimodalities, or a crisis rooted in the presumed absence or inadequacy of appropriate literacies threatening the foundations of our civilization and polity (Graff and Duffy, 2007; Graff, 1995a).[2] Reflecting more of the historical legacies of literacy and certain powerful literacy narratives than he acknowledges, Leon Lederman (2008, p. 36), director emeritus of the Fermi National Accelerator Laboratory, writes in an editorial in *Science News*, "In a world in which illiteracy is the shame of societies where it is found, science illiteracy is increasingly disastrous. And wherever it is measured, this illiteracy rate is 90 to 95 percent." "Science literacy" is only one of many examples. Yet its implicit significance and presumed trajectory need no extended argument or explanation. In itself, it constitutes a narrative, an interdisciplinarity narrative.

In this typical formulation, literacy studies embraces two more-or-less opposing positions: that of "many literacies" *and* that of dangerously low levels of literacy, their causes and their consequences. When conceptualized complexly—not the most common practice—their contradictory relationships form part of our subject of inquiry and part of the challenge for explication and explanation.[3]

The difficulties and the potentialities attendant with literacy gave rise to a field of literacy studies during the last one-third to one-quarter of the twentieth century.[4] Sociolinguist David Barton (2007, p. 23) relates, "The meaning of the word literacy is to be found not just by examining dictionary entries. It has become a unifying term across a range of disciplines for changing views of reading and writing; there has been such a growth of study in the area that is now referred to as Literacy Studies or the New Literacy Studies."[5]

Literacy studies developed as an *interdisciplinary* field of study and knowledge, the theme of this exploratory essay. Barton (2001, p. 93) further notes, "In many ways Literacy Studies grew out of a dissatisfaction with conceptions of reading and writing which were prevalent in education in all areas, from early childhood reading to adult literacy programmes: these were conceptions of reading and writing which were based on over-simplistic psychological models. The critique has been made from a range of disciplinary vantage points and in a range of ways...."[6] From "dissatisfaction" and "over-simplistic models" to criticism from multiple disciplinary "vantage points" and "ways": This is one of the principal paths to the development of areas of interdisciplinary study and interdisciplines. Exploring the strengths and weaknesses of this path to interdisciplinarity within the context of both literacy studies and interdisciplinary studies constitutes the fundamental task of this essay.

Not surprisingly, tensions between the principal disciplines and their contributions to an interdiscipline mark the dynamics of change and development. The most common and perhaps most notorious is the clash between the cognitive/psychological in psychology (and sometimes also in literature, history, linguistics, or philosophy), *and* social/contextual approaches in anthropology, sociology, linguistics, and history. These differences often parallel the conflicts between "strong" or "great divide" theories *and* practice/contextual understandings. More practically but no less important is the long struggle between departments of English and colleges of education over institutional "ownership" of literacy. These recognitions remind us that efforts at interdisciplinarity are inseparably part of the processes of disciplinary formation, maintenance, and shifts themselves, not a later or separate movement.[7]

The perspective outlined here also highlights key factors among the critical elements that contributed to the decline of an earlier consensus. That understanding–indeed, faith—was rooted in an integrative and "over-simplistic psychological" narrative that promulgated the universal unmediated and transformative, epoch-making power of writing and/or reading—literacy—(what Brian Street calls "the autonomous model" of literacy), and stimulated the search for alternatives. Brockmeier and Olson (2002, pp. 6-7) summarize evocatively,

> a theory of literacy was outlined that made strong claims for the cultural and cognitive implications of writing. It was argued that alphabetic literacy is a unique technology of representation and communication which has been of fundamental importance for the development of Western culture. According to this theory, oral language and written language are intellectual technologies which are causally responsible of two different types of culture, cultures of orality and of literacy. Some critics of the "literacy hypothesis" thus spoke of a "great-divide theory" (Finnegan). The watershed, to stick to the metaphor, between speech and writing, oral and literate culture was the invention (or, once it was invented, the introduction) of the alphabet....

According to this version of the "received wisdom," the consequences were epochal and without limits. "Patently, the domain of culture upon which literacy was expected to have its impact was exceedingly broad."

> Literacy was claimed to impinge upon the entire gamut of cultural phenomena from the intellectual to the aesthetic and political, including the production of science, philosophy, history, literature, art, and religion, as well as the institutions of education, documented law, and democratic forms of social organization. Further, literacy was seen as having an impact on the individualism of modern Western thought along with forms of mentality (rational and logical), cognition (conceptual and analytical), memory (objective and accumulative), as well as forms of communication (decontextualized and emotionally distanced) and grammar (reflective and prescriptive). Here, the vision of culture that unfolded with literacy, printing, and the alphabet, merged with the idea of civilization in general.[8]

Alternatives that arose to counter this understanding include Barton's Literacy Studies or New Literacy Studies, or Brian Street's "ideological model" of literacy, claiming authority in part by the act of naming. How often do incipient interdisciplines proclaim or identify themselves as "new"? It is no coincidence that the earlier dominance of "strong theories," "great divides," or dichotomous understandings of literacy had no need for a nominal cover like "literacy studies." Literacy was unreflectingly incorporated into the principal narratives of the rise of the West and the triumph of democracy, modernization, and progress. Indeed, literacy was equated with those qualities, each seemingly the cause of the other in confused causal order. Regardless of confusion, the qualities presumed for modern civilization and for literacy became interchangeable.[9]

No less coincidental is that the search for confirmation of grand theories of literacy and their "consequences," in Goody's and Watt's original formula, ironically did more to fuel skepticism and the search for more specific and documented contextual interpretations. (This was revised to "implications," by Goody in response to criticism.) That shift, in turn, led to new and different findings, and orientations, that contributed to bringing literacy studies explicitly to the realm of interdisciplinarity research.[10]

Interdisciplinary literacy studies thus developed from different methods and sources, and different presuppositions and expectations. As suggested by Brockmeier and Olson, "over-simplistic psychological" notions were often rooted in reductive great leaps across relatively rarified cognitive and philosophical artifacts. Radical dichotomies substituted for dynamics of social and cultural change. Generalizations without qualification were applied without hesitation to large numbers of persons. And the dynamics of literacy itself were reduced to cartoonish images of literacy versus orality and print versus manuscript.

In contrast, across the sweep of the twentieth century, empirical and critical studies in oral literature, folklore, psychology, anthropology and archaeology, linguistics, philosophy, sociology, classics, and history began to tell different and more variegated stories. They turned to more direct evidence of literacy's development, distribution, and uses via case studies, ethnographies, and histories that gave more attention to matters of practice and social context. Sources and subjects were approached and read more carefully and critically. Ironically, New Literacy Studies scholars over the past three or four decades only slowly rediscovered the truly groundbreaking work earlier in the century of oral literature researchers who climbed mountains in Eastern Europe from the 1920s to record performances, constructing "Singers of Tales," as Milman Parry and Albert Lord famously dubbed them, and comparing oral narratives (Lord, 1960, 2000; Parry, 1971). No less momentous but often neglected is the dynamic activism of the cultural-historical psychology of Lev Vygotsky, Alexander Luria, and their colleagues from the 1930s.[11] So much richer than the modernization studies of American sociologists after World War II, this work seems destined for repeated rediscovery.

That phenomenon may also be a stop on paths to interdisciplinarity, constituting a step forward accompanied by a constraining half-step backward.[12]

By and large, these approaches and their appropriation for literacy studies derived from several distinct disciplines, in particular anthropology, linguistics, and cognitive psychology. Through these origins or sources, literacy studies represents a search for a different but common or shared place amid the disciplines, and often outside the walls of colleges and departments of education and/or psychology. More implicitly, that place ideally should be outside the blinders of Western civilization. Literacy studies turned toward anthropology, linguistics, and cognitive (psychology) studies, with strong assistance from history, classics, and most recently cultural studies.

Brian Street (1993, p. 1) articulates a credo and point of origin for the New Literacy Studies:

> The field of literacy studies has expanded considerably in recent years and new, more anthropological and cross-cultural frameworks have been developed to replace those of a previous era, in which psychologistic and culturally narrow approaches predominated (as they arguably still do in much educational and developmental literature). Where, for instance, educationalists and psychologists have focused on discrete elements of reading and writing skills, anthropologists and sociolinguists concentrate on literacies—the social practices and conceptions of reading and writing. The rich cultural variation in these practices and conceptions leads us to rethink what we mean by them and to be very wary of assuming a single literacy where we may simply be imposing assumptions derived from our own cultural practice onto other people's literacies. Research in cultures that have newly acquired reading and writing draws our attention to the creative and original ways in which people transform literacy to their own cultural concerns and interests.[13]

David Barton (2007, p. 24) speaks more specifically to certain central threads of interdisciplinary literacy studies and the making of an interdiscipline of literacy studies: "A key to new views of literacy is situating reading and writing in its social context... people in different disciplines has been moving in the same direction. ... three important academic studies, the work of Sylvia Scribner and Michael Cole, Brian Street, and Shirley Brice Heath.... In their different ways they provide three threads to weave together to represent the beginnings of literacy studies and they have become classics in the field." Psychologists Scribner and Cole wrote *The Psychology of Literacy* (1981); anthropologist Street, *Literacy in Theory and Practice* (1984); and sociolinguist Heath, *Ways with Words: Language, Life and Work in Communities and Classrooms* (1983). As classics, they became powerful signposts and markers. Barton

(2007, p. 24) elaborates, "They are part of different research traditions but they actually have a great deal in common. All three academic studies looked at particular societies in detail, examining different groups within a society and how they use literacy. They start from everyday life and what people read and write. They observe closely and they are willing to make use of a wide range of evidence.... Part of what comes with these studies is a recognition of the complexity of the idea of literacy and the fact that much of our understanding of it is not obvious. This leads to new definitions of literacy." History, represented by my *The Literacy Myth: Literacy and Social Structure in the Nineteenth-Century City* (1979, 1991), is one missing link. In these charter statements, there is no room for precedents or longer-term perspectives.

Nevertheless, these are important observations. Implicit in Barton's words are both the possibilities and the complications for literacy studies' turn (necessarily incompletely) toward interdisciplinary studies. The impact of both similarities and differences in "research traditions" demands more attention, especially with respect to the institutions and traditions of disciplinarity and changing sociocultural currents regarding literacy and its imperatives. However ironic, literacy studies lacks a memory and a sense of its own history or genealogy. Neither Barton nor Street casts their gaze much before the recent past, not even to the middle decades of the twentieth century, let alone earlier. Neither Street nor Barton is much concerned with the institutional, intellectual, or cultural context of either older or more recent literacy studies. Interdisciplinary studies of literacy would benefit from knowledge of, at least, the history of specific fields, disciplines, and interdisciplines.[14]

Regardless, literacy studies simultaneously seeks to distinguish and differentiate itself in an effort to integrate, synthesize within clearer limits, and re-bound major components of the "new" field. Along with other interdisciplines, literacy studies developed and grew both within disciplines and across them, sometimes building toward interdisciplinarity, sometimes developing separately.[15] Both efforts influenced interdisciplinary movements, together constituting contradictory influences on the field's integration and differentiation. This mode of inter/disciplinary development can risk a linear, progressive, or almost teleological epistemology and explanation for the rise and effects of literacy itself as well as interdisciplinary literacy studies. For example, the more one looks, the more literacy, or literacy practices, one finds, often in complex cultural and communicative contexts. This may be accompanied by a tendency to see "more" literacy leading to more and greater effects, in part by blurring distinctions between individual, collective, and societal impacts, shifting ideologies, causes and effects, and expectations. Developments within several disciplines at once only exacerbate these complications.[16]

Theories of modernity and post-modernity create anticipations of soaring needs for literacy/literacies that sometimes exceed those that can be estimated or measured empirically, or attained popularly. At times the opposite—the limits of literacy—seems at least as compelling. Modernization models do this in part by projecting incomplete or erroneous narratives (and images) of the past on to the future.[17] Ironically, constructing a separate, recognized field of literacy studies runs the risk of reifying Street's "autonomous model" of transformative unmediated literacy. Yet when literacy studies initially sought confirmation of "strong theories" and "great divides," more was learned about the specific contexts of literacy's uses and influences. There is also a danger of exaggerating the import of a new field of study striving for and promoting its case for recognition and institutional place. This, too, is a common component of paths to interdisciplinarity.

Interdisciplinary Studies

My approach to, and strong presumptions about, the social history of interdisciplinarity in my current research project, *Undisciplining Knowledge: Pursuing the Dream of Interdisciplinarity,* contrasts with most writing in this area. It begins with the argument that interdisciplinarity is a central part of the historical process of the making and ongoing reshaping of modern disciplines since at least the mid- to late nineteenth century. Contrary to many notions, interdisciplinarity is inseparable from the disciplines, neither a rejection nor opposition or circumvention, neither an end run nor an end-point or end-game. Nor is it primarily a post-World War II or more recent development as implied by Barton, Street, or many others. *Undisciplining Knowledge* seeks to demonstrate historically that the organization, structures, production, and dissemination of knowledge around universities, disciplinary departments, and research institutes, especially in the United States and the modern West more generally, give rise to interdisciplinary efforts and movements across the expanse of fields over time. Interdisciplinarity is a (historical) construct that varies by field and also by time, place, relationships, and circumstances. As educational and research institutions have changed over time and space, so too have interdisciplines and disciplines in various ways that demand to be charted comparatively.

Literacy studies' relatively recent rise and race for recognition is a case in point. But so too are the important historical developments that are often obscured. Among the many contributions from recent studies in the history of literacy are important lessons for the present and future (Graff, 1995a, 1995b).

Although their presentation requires a lengthy critical discussion, even a short listing of the variety of major explanations/descriptions found in the literature, ascribed for the construction of interdisciplines, suggests the breadth, depth, and complicated, contradictory nature of the process, structures, dynamics, and narratives. They include evolutionary progressive, functional, structure and process, market-driven, specialization, novelty, fission or fusion, collective movement, boundary-making and maintaining, conflict, internalist and externalist among other models or approaches. They are suggestive, but none is particularly historical or comparative.

Literacy studies, and interdisciplinary studies, can be better understood with more attention to a longer chronological span of intellectual and sociocultural development and a broader, more dynamic focus on its place and play among a wide array of disciplines and institutional locations (subfields in disciplines or interdisciplines that deal with literacy include reading, writing, child-and human development, cognitive studies, comparative and development studies, communication or media studies). "External" factors and developments—social, cultural, political, economic—that is, external to the normal workings of a discipline or field, such as war-time needs, consequences of global cross-cultural contacts and colonialism, "discovery" of new social problems—combine, often contradictorily, with shifting currents within and across disciplines. They may then stimulate changing views that, in the context of universities and their organization of knowledge, lead to criticism, different assertions, and sometimes institutional articulations both within and outside the "boundaries" of departments or divisions that take the name of interdisciplinarity.[18]

A more complete and useful approach to literacy studies, one that also deepens our understanding of interdisciplinarity, begins no later than the 1920-1930s (as above). It looks back carefully to the period spanning the mid-eighteenth century through the early twentieth century. Ideally, it embraces a longer (if briefer) glance back to the Renaissance and also classical antiquity. There it locates in historical context the dynamic building blocks for our expectations, understandings (including theories and policies), and institutions that culminate in modern literacy(ies) and their travails, and literacy studies.

Modern arrangements and judgments grew from the foundational (if sometimes contradictory) currents of Enlightenment emphases on human malleability, perfectionism, learning capabilities, environmentalism, and institutionalism. They were partly reinterpreted by Romanticism's deeply divided recognition of the power and significance of the "other," the alien or primitive within ourselves and in "strangers," both within the modernizing West and in "newly discovered" regions. Questions about language and order lay at the core of both. The beginnings and foundations of literacy studies also lay in "civilization's" confronting many "Wild Child[ren]" (*enfants savage*), noble or savage; South Sea islanders who confronted explorers; missionaries (whose work in creating alphabets and written languages initially to "translate" the Bible in aid of their proselytizing is fundamentally a part of literacy studies and linguistics); colonizers and colonists. They all deployed early (and later) modern notions of Western literacy and its expected influences in their efforts at expansion, "conquest," and domesticating and elevating the primitive and different.

Charles Dickens and Henry Mayhew taught that the "other" was also close at home especially in the swelling cities of the "modernizing West," sharing the difference, deviance, and deficiency of those much further away. Those nearby could be more threatening than those farther afield. In anthropology and the arts, the primitive and the oral were grounds for celebration at times, compromising wholly positive associations of literacy and negative associations of illiteracy. Strong currents from the Enlightenment and Romanticism intertwined, sometimes contradicting but sometimes supporting expectations about progress and modern development.[19]

From earlier eras, including the Renaissance and classical antiquity, came haltingly at first the conviction that writing, and reading it, were, at least in some circumstances, superior to other means of communication, especially the oral. On one hand, this was a functional development, but, on the other hand, personal and eventually collective cognitive change might follow, some persons of influence thought. So commenced *early* literacy studies. The first general uses derived from the needs of religion, government, and commerce. That was followed slowly by a faith in the powers of formal instruction in places called schools, initially first for the relatively few, primarily boys. Some agendas stressed socialization for citizenship and its correlates; others emphasized literacy as useful or necessary practices or abilities. Over time, places for instruction expanded to include many more and to focus especially on the young. In these formulations, literacy stood at the center of training that embraced social attitudes and control, and civic morality, along with at least rudimentary intellectual practice, and training in skills for productive contributions to economy, polity, and society. The tools began with simplified alphabets that helped to link signs and sounds to words and sentences, and expanded to include paper, pens, and various means of reproducing and circulating texts that were first handwritten and later printed. The superiority of technology and the inferiority of the "unlettered" stood as certainties, framing constructions of literacy. Literacy's story, right or wrong, came to occupy the center (though often implicitly) of the rise of civilization and progress in the West.

These elements became inseparable as they joined capitalism's relentless efforts to remake the world—and the word, written or printed—in the image of the marketplace and its institutions (with other images), and to remake the young, in particular, for the strange new world. They mark, and also serve as representations of literacy in the traditions that emerged to study and understand literacy from the Renaissance (or earlier) forward. Not surprisingly, the development and institutionalization of disciplines in the nineteenth- and twentieth-century Western university incorporated the understandings of literacy to which they were the heirs, especially but not only in the social sciences—anthropology, linguistics, psychology—and the humanities—classics, history, literature, philosophy, politics. Early relationships resist efforts at change. The resulting disciplinary fragmentation, as discussed in this essay, not only contributes to efforts to build interdisciplinary literacy studies, but also limits them. They also underwrote the many contradictions—what I call "the literacy myth," for one—in the place of literacy in Western cultures, and the lives of many persons yesterday and today.

Interdisciplinary possibilities and limits on opportunities stem from the interplay within and across what I call "disciplinary clusters." (The humanities, arts, social sciences, and basic sciences constitute major disciplinary clusters.) No less important is the sometimes very dynamic interplay—critical and complementary—between disciplines. Of this, the key disciplines of anthropology, linguistics, and psychology provide powerful examples. Among them, orality and oral literature, everyday and privileged writing practices, the ubiquity of "reading" across multiple media, and the search for cognitive and noncognitive "implications" of literacy are telling. So, too, is literacy's active presence as values, ideology, and both cultural and political capital. Destabilizing times can become opportunities to advance or to fall from favor for disciplinary approaches, and moments for interdisciplinary movements.[20]

For literacy studies across the last two centuries at least, one of the most powerful forces has been the fear, and often the certainty, that literacy is declining (or not rising), and with it, families, morality, social order, progress, and socioeconomic development are also declining. This accompanied one of the most momentous transformations in the history of literacy and its study: from a "premodern" order in which literacy was feared and (partly) restricted, to a more modern order in which illiteracy (or literacy gained outside of formal institutional controls) is feared. When taken comparatively, and further heightened by international conflict or competition (most famously perhaps in France's defeat by Prussia in the 1870 Franco-Prussian War), social disorder and division, international migration of "aliens," declining fertility and rising mortality, failure for "human capital" to grow, and similar circumstances, literacy levels become flashpoints for study and action to reverse the dreaded tide. Schools and popular culture attract attention which has in turn the potential to propel disciplinary action and conflict, and, sometimes, interdisciplinary efforts. The apparently endless "crisis" of literacy in the mid- to late-twentieth century is inseparable from Cold War anxieties, global economic restructuring and collateral social and cultural change, communicative and media transformation, and both new and persisting inequalities. Seemingly unprecedented "social problems" become calls for and stimulants of interdisciplinary "solutions." Literacy's role as either or both cause or consequence is very tricky to unravel, a complication in literacy studies' development.

For literacy studies, these complications often impinge on one or another of the "great divides" prominent among approaches that see literacy—almost by its very "nature"—as universal, unmediated, and transformative in its impact. Often cited are reading or writing as "technology of the intellect," the power of the Greek alphabet, the impact of print, cognitive shifts from writing or reading, and the like. Constructing this tradition of study and understanding was relatively uncomplicated.[21] In recent decades, however, others have emphasized increasingly the sociocultural influences and contextual effects from literacy. Among the elements stressed are psychological theories, schools and other environments; families and communities, cultures of practice, practice and use of reading and writing.

In the second half of the twentieth century, in conjunction with other disciplines and interdisciplines, literacy studies has taken social, contextual, cognitive, linguistic, and historical, among other "turns." With the turns came the adoption of signifying French theorist "godfathers" from Levi-Bruhl and Levi-Strauss to Pierre Bourdieu and Bruno Latour. These developments at times interact with and deepen conflicts among disciplines and promote interest in interdisciplinary resolution.[22]

Literacy studies' paths are revealing. Recent years witness an emphasis on the everyday and the practical, including the concept of practice itself. This led to an effort at overturning the dominance of grand theories that stressed the universal importance of the written over the oral, the printed over the written, the literate over the unlettered and untutored. Practice and context, explored in a variety of contexts and traditions, replaced presumptions of the unmediated powers and advantages of literacy. In part, literacy studies' emerging interdisciplinarity stemmed from perceptions of the inadequacy of earlier conceptualizations and presumptions, the search for new methods and sources on which to base a major revision, and reactions to it.

Successful construction of recognized interdisciplines is *not* the most common consequence of developments and changes in the disciplinary process. Although success or failure can be hard to determine, literacy studies is no exception. Some observers refuse the interdisciplinary mantle to literacy studies because of a general absence of Departments of Literacy Studies, despite many centers and programs.[23] Adding to the complexity and grounds for confusion is the fact, on the one hand, that interdisciplinarity can be strikingly different, say, in the sciences or technology fields than in the humanities or social sciences.[24] On the other hand, disciplines and interdisciplines are not synonymous forms of organization or production. They differ considerably from each other, both within and across disciplinary clusters, from history to physics or the arts. Consequently, while most programs and the occasional department of literacy studies are often in colleges of education, there are also programs, concentrations, or definite interests in the social sciences and humanities, with either or both institutional location or intellectual foundation. A few programs reach for the mantle of science.[25] In other words, understanding literacy studies calls for a critical perspective derived from interdisciplinary studies along with a comparative and historical view. At the same time, literacy studies provides a valuable case study that tests our understanding of interdisciplinarity.

Claims and conflicts about interdisciplinarity are almost as frequent and strong as those about literacy(ies). In a mix of recurring and current issues, intellectual and professional issues associated with the organization and production of knowledge prompt periodic debates over the promises and perils, including the faddishness and, of course, the definitions of interdisciplinarity. The spectrum is wide but not straight. It embodies both light and darkness.[26] For example, Guy Michaud (1972) asserts, interdisciplinarity "is a way of life. It is basically a mental outlook which combines curiosity with open-mindedness and a spirit of adventure and discovery," while Georges Gusdorf (1977, p. 580) declares, "The appeal to interdisciplinarity is seen as a kind of epistemological panacea, designed to cure all the ills the scientific consciousness of our age is heir to ... [although] even those who advocate this new image of knowledge would find it hard to define." On the other hand, Marc De Mey (1982, p. 140) states, "Interdisciplinarity is an ambivalent term in science.... For practical problems it is considered valid and unavoidable but for theoretical purposes in science, interdisciplinarity is handled with great caution and even with suspicion." Others see an affinity between the sciences and interdisciplinarity (Weingart and Stehr, 2000).

Neil Smelser (2004, p. 52) writes more expansively:

> My own sense is that this positive aura—which has a staying power even though the positive consequences of interdisciplinary activity remain unknown—retains its appeal on account of its connection with quasireligious and quasicommunal imagery. Interdisciplinarity is powerful because it promises to be an antidote to the disenchantment with specialization and fragmentation of knowledge, and because it evokes an unspoken but persistent romance with the idea of the unity of knowledge.... Interdisciplinary thus bears some of the marks of a utopian ideology and social movement.

Smelser continues, "On closer examination, moreover, interdisciplinarity reveals a darker, more negative side. We smile on it in principle and frown on it in practice. Our reward system discourages it."

Then, there is the evangelical chapel of transdisciplinarity. The First World Congress of Transdisciplinarity (Portugal, 1994) adopted a charter with fifteen articles "which comprises the fundamental principles of the community of transdisciplinary researchers, and constitutes a personal moral commitment, without any legal or institutional constraint." The charter (1998) enunciated a "transdisciplinary vision."

Claiming a high middle (if slightly evasive) ground, Marianna De Marco Torgovnick (1996, p. 282) avers, "Interdisciplinarity has no promises to keep and none to break. It is not a mantra or a magic potion. Work that cuts across areas of study is as good or as bad as the individual books and articles that do it. Certainly, working across disciplines is not the only or even always the best way to do scholarly work." Whereas some see it as the easy way out of hard problems, English and sometimes law professor Stanley Fish (1989) famously declared "Being Interdisciplinary Is So Very Hard to Do."[27] Across the steep discursive mountains and deep canyons between disciplines and interdisciplines, there is room to play, including the spaces occupied by literacy studies. That is another part of the paths to and from interdisciplinarity.

That literacy studies and interdisciplinary studies have a number of attributes in common raises important questions about these distinctive fields and their relationships. Both stimulate strong sentiments of allegiance and dissent. Both are linked inextricably with disciplinary "boundary issues."[28] Arguments for and against interdisciplinary programs mirror the sometimes utopian or otherwise extraordinary dreams that interdisciplinarity represents to many inside and outside the academy, but to others the dystopian nightmares. Paralleling claims about the powers of literacy and imperatives of literacy studies, they are long on repetition of strong claims, or their denial. They are short on focus, key distinctions and qualifications, and historical, temporal, and institutional context. Despite significant and sometimes urgent questions and issues, and an identifiable body of writing (often either polemical or technical), interdisciplinarity is poorly grasped and often misunderstood. So too is literacy studies. What at first appear to be substantial literatures, on closer inspection reveal themselves riven by a distorting, disorienting, and exaggerating positive *or* negative discourse about multi-, pluri-, inter-, and transdisciplinarity, even anti- or adisciplinarity.[29]

Magnifying and denying myths mark both interdisciplinary studies and literacy studies.[30] Conceptual, evidentiary, and interpretive contradictions complicate efforts to understand them. Most views are also truncated chronologically to a constricting association with the post-World War II era, often later for literacy studies, the 1970s-80s, which is too late.

Barton's and Street's emphasis on "over-simplistic psychological models" shifts attention away from the *re*discovery of frequent illiteracy among soldiers in the West, and its powerful relationship to social class, race, and geography in the United States, and elsewhere. It also distracts from observing how the understanding and promotion of literacy for development became a weapon in the Cold War between the Western and Eastern blocs, regarding the foundations of democracy, international competition, and both the theories and data to support the presumed relationships.

At issue was the reconstruction of postwar Germany, Japan, and the Soviet Union as more (or less) democratic, and the roles that education and print—textbooks and beyond—should play. The future of democracy in the West itself was also at stake, threatened by "the authoritarian personality" and more. No less important was the future of the lesser-developed, or under-developing nations, as they were represented. Political ideology and attitudes mattered, and literacy and schooling commanded attention as vehicles. The search for modern personality types helped to shift ostensible attention away from the Western and especially the American need for markets and materials, inseparable from political allegiance. Modernization theory became the banner for Western democracies in their struggles with communism. Consequently, they strived to export plans for literacy *and* attitudes—including school systems and print materials—along with other goods and services. Studies like Daniel Lerner's (1965) *The Passing of Traditional Society* or the more statistically oriented *Becoming Modern* by Inkeles and Smith (1974) used literacy among their key variables. Their measures were weak; findings and arguments were often unpersuasive. They also confused attitudes with skills, much as they did with their concepts of development, including political development. Literacy studies was socially relevant and worth a struggle, as literacy took its place in a privileged list along with democracy, communications, economic productivity, cultural development, social mobility, and social order and stability, in sometimes contradictory connections. For literacy studies, these relationships were not new; nor were perceptions that literacy was at issue in threats to civilization in the West. Although a boost to literacy studies, interdisciplinary literacy studies lacked, and still need a historical foundation.

For interdisciplinary studies in general, the biological or physical sciences *or* the behavioral sciences or cognitive science stand on top, slighting the humanities, historical and social sciences, and many professional programs.[31] For literacy studies, emphasis and a struggle for dominance come from anthropology, psychology, and linguistics, amid confusion over the proper disciplinary (or interdisciplinary) place for the critical (re)consideration of reading and writing to occupy. The search for understanding and applications to the contemporary literacy scene within the domain of Education has mixed results and raises other issues regarding location and disciplinary status or power.

The lines between disciplines and across them are less clear than we are trained to expect. Perceived overlap leads to competition as well as collaboration. There are linguists, for example, in anthropology, psychology, English, and education departments. English has long claimed (if somewhat incompletely and inconsistently) a special relationship with reading and writing via tutelage and practice, but more formally through subdisciplines like Rhetoric and Composition. During the last 5-10 years, RC programs, as they are called, began to rename and sometimes reframe themselves as RCL—"L" for literacy. This act represented what I call "the lure of literacy" for currency and relevance, and enrollments and funding. English and literature departments are also (at least sometimes) home to other elements of interdisciplinary literacy studies, including oral literature, folklore, popular culture, graphic literature, film, linguistics, as well as variations along the lines of writing and reading. Seldom do they work closely together or build interdisciplinarity within their space.

At The Ohio State University, since 2004, my own work focuses on constructing what I call the LiteracyStudies@OSU initiative, an experiment in campus-wide interdisciplinary program development in theory and practice.[32] (See figures in chapter 8.) The program's multi-level and multi-centered hallmarks are historical, comparative, and critical. These building blocks integrate a series of public programs, faculty and graduate student seminars in literacy and the history of the book, a Graduate Interdisciplinary Specialization or minor open to all graduate students, and other student, faculty, and staff activities. Our cross-university breadth with primarily horizontal connections is unprecedented and path-breaking. Faculty, staff, and students across OSU's 18 colleges (with more than 90 graduate programs) have participated in one or more programs. Informal and formal linkages dot the huge campus. Worthy of attention in its own right, both the successes and the constraints on interdisciplinary development are provocative. (See figures in chapter 8 for LS@OSU program.)[33]

Literacy Studies and Interdisciplinary Studies

Interdisciplinary literacy studies continues to struggle with foundational dichotomies—the making of myths—between oral and literate, writing and print, print and electronic, and literacy as transformative—that continue to guide and divide opinion and orient studies. Consequently, the longstanding neglect of rich research on orality and oral literature is almost as much a mark of the limits of many interdisciplinary endeavors as of the power of disciplines. The proponents of the New Literacy

Studies have not reclaimed Lord or Parry or Vygotsky. The persistence and importance of orality is regularly rediscovered across disciplines. The heterogeneity of constructions of the cognitive domain also plagues literacy studies, another instructive matter of connections.

More generally, we confront the antimonies of interdisciplinary studies. They are mirrored in literacy studies. To begin, there is the swamp of confusing, conflicting, contradictory definitions. They come in many versions, including disciplinary, multidisciplinary, pluridisciplinary, interdisciplinary, and transdisciplinary; indiscriminate interdisciplinarity (hodge-podge, cafeteria-style), pseudo-interdisciplinarity, auxiliary inter-disciplinarity, composite interdisciplinarity, supplementary interdiscipli-narity, and unifying interdisciplinarity. *Or* nondisciplinary, adisciplinary, antidisciplinary. metadisciplinary. supra-interdisciplinary, omnidisciplinary, trans-specialization, and post-disciplinary. Leaving aside the transcendent disciplinarities (that is, those *beyond inter*disciplinarity), the distinctions between interdisciplinary and non- or adisciplinary blur disturbingly. The unceasing proliferation of hyphenated-disciplinaries is silly, even funny, but its negative impacts do not stop there. To too many persons, the number of disciplines somehow brought together is the magic potion, rather than such alternatives as the nature of the inquiry, the elements of disciplines brought together, or the questions asked.[34](See Figure 7.1.)

For many interested people, interdisciplinarity represents synthetic and integrative general education (sometimes called IDS) in major clus-ters of the curriculum or the search for unification across broad realms of knowledge, This is especially but not only the case for those who claim the mantle of science as a foundation for interdisciplinarity (to a lesser extent in philosophy or literature) (Klein, 1990, 1996, 2005). At the same time, interdisciplinarity to other observers and practitioners is basic and foundational, while to yet others it is specialized and advanced (sometimes termed IDR). For the first group, instruction in general educa-tion takes a higher priority; to the second, sophisticated research and the difficult interpretation of its results rules. Literacy studies at times seems to aspire to the former. One traditional narrative of (Western) civiliza-tion is logos centric, with literacy as engine of modernizing changes. But literacy's study and understanding tends to contribute more to the latter, however ironically or contradictorily. This is the advanced track, more closely aligned to specialization or fragmentation of knowledge, not general education or unification. Claims of interdisciplinary syn-thesis or integration are often asserted; yet they need to be read within specialized research areas.

Figure 7.1
Types of Interdisciplinarity: 57 Varieties Or ?:
Terms of Endearment, or Not? and Explaining Interdisciplinarity

UNESCO 1972
Discipline
Multidisciplinary
Pluridisciplinary
Interdisciplinary
Transdisciplinary
Source: Centre for Educational Research and Innovation (CERI), *Interdisciplinarity: Problems of Teaching and Research in Universities*, report based the results of a Seminar on Interdisciplinarity in Universities, organized by CERI in Collaboration with the French Ministry of Education at the University of Nice, Sept 7-12, 1970 (1972).

Heckhausen
Disciplinarity
Interdisciplinarity
            Indiscriminate interdisciplinarity
                        Hodge-podge, cafeteria-style
            Pseudo-interdisciplinarity
            Auxiliary interdisciplinarity
            Composite interdisciplinarity
            Supplementary interdisciplinarity
            Unifying interdisciplinarity
Source: Heinz Heckhausen, "Discipline and Interdisciplinarity," in CERI, *Interdisciplinarity: Problems of Teaching and Research in Universities*. Paris (Organisation for Economic Co-Operation and Development, 1972), 83-89.

UNESCO 1998
Transdisciplinarity
Charter of Transdisciplinarity
Source: UNESCO, Division of Philosophy and Ethics, *Transdisciplinarity: "Stimulating Synergies, Integrating Knowledge,"* 1998.

Boden, six types of interdisciplinarity
            Encyclopaedic
            Contextualizing
            Shared
            Co-operative
            Generalising
            Integrated
Source: Margaret A. Boden, "The Character of Interdisciplinarity," in Richard Cunningham, ed., *Interdisciplinarity and the Organisation of Knowledge in Europe.* Luxembourg: Office for Official Publications of the European Communities, 1999, 13-24.

Raymond Miller, approaches to interdisciplinarity
Multi-disciplinary
Cross-disciplinary

Figure 7.1 (cont.)

Trans-disciplinary
Source: Raymond C. Miller, "Varieties of Interdisciplinary Approaches in the Social
Sciences: A 1981 Overview," *Issues in Integrative Studies*, 1 (1982), 1-37.

Louis Menand
Disciplinary
Interdisciplinary
Postdisciplinary
Antidisciplinary
Source: Louis Menand, *The Marketplace of Ideas.* ACLS Occasional Paper, no. 49, 2001.

Others.....
Cross-disciplinary
Linear interdisciplinarity
Method interdisciplinarity
Restrictive interdisciplinarity
Problem interdisciplinarity
Border interdisciplinarity
                Interdisciplinarity of neighboring disciplines
Structural interdisciplinarity

Nondisciplinary
Adisciplinary
Antidisciplinary
Metadisciplinary
Supra-interdisciplinary
Omnidisciplinary
Trans-specialization
Post-disciplinary

Integration
Integrative
Unification

Specialization
Basic, general, foundational
Specialized
Complex
Complexity
Hybridity
Transdisciplinarity
Critical interdisciplinarity
Integrative interdisciplinarity
Disciplined interdisciplinarity
Multi-modality

Striving for recognition, literacy studies occupies ambiguous ground both disciplinarily and interdisciplinarily. In part, this is a question of location. But it is also a question of status. The "rise" of literacy studies, part of its generally successful emergence and development (within limits), contributes to its presence in many academic departments and disciplines. This holds for education, the social sciences, and the humanities, but usually to a lesser extent also in the sciences, medicine, public health, the law, and business.[35] This pattern is problematic in some critical respects. In the pantheon of disciplines, centers of interest in literacy studies do not usually rank highly.[36] That literacy, for good reasons, is often seen as basic or elementary does not boost its standing. By reputation, it is often viewed as inseparable from Education.

Mainly in Education has literacy studies achieved institutionalization as an interdisciplinary unit, in the form of departments, degree programs, or areas of concentration often under the name/rubric of "Literacy, Language, and Culture," sometimes complemented with a research, outreach, or service center.[37] Both "literacy" and "interdisciplinary" at times become promotional labels: new, relevant, sexy—in academic terms—and appealing for applied and practical reasons to citizens, governments, corporations. Perceptions of crises or at least serious problems with popular literacy abilities add to this mix. Such promotion, which is less problematic in professional schools, aims to benefit programs and their home departments, colleges, or universities. It also can provoke negative reactions from more traditional faculty in the arts and sciences. A sometimes unstable mix of sexiness, practicality, and applied "science" paves certain paths to interdisciplinarity, with ambivalent (or negative) responses by others within universities.

Of course, literacy studies is often an active presence in departments that are home to the disciplines that are most often identified as predominant contributors to the New Literacy Studies or literacy studies more generally. These are the social sciences of anthropology, linguistics, and psychology. At one time or another, each of these disciplines has claimed the status of a science, applied if not always "pure" or "basic." Psychology, followed by linguistics, exhibits the greatest ambitions, with strong interests in reading, writing, development, and cognition. All three stress contemporary and sometimes comparative relevance, usually reserving the strongest claims for the perspectives, methods, and theories of their own discipline, even when also proclaiming their interdisciplinarity. Practitioners in these fields often occupy central places in interdisciplinary literacy centers, programs, or concentrations in Education.

That interdisciplinarity is often deemed best-suited to "solving problems" that fall outside the domain, traditions, or intellectual resources of any given discipline is commendable to some but damning to others. This is no less true for literacy studies with its strong affinities to the practical and applied. While the interdiscipline has serious interests in theory and knowledge generation about the uses and influences of literacy, social and geographic variation, or multiple literacies, practice, problem, and applied studies are very common. Barton (2001, p. 93) observes, "Within education, Literacy Studies sometimes supports particular pedagogical practices...."

In *Chaos of Disciplines* (2001, p. 134), sociologist Andrew Abbott argues that "interdisciplinarism has generally been problem driven, and problems ... have their own life cycle. There is ample evidence that problem-oriented empirical work does not create enduring, self-reproducing communities like disciplines, except in areas with stable and strongly institutionalized external clienteles like criminology." Abbott points toward one perspective on paths toward interdisciplinarity for literacy studies. Perhaps only with respect to Education does literacy studies have a "strongly institutionalized external clientele...." Perhaps others remain to be developed. The field of play is potentially broad. On the one hand, if Abbott is correct, there *are* opportunities for literacy studies to develop as interdisciplinary, within limits. This would build upon its dimensions that are "problem driven." They in turn may include larger questions of theory, comparison, connections, and even history, in addition to matters of contemporary relevance or application. On the other hand, such interdisciplines are likely to be shorter-lived, not "enduring, self-reproducing communities." That might be a very useful, potentially liberating path.

Likening interdisciplines to disciplines, and to each other, in search of similarities, our common, even reflexive practice, may mislead more than clarify. Interdisciplinary developments follow different paths toward a variety of institutional, intellectual, and societal ends, different timelines and lifetimes. They may prove influential without attaining the niche and continuity of disciplines. That is one of their strengths whose understanding may carry benefits. If this is, in fact, the case, it may carry powerful implications for literacy studies and for interdisciplinary studies.[38]

Notes

1. My own *definition of literacy* emphasizes literacy as the ability to read—make and take meaning—and the ability to write—express understanding and make other

communications—and their metaphors and analogies across distinct media and modes of communication.

For me, *interdisciplinarity is defined* by questions and problems and the means developed to answer them in new and different ways that are constructed or built on or from elements from different disciplines. This might involve approaches, methods, theories, orientations, comparisons, understandings, or interpretations. I emphasize the former—questions and problems, not the disciplines.... Or to put it another way, interdisciplinary defined or realized comes from fashioning interdisciplinarity via method, theory, conceptualization to form a new and distinct approach or understanding derived from or based on aspects of different disciplines. This will differ by discipline and disciplinary clusters. Interdisciplinarity is not a matter of the number of disciplines. Therefore, there is no need to "master" two or more disciplines, as more than a few pundits have asserted.

2. The subject of this essay, it should be clear, is literacy studies, not literacy itself. Although they are inseparable, they are not the same.

3. See the literature on New Literacy Studies including Bartlett, 2003; Barton, 2001, 2007; Collins and Blot, 2003; Gee, 2007; Lankshear, 1999; Stephens, 2000; Street, 1984, 1993, 1998; Street and Besnier, 2004; also Graff, 1995a, 1995b.

4. Scott Frickel (2004, p. 269): "Interdisciplines are hybridized knowledge fields situated between and within existing disciplines (Klein 1996). Like disciplines, interdisciplines are sites of institutional conflict. Their formation involves disputes over access to organizational, technical, financial, and symbolic resources, and their stabilization reflects a reordering of theoretical loyalties, epistemic assumptions, research practices, standards of evidence, and professional credibility and identity. But unlike disciplines, whose "maturity," coherence, or status within the broader academic field is often judged in terms of the strength or hardness of professional boundaries, interdisciplines maintain themselves through interactions with other fields and thus require boundaries that are *intentionally permeable....*"

5. Barton (2007) himself examines dictionary definitions of literacy. See also Barton, 2001; Brockmeier, Wang, and Olson, 2002; Collins and Blot, 2003; Olson, 1988, 1994; Street, 1984, 1993, 1998.

6. Compare with Street; 1984; Collins and Blot, 2003; see also Graff, 1995a, 1995b; Olson, 1988, 1994; Lankshear, 1999.

7. This occurs in a variety of forms and locations. In general, see Klein, 1990, 1996. 2005; Davidoff; et al, 1993. For literacy studies, compare the work cited below of Goody and Olson with Street, Graff, and Barton.

8. See also Goody, 1968, 1979, 1986, 1987; Goody and Watt, 1968; Havelock, 1976a, 1976b, 1982; Brockmeier et al, 2002;Greenfield, 1972; McLuhan, 1962;Olson, 1988, 1994; Ong, 1982; Tannen, 1981; Cole, 1996; Scribner and Cole, 1981; Halverson, 1991, 1992; Heath, 1983; Lord, 1960, 2000; Parry, 1971.

9. See Goody and Havelock in References; compare with Harris, 1989; Clanchy, 1979, 1993. See now Clark, 2007. Post –World War II studies include Lerner, 1965; Inkeles and Smith, 1974. See also Olson, 1994.

10. See Goody and Watt in Goody, 1968, pp. 27-68. That article was first published in 1963. Goody's Introduction to this volume was entitled purposefully imprecisely "The Implications of Literacy." For tensions in the field, see Goody, 1968; Halverson, 1991, 1992; New Literacy Studies in general; Graff, 1979, 1987, 1995a, 1995b.

11. See Cole, 1996; Wertsch, 1985. Steve Witte also worked for their rediscovery.

12. Lerner, 1965; Inkeles and Smith, 1974. Among others, see Scribner and Cole, 1981; Heath, 1983; Street, 1984. See also McLuhan, 1962; Ong, 1982.

13. See Street and his critics, Bartlett, 2003; Brandt and Clinton, 2002; Collins and Blot, 2003; Collins, 1995; Maddox, 2007; Reder and Davila, 2005; Stephens, 2000.

Neither Barton nor Street employs historical perspective on the relevant fields; their focus can be very narrow—a sign of striving for distinction as interdisciplinary. At times, they seem to presume the dominance of linguistics or anthropology that is implied.

14. See for example ENG 750 Introduction to Graduate Studies in Literacy syllabus. This is a required core source in the Graduate Interdisciplinary Specialization at Ohio State University. For studies of disciplines, see Klein and Davidow, cited above; Abbott, 2001; Allen, 1975; Cole, 1996; Dogan and Pahre, 1990; Frank, 1988; Frickel, 2004; Kaestle et al, 1991; Lankshear, 1999; Timothy Lenoir, 1997; Peters, 2005; Smelser, 2004; Smith, 2006; Weingart and Stehr, 2000.

15. See Graff, 1995b. There are excellent examples in history, economics, education, and rhetoric and composition.

16. See for example Clanchy, 1979, 1993; Heath, 1983; Barton et al, 2007; Barton and Hamilton, 1998.

17. See Pattison, 1982; also Graff, 1979, 1991, and some of the responses to it.

18. Not discussed here but important are issues of interdisciplinary activity and establishment *before* interdisciplinary is recognized and at least struggles to be institutionalized within universities. The accepted narrative of origins takes a supposedly early use of the word "interdisciplinary" at a meeting at the Social Science Research Council in New York in the late 1920s as the initiation of its arrival on the academic scene. See Frank, 1988.

    While being aware of the dangers of anachronism, we need not wait so long to look for and find recognizable interdisciplinary at play. Important examples include the fields of biology, genetics, biochemistry, and efforts, say, in sociology in the nineteenth century and the mid-twentieth. We must beware of romanticizing pre-modern university organization of knowledge as interdisciplinary or "before the fall." Nondisciplinary does not equal interdisciplinary.

19. On non-literate and preliterate, see Duffy, 2007.

20. Good examples are the field of education, and the long-standing and persisting conflicts among those who endorse reading's and writing's special affinities to cognitive development and "cultures" of reading and/or writing, as opposed to those who emphasize social context and practice. For recent efforts to go beyond a dichotomy, see Brandt and Clinton, 2002; Collins and Blot, 2003.

21. For more complications, see Brockmeier et al, 2002; Olson, 1988, 1994; Goody after the 1970s; Halverson, 1991, 1992; Kaestle et al, 1991; Graff, 1995a, 1995b; Graff and Duffy, 2007; New Literacy Studies more generally.

22. See and compare, for example, the work of Goody and Olson with Cole and Street. See also Brandt and Clinton, 2002.

23. Alternative locations for literacy studies include departments—disciplinary and interdisciplinary—centers, programs, committees, degrees, subgroups in departments or colleges, etc. Ph.D. programs include Language, Literacy and Culture at UC-Berkeley in Graduate School of Education; Language and Literacy Studies in Education at UC-Santa Cruz; Ph.D. in Literacy Studies in the Department of Literacy Studies, Education, Hofstra University; Ph.D. in Language, Literacy, and Culture, Education, University of Iowa; Ph.D., Department of Counseling, Leadership, Literacy, and Special Education, Lehman College, CUNY (with a link to disabilities); Language and Literacy Education Concentration, Rutgers Graduate School of Education; Ph.D. in Culture, Literacy, and Language, Division of Bi-cultural-Bilingual Studies, College of Education & Human Development, UT-San Antonio; Graduate Program Area of Study, Literacy Studies, Department of Curriculum and Instruction, School of Education, University of Wisconsin-Madison. In addition, graduate minor in literacy and rhetorical studies, University of Min-

nesota; Graduate Studies in Composition, Rhetoric, and Literacy Studies, MA & Ph.D., University of Oklahoma; Ph.D. in Rhetoric, Composition, and Literacy, Ohio State University; also at OSU Graduate Interdisciplinary Specialization in Literacy Studies open to all graduate students at OSU. See figures in chapter 8 for this program.

Examples in detail:

Reading/Writing/Literacy, in Language and Literacy in Education Division: University of Pennsylvania. "The RWL Program is guided by four principles. First, it is interdisciplinary because literacy, language and culture are studied from sociocultural, cultural, psychological, historical, linguistic, and literary perspectives. Second, the program is inquiry-based, intended to raise questions about the relationships among theory, research, policy and practice. Third, it focuses on diversity and on urban settings, and the contexts of different schools, communities, families and cultures. Fourth, educational institutions are sites to work for social justice, transformation and equity."

New Interdisciplinary Ph.D. in Literacy Studies, 2008, Middle Tennessee State University claims interdisciplinary breadth and basis in science. Apr 30, 2008 press release: "School psychologists, speech-language pathologists, reading teachers, classroom teachers and school administrators at all levels will be among those enrolling at MTSU's new Ph.D. in Literacy Studies degree. The program will come face to face with why the National Assessment of Education Progress consistently shows that an average of four out of 10 children fail to read at grade level by fourth grade.

"The interdisciplinary doctorate is based on the idea that narrow expertise in a single area does not equip graduates to understand the many factors that support successful literacy. The new doctorate is a first-of-its-kind partnership that has emerged from the Center for the Study and Treatment of Dyslexia at MTSU, a hands on learning lab that may be the only one of its kind in the nation. The Dyslexia Center is a unit within the School of Education and Behavioral Science where professionals with different backgrounds work together to improve educational outcomes for children with dyslexia. The doctorate has been shaped and will be governed by faculty representing several academic departments: educational leadership, elementary & special education, dyslexic studies, psychology, sociology, English (linguistics) and communication disorders."

Some are research, some are teaching; some are other practitioners.

24. In the humanities and social sciences, there is nothing like the hybridity or conjoint compounding of biochemistry and other compounds linking biology, chemistry, physics, for example, or the development of technical fields across or between science and engineering.

25. Middle Tennessee State University doctoral movement is based on shifting from dyslexia to Literacy Studies, with the claim to science both implicit and explicit.

26. For example, see Klein, 1990, 1996, 2005; Davidow et al, 1993; Weingart and Stehr, 2000.

27. See also quotation from Julie Stone Peters that begins this essay.

28. Increasingly, I have doubts and discomfort about usefulness of the notion of "crossing boundaries" as a guideline, a mode of discourse, or a governing metaphor. There may be a necessary amount of permeability on the edges or perimeter of most disciplines, and that may well be part of the nature or order of disciplinarity itself. Boundaries are so slippery that caution is the best practice. To focus on

boundaries perhaps also unduly limits the interactions and relationships open to interdisciplinarity.

29. There is a need for a sophisticated and comparative study of the discourse of interdisciplinarity. Many of us comment on it but there is little deep probing. This is a trickier problematic than it is often expected to be.

30. See Graff & Duffy, 2007. See also, on the one hand, Goody in general; Olson, 1994; on the other hand, Street, Barton; also Halverson, cited herein. More or less in between are Collins & Blot, 2003; Brandt & Clinton, 2002; Graff, 1995b.

31. This is complicated and well worth study in its own right.

32. For LiteracyStudies@OSU, see http://literacystudies.osu.edu/. See also my essay, "Literacy Studies @ OSU in Theory and Practice," presented to the Conference on College Composition and Communication annual meeting, New Orleans, 2008. See also chapter 8 below.

33. That LS@OSU resides in the English department (within the former College of Humanities, and also in the Institute for Collaborative Research and Public Humanities) is partly a matter of chance and partly one of strategic thinking. It is not an outgrowth of disciplinary attributes or affinities. (No more, that is, than that our only major public conflicts are with the College of Education and Human Development, who claimed "ownership" of literacy.) Appropriately, the Office of Academic Affairs declared that literacy is a university-wide matter. The lessons for interdisciplinary literacy studies are ambiguous. A stable base with sufficient resources, wide-ranging goals, good advisors, interested and varied audiences and potential participants, and lots of energy may be more important than which disciplines lead and which ones follow. That LS@OSU is led by a social historian is probably more important.

34. See above, Fish, 1989; Smelser, 2004; Dogan and Pahre, 1990.

35. Science seems to have its own path(s) to interdisciplinarity. See Smith, 2006; Weingart and Stehr, 2000, among others. As suggested by the statements in support of or in opposition to interdisciplinarity quoted earlier, some see science as allied closely, even fundamentally connected, with at least some forms of interdisciplinary. Others find it firmly opposed or resistant. The contradictions evoke the antimonies of interdisciplinarity as they relate to disciplinary clusters. Natural science is also home to such conjointly constructed or compounded interdisciplines as biochemistry and other compounds linking biology, chemistry, physics, and, recently, technology fields. The social or human sciences lack that kind of compound.

   Interdisciplinarity in biology, for example, looks and proceeds, and has contributed historically, very differently than interdisciplinarity in history or anthropology or geography. Historian of biology Garland Allen (1975) suggestively calls twentieth-century biology itself "a convergence of disciplines." On disciplines in science, see Lenoir, 1997. Similarly, when social scientists and natural scientists talk about laboratories and experiments, what they have in mind and what they expect to happen there is likely to differ greatly. Replication in the social sciences shares more metaphorically than materially with replication in natural science. This is part of common confusion with respect to interdisciplinarity, and perhaps disciplinarity, practice, meaning, discourse, location, and evaluation across clusters.

36. The sense of an implicit contradiction here is very real.

37. In addition, the accurate measurement of literacy levels with "hard" data is a perennial quest but probably an impossible dream. That, of course, doesn't limit generalizations or judgments. Research in different dimensions of literacy studies proceeds very differently. Psychologists including "cognitive scientists" and economists, in particular, seek the status of science within the domains of reading and writing as cognition for the former, and "human capital" for the latter. They

design their research to construct numerical data, often conducting experiments. Disability researchers increasingly join them. Discourse studies; ethnographies, and case studies of literacy practices, written or recorded testimonies including life histories, and other studies of the acquisition, uses and value, impact, or ideologies of reading and writing, quantitative or qualitative, occupy other researchers across the human and social sciences including education and professional studies. Each of the two divisions constructs its vision of interdisciplinary in accord with these distinctions.

The imprecision of literacy's definitions and measures adds a certain vagueness that may facilitate its general appropriation for many incommensurate ends (for example, as one of a number of factors in a statistical manipulation, say, to explain economic growth or fertility levels). At the same time it counters efforts to gain higher marks for the field when compared to other research of a more scientific or prestigious bent. Literacy studies has seen limited development in neuroscience and the more experimental domains of cognitive science, despite proclamations of their great value. Studies of disabilities and deficits are more common.

Another sign of literacy studies' emergence with limits on its status follows from the ubiquity of literacy as a factor—a "variable," independent or dependent—commonly employed in a wide range of studies across disciplines. Imprecision combines with a general but typically vague sense of its actual importance to simultaneously encourage the use of literacy data inconsistently, sometimes as indicators of schooling, training; or skills, but also with respect to attitudes, values, morality, or experience; symbolically or materially. Sometimes deemed "human capital," the answer to the basic question "what does it mean to be literate?" is seldom satisfying. Yet, the simple fact that both notions and theories of civilization, progress, development, modernization, and so on, include literacy among their ingredients enhances its appeal despite the limitations. See Graff, 1979, 1995a, 1995b; Graff and Duffy, 2007.

The order of the terms Literacy, Language, and Culture and the acronyms varies from program to program, regarding the place, for example, of anthropology, linguistics, or psychology.

38. That this constructive consequence is not literacy's alone is suggested by the history of nanotechnology and perhaps materials science more broadly. I plan to consider that in *Undisciplining Knowledge*.

References

Abbott, Andrew, 2001. *Chaos of Disciplines*. Chicago: University of Chicago Press.

Allen, Garland, 1975. *Life Science in the Twentieth Century*. New York: John Wiley.

Bartlett, Lesley, et al, 2003. "Social Studies of Literacy and Comparative Education: Intersections," *Current Issues in Comparative Education*, Teachers College, Columbia University, 5, 2.

Barton, David, 2001. "Directions for Literacy Research: Analysing Language and Social Practices in a Textually Mediated World," *Language and Education*, 15: 92-104.

———, 2007. *Literacy: An Introduction to the Ecology of Written Language* 2nd ed. Oxford: Blackwell.

Barton, David, et al, 2007. *Literacy, Lives and Learning*. London: Routledge.

Barton and Mary Hamilton, 1998. *Local Literacies: Reading and Writing in One Community*. London: Routledge.

Brandt, Deborah and K. Clinton, 2002. "Limits of the Local: Expanding Perspectives on Literacy as a Social Practice," *Journal of Literacy Research*, 34: 337-356.

Brockmeier, Jens, Min Wang, and David R. Olson, eds., 2002. *Literacy, Narrative and Culture*. Richmond, Eng.: Curzon Press.

Charter of Transdisciplinarity,1998. UNESCO, Division of Philosophy and Ethics, Transdisciplinarity: "Stimulating Synergies, Integrating Knowledge."

Clanchy, Michael, 1979, 1993. *From Memory to Written Record: England, 1066-1307*. Oxford: Blackwell.

Clark, Gregory, 2007. *A Farewell to Alms: A Brief Economic History of the World*. Princeton: Princeton University Press.

Cole, Michael, 1996. *Cultural Psychology: A Once and Future Discipline*. Cambridge, Mass.: Harvard University Press.

Collins, James, 1995. "Literacy and Literacies," *Annual Review of Anthropology*, 24: 75-93.

Collins, James and Richard K. Blot, 2003. *Literacy and Literacies: Texts, Power, and Identity*. Cambridge: Cambridge University Press.

Davidow, Ellen Messer, David R. Shumway, and David J. Sylvan, 1993. eds., *Knowledges: Historical and Critical Studies in Disciplinarity*. Charlottesville: University Press of Virginia.

De Mey, Marc, 1982. *The Cognitive Paradigm: Cognitive Science, a Newly Explored Approach to the Study of Cognition Applied in an Analysis of Science and Scientific Knowledge*. Dordrecht: D Reidel Publishing Co.

Dogan, Mattei and Robert Pahre, 1990. *Creative Marginalization: Innovation at the Intersections of the Social Sciences*. Boulder: Westview.

Duffy, John, 2007. *Writing from these Roots: Literacy in a Hmong-American Community* Honolulu: University of Hawaii Press.

Fish, Stanley, 1989. "Being Interdisciplinary Is So Very Hard to Do." *Profession 89*, Modern Language Association, 15-22.

Frank, Roberta, 1988. "'Interdisciplinarity': The First Half-Century," in *Words for Robert Burchfield's Sixty-Fifth Birthday*, ed. E.G. Stanley and T.F. Hoad. London: D.S. Brewer, 91-101.

Frickel, Scott, 2004. "Building an Interdiscipline: Collective Action Framing and the Rise of Genetic Toxicology," *Social Problems*, 51, 2: 269-287:

Gee, James, 2007. "The New Literacy Studies and the 'Social Turn,'" http://www. schools.ash.org.au/litweb/page300.html 12/28/2007.

Goody, Jack, ed., 1968. *Literacy in Traditional Societies*. Cambridge: Cambridge University Press.

Goody, Jack, 1979. *The Domestication of the Savage Mind*. Cambridge: Cambridge University Press.

———, 1986. *The Logic of Writing and the Organization of Society*. Cambridge: Cambridge University Press.

———, 1987. *The Interface Between the Written and the Oral*. Cambridge: Cambridge University Press.

Goody, Jack and Ian Watt, 1968. "The Consequences of Literacy," in *Literacy in Traditional Societies*, ed. Goody. Cambridge: Cambridge University Press, 27-68.

Graff, Harvey J., 1979, 1991. *The Literacy Myth: Literacy and Social Structure in the Nineteenth-Century City*. New York: Academic Press, Transaction.

———, 1987. *The Legacies of Literacy: Continuities and Contradictions in Western Society and Culture*. Bloomington: Indiana University Press.

———, 1995a. "Literacy, Myths, and Legacies: Lessons from the History of Literacy," in *The Labyrinths of Literacy*. Pittsburgh: University of Pittsburgh Press, Composition, Literacy, and Culture Series, 318-349.

———, (1995b) "Assessing the History of Literacy in the 1990s: Themes and Questions," In *Escribir y leer en Occidente*, ed. Armando Petrucci and M. Gimeno Blay Valencia, Spain: Universitat de Valencia, 5-46.

Graff, Harvey J. and John Duffy, 2007. "Literacy Myths," *Encyclopedia of Language and Education*, 2nd ed., Vol. 2 Literacy, ed. Brian V. Street and Nancy Hornberger Berlin and New York: Springer, 41-52.

Greenfield, Patricia, 1972. "Oral or Written Language: The Consequences for Cognitive Development in African, the United States and English," *Language and Speech*, 15: 169-178.

Gusdorf, Georges, 1977. "Past, Present, and Future in Interdisciplinary Research," *International Social Science Journal,* 29.

Halverson, John, 1991. "Olson on literacy," *Language and Society*, 20: 619-640.

———, 1992. "Goody and the Implosion of the Literacy Thesis," *Man,* 27: 301-317.

Havelock, Eric, 1976a. 1963. *Preface to Plato.* Cambridge, Mass.: Harvard University Press.

———, 1976b. *The Origins of Western Literacy.* Toronto: OISE.

———, 1982. *The Literate Revolution in Greece and its Consequences.* Princeton: Princeton University Press.

Harris, William V., 1989. *Ancient Literacy.* Cambridge, Mass.: Harvard University Press.

Heath, Shirley Brice, 1983. *Ways with Words: Language, Life and Work in Communities and Classrooms.* Cambridge: Cambridge University Press.

Inkeles, Alex and David Horton Smith, 1974. *Becoming Modern: Individual Change in Six Developing Countries.* Cambridge, Mass.: Harvard University Press.

Kaestle, Carl F., Helen Damon-Moore, Lawrence C. Stedman, Katherine Tinsley, and William Vance Trollinger, Jr., 1991. *Literacy in the United States: Readers and Reading since 1880.* New Haven: Yale University Press.

Klein, Julie Thompson, 1990. *Interdisciplinarity: History, Theory, & Practice.* Detroit: Wayne State University Press.

———, 1996. *Crossing Boundaries: Knowledge, Disciplinarities, and Interdisciplinarities.* Charlottesville: University Press of Virginia.

———, 2005. *Humanities, Culture, and Interdisciplinarity: The Changing American Academy.* Albany: State University of New York Press.

Lankshear, Colin, 1999. "Literacy Studies in Education: Disciplined Developments in a Post-Disciplinary Age," in *After the Discipline: The Emergence of Cultural Studies*, ed. Michael Peters. Amherst, Mass.: Bergin and Garvey.

Lederman, Leon, 2008. editorial in *Science News*, 173 (May 10, 2008), p. 36.

Lenoir, Timothy, 1997. *Instituting Science: The Cultural Production of Scientific Disciplines*. Stanford: Stanford University Press.

Lerner, Daniel, 1965. *The Passing of Traditional Society: Modernizing the Middle East.* New York: Free Press.

Lord, Albert B., 1960, 2000. *The Singer of Tales.* Cambridge, Mass.: Harvard University Press, 1960, 2nd ed.

Maddox, Bryan, 2007. "What can ethnographic studies tell us about the consequences of literacy?" *Comparative Education*, 43: 253-271.

McLuhan, Marshall, 1962. *The Gutenberg Galaxy: The Making of Typographic Man.* Toronto: University of Toronto Press.

Michaud, Guy, 1972. "General Conclusions," Centre for Educational Research and Innovation (CERI), *Interdisciplinarity: Problems of Teaching and Research in Universities*, report based the results of a Seminar on Interdisciplinarity in Universities, organized by CERI in Collaboration with the French Ministry of Education at the University of Nice, Sept 7-12, 1970 (OECD), 281-286.

Olson, David R., 1988. "Mind and Media: The Epistemic Functions of Literacy," *Journal of Communication* 38: 27-36.

———, 1994. *The World on Paper: The Conceptual and Cognitive Implications of Reading and Writing.* Cambridge: Cambridge University Press.

Ong, Walter, 1982. *Orality and Literacy*. London: Methuen.

Parry, Adam, ed., 1971. *The Making of Homeric Verse: The Collected Papers of Milman Parry*. Oxford University Press.

Pattison, Robert, 1982. *On Literacy: The Politics of the Word from Homer to the Age of Rock*. New York: Oxford University Press.

Peters, Julie Stone, 2005. "Law, Literature, and the Vanishing Real: On the Future of an Interdisciplinary Illusion," *PMLA* 120: 442-453.

Reder, Stephen and Erica Davila, 2005. "Context and Literacy Practices," *Annual Review of Applied Linguistics*, 25: 170-187.

Scribner, Sylvia and Michael Cole, 1981. *The Psychology of Literacy*. Cambridge, Mass.: Harvard University Press.

Smelser, Neil J., 2004. "Interdisciplinarity in Theory and Practice," in *The Dialogical Turn: New Roles for Sociology in the Postdisciplinary Age*, ed. Charles Camic and Hans Joas. Oxford: Rowman and Littlefield, 43-64.

Smith, Barbara Herrnstein, 2006. *Scandalous Knowledge: Science, Truth and the Human*. Durham, NC: Duke University Press.

Stephens, Kate, 2000. "A Critical Discussion of the 'New Literacy Studies,'" *British Journal of Educational Studies*, 48: 10-23.

Street, Brian, 1984. *Literacy in Theory and Practice*. Cambridge: Cambridge University Press.

————, 1993. "Introduction: The New Literacy Studies," in *Cross-Cultural Approaches to Literacy*, ed. Street. Cambridge: Cambridge University Press, 1-21.

————, 1998. "New Literacies in Theory and Practice: What are the Implications for Language in Education," inaugural professorial lecture, King's College London 19 October 1998.

Street, Brian V. and Niko Besnier, 2004. "Aspects of Literacy," *Companion Encyclopedia of Anthropology*. London: Routledge, 527-562.

Tannen, Deborah, 1981. "The Myth of Orality and Literacy," in *Linguistics and Literacy*, ed. William Frawley. New York: Plenum Publications, 37-50.

Torgovnick, Marianna De Marco, 1996. "Defining Interdisciplinarity," *PMLA* 111, no. 2 (Mar.), 282.

Weingart, Peter and Nico Stehr, eds., 2000. *Practicing Interdisciplinarity*. Toronto: University of Toronto Press.

Wertsch, James V., 1985. *Vygotsky and the Social Formation of Mind*. Cambridge, Mass. Harvard University Press.

8

LiteracyStudies@OSU as Theory and Practice

Introduction

Question: What happens when you cross a 50-some-year old social historian who is a recognized authority on the history of literacy and who has long pursued interdisciplinary programs and their development, with a faculty position as Ohio Eminent Scholar in Literacy Studies (and Professor of English and History), a huge Department of English, an Institute for Collaborative Research and Public Humanities, and a mega-university in the middle of Ohio in the early twenty-first?

Answer: You get LiteracyStudies@OSU, a campus-wide interdisciplinary initiative and an experiment in university-wide interdisciplinarity. You get a series of remarkable transformations, challenging relationships, and complicated questions. And a potentially unique case study in the sociology of interdisciplinary knowledge and organization, with some general lessons to draw. All in a few years beginning in 2004.

When I decided to accept the position of the inaugural Ohio Eminent Scholar in Literacy Studies at The Ohio State University in 2004, I had in mind an experiment—something very different for OSU and almost everywhere else; something very different for me: building and crafting a unique, university-wide, integrated interdisciplinary program.

The story of LiteracyStudies@OSU raises many issues and questions, and matters of both theory and practice. Among the key elements:

- The question of interdisciplinarity
- The question of literacy studies, and their relationships.[1] [note similarities]

141

- The complicated opportunities and contradictions of OSU
- The problem(s) related to LS@OSU as an experiment personally and professionally, institutionally, pedagogically

The Road to Ohio State

I was not attracted initially to a position at Ohio State. The OSU English Department's interest came as a surprise. The notion of a position in literacy studies in a very large English Department in a huge university in the Ohio heartland did not appeal to me. Although I had long taught graduate courses in different departments and colleges on the history of literacy (and had only the year before taught a graduate seminar on the history of growing up in the English doctoral program at the University of Texas at San Antonio, and a graduate seminar on the history of literacy the previous year, in the doctoral program in Bilingual and Bicultural Studies), and presented lectures when invited, I was not planning new research on literacy. I had more or less left active primary source-based studies of literacy.[2] For some time, my focus had shifted to the history of children, adolescents, and youth—the history of growing up—and the history of cities and urban culture. As my experimental history of Dallas, Texas neared completion, I was considering beginning a new research project on the social history of interdisciplinarity.[3]

Based in part on a visit to OSU for a conference in 1978, I had reservations about the university as a home for my scholarly work. In addition, I could not imagine myself or Vicki Graff finding Columbus sufficiently urban to transplant ourselves into wintery central Ohio, leaving lovely, multicultural and gastronomic San Antonio.

As I prepared for what would be the first of six visits before I moved to Columbus in August, 2004, I explored the stack of items sent to me and the university's website. The size of OSU—about 55,000 students—was not an attraction. It ran counter to my educational values and presumptions about teaching and learning. The eighteen colleges seemed poorly connected, even those representing parts of the federated fragments of a traditional college of arts and sciences. The number, size, and reach of interdisciplinary programs were relatively small. I had my first inkling of a phenomenon called "silos"—apparently autonomous large disciplinary departments, nestled into seemingly separate colleges comprised of disciplinary departments.[4] Not only were the arts and sciences separated into different units, but so too were the biological, physical, and social sciences. This seemed to run contrary to the perquisites for building communication, cohesion, and integration, let alone the interdisciplinarity for which I searched.[5]

But as I continued to explore, I received two positive stimuli. One was the quality of the faculty in many departments, including a number of people who I knew. The second I found in the university's mission statements: After skimming through an unexceptional Academic Plan, I found an Affirmative Action plan that seemed to have both originality and force. Then I discovered that, unlike the situation in most states, OSU, Ohio's land grant institution, was the state's Research I and its Comprehensive university. That was interesting. And more than interesting was the seriousness with which OSU embraced its mission toward Outreach and Engagement. Rhetoric and reality could clash, of course. A substantial number of units were dedicated at least in part to bridging some of the gaps between research and teaching, and contributing to the welfare of the citizens of Ohio and elsewhere. There were dangers of course. They included parochialism, and reducing the focus solely to the state economy or narrowly defined corporate development. At the same time, there were real possibilities.

My initial sense of possibilities deepened with my recognition of widespread interest in my work. This was evident not only in English, the location of the state-funded Ohio Eminent Scholar in Literacy Studies position and one obvious base for development, and my own discipline of history, but broadly across the humanities, education, and social sciences. Not surprisingly, there was broad interest in and concern about "literacy"—often ill- or undefined—in many units of the huge university including the professional schools. That interest sometimes included my scholarly work in the history of children and youth, and in urban history.

Across several visits, I probed the definition and expectations for the position itself and the possibilities for expansive development of what I called "literacy studies." I was aware of the need to "name" the field. While not a rare descriptor, "literacy studies" has not achieved even rhetorical hegemony. It is a peripatetic field, unstable and in flux. Across universities, when it or a synonymous descriptor is identified, literacy studies' location ranges from Education—sometimes a department, more often a program—to English. It is often but not always associated with composition, rhetoric, and/or writing programs whose own locations vary.[6] Nevertheless, it was important to differentiate those who studied literacy—comparatively, critically, historically—from those who taught reading and writing in any media. The power of *explicit* identity/identification, location, and relationships, I recognized, was inseparable from naming.

I also probed the probable life of a historian in a department of English. No matter how many different ways I asked, the consistent answer was that the definition and scope of the position rested firstly with the incumbent—a rare opportunity and a great challenge. That openness was a major factor in my decision to relocate to an English department in Ohio. It has been mostly true, more or less. But that does not resolve all questions of identity, location, and relationships, which can get very difficult.

In subsequent visits, I learned about the breadth and depth—and conflicts—of interests in literacy and interdisciplinarity across OSU. Conflicts ranged from different definitions or lack of definitions of literacy to different approaches and politics of literacy and "ownership" issues. From the time I set foot in Columbus in January, 2004, I encountered a number of surprises, many of them the roots of possibilities for academic development including locations, relationships, spaces—and some warnings for the future—and others for life in the city.

Good fortune brought OSU's exceptional Institute for Collaborative Research and Public Humanities early to my attention. The Institute's medievalist director, Chris Zacher, took on the task of showing me urban Columbus. This instructive tour began with Chris informing me that his daughter, then a doctoral student in Education at UC-Berkeley, was a big fan of my work.[7] The tour ended at his own house, close to the OSU campus, with him telling me that the house next door was for sale. It might even be big enough for my books. We laughed. Four months later we bought the house next door (7 blocks from my office) and eight months later. LiteracyStudies@OSU began as a working group of the Institute (with additional support from the College of Humanities and Department of English). In recognition of my belief that the humanities should hold a central place in the university and of the encouragement of interdisciplinary and collaborative work that the Institute fosters, it has remained our OSU home.

Before Ohio State: Searching for Interdisciplinarity

My decision to seize the rare opportunity offered by the Ohio Eminent Scholar position was based on many professional and personal considerations, rooted in my intellectual biography and pedagogical goals, and shaped, refined, or redefined by my prior experiences as a student and as a professor. To simplify a long, complicated personal narrative, they pivot around my coming of age in the 1960s and 1970s, belief in the relevance of critical new historical scholarship to the present and future, pursuit of interdisciplinarity, and connections among these elements. My introduction as an undergraduate history and sociology student at Northwestern University, followed by graduate training in the then "new social history," one of the conceptually, methodologically, and topically "new histories" that stimulated strong responses positively and negatively in the period, led to a long-term commitment to interdisciplinary research, teaching, and writing.[8] Contemporary efforts to probe the past in new ways to better understand and confront the problems of the present left a lasting impression.[9]

As I have written elsewhere,

> Within a global context, social upheavals at home stimulated interests in new histories and social science history. "The political conflict of the 1960s created new historiographic energies and directions," Ross emphasizes. The civil rights movement, the Vietnam War, women's and youth movements, and changes in higher education shattered the "American moment" and its faith in the virtues of consensus. The post-World War II democratization of higher education opened the historical profession to men and increasingly women, making it more representative of American society. From the New Left, the profession gained a wider range of radical views, that embraced liberal democratic, populist, Marxist, feminist, and contemporary radical traditions. "It produced a socio-cultural history that focused on the 'inarticulate,' the working class, racial minorities, and women, those who had been marginalized in American history and left out of its historiography."

Personal experience and professional training and development reciprocally shaped and reshaped each other.[10]

Retrospectively, neither my research and teaching concentrations on literacy, children and youth, and cities is surprising, given the concerns of the times. Nor are my persistent efforts in research and teaching and also in program development to develop new interdisciplinary approaches to their study and teaching. Both a cause and consequence of my graduate studies, these currents not only influenced the subjects I examined, the methods and theories to which I turned, and the critiques to which I contributed. They also contributed to the programs I worked to develop and also the universities in which I spent many years, teaching courses under different disciplinary, departmental, degree, and interdisciplinary rubrics (including History, English, Education, Humanities, Social Sciences, Urban and Policy Studies, Bilingual and Bicultural Studies, Comparative Studies, among others). The paths I traveled from home to university and then to graduate studies and several professorships may seem incongruous or curious. But retrospectively, I see patterns in the practice. The study, teaching, and promotion of interdisciplinary history unite them.

My interest in the history of literacy began in graduate school where I was trained in the new social and social-science influenced history and studied the history of education, urban history, and social history.[11] My focus on literacy also reflected the powerful criticisms of schools and hopes for reform of the era. Major voices included Paulo Freire, Ivan Illich, Paul Goodman, Jonathan Kozol, and Herbert Kohl, among others.

My initial intention in selecting the University of Toronto for doctoral work was to concentrate in modern British history. Undergraduate research had led to an interest in the anti-socialist response to the first Labour Party government in 1924. I imagined fashioning a new approach rooted in social psychology and sociology.[12]

A variety of factors led to a major shift in focus. Partly pushed and partly pulled by intellectual and social currents, I turned to the exciting combination of the history of education and the new social history, dividing my program of study between the Department of History and Philosophy of Education where Michael B. Katz was leading foundational work in Canadian and American urban and social history, and the Department of History where historians of the U.S., Canada, and Europe all stimulated my interests and influenced my approach and understanding, together leading me to the "new" social and cultural histories, social science history, quantitative history, history of population and social structure, history of families and children, history of literacy and education, among the exciting threads of the moment. They also aligned my interests with issues of theory and method across the humanities and the social sciences. [13]

My first paper on literacy—exploring the usefulness of the Canadian census of 1861—was written in Katz's course on urban social structure which required a quantitative project derived from his developing database. That paper led to an M.A. thesis, and in time a dissertation and first book set in a comparative, trans-Atlantic framework and an original effort to explore and expose what I called *The Literacy Myth: Literacy and Social Structure in the Nineteenth Century*, the disjunction between the rhetoric of literacy's importance in a modernizing world and the reality of its impact for individuals. Important matters of theory and practice, past and present, and their intersections came together in this study.[14]

The mid-1970s were a grim period for graduate students seeking tenure-track positions in North American universities. That I was seeking a nontraditional, interdisciplinary job for a fledgling social, urban, and educational historian was both a help and a hindrance, the fate of my job applications and interviews confirmed. Interdisciplinarily, I applied for positions in history, education, sociology, social science, humanities. This was also a time at which U.S. citizens were no longer the object of desire as professors for Canadian universities, as they had been for more than a decade earlier. One clear option was blocked.

In these circumstances, the nondepartmental College of Arts and Humanities at the newly expanding University of Texas at Dallas, situated in Richardson, the first suburb north of the city of Dallas, was attractive. Although I was hired following an interview in a Toronto airport hotel, never having seen Dallas or Texas, its intellectual and pedagogical prospects appeared almost unlimited. At least, that's what sold me on the adventure.

UT-Dallas grew from an unrealized Graduate Center for Advanced Study in the Southwest.[15] This project of regional development owed much to the efforts of Dallas-area high tech interests like Texas Instruments. When SCAS became UTD in the late 1960s, it was predominantly a graduate university in the sciences with emphasis on geoscience, computer science and electrical engineering, space science, and biology. Charter documents with the State of Texas mandated expansion into an upper-division and graduate institution in 1975. I was one of about 120 new, largely junior faculty who came together with the explicit command that we make a university, with interdisciplinarity held out as an exemplar and undefined guiding light. This was an impressive, very talented group. We founded novel programs but our achievements were limited and contradictory.

In retrospect, it is clear that interdisciplinarity was more a rhetorical mantra than a plan. In practice, it signified the absence of disciplinary departments (except in the sciences where disciplines functioned like departments with budgets, faculty governance, etc., without their formal existence). Interdisciplinary also meant that undergraduates had to complete one or sometimes two courses (with at least one outside their major area) drawn from a rather ungainly roster of courses called Interdisciplinary Studies or IS courses. Often, proposing a course was simply a question of listing or naming two disciplines. There were few designated interdisciplinary programs.

At first, interest in interdisciplinarity influenced hiring, up to a point. The match between faculty expertise and student interest was uneven. For example, there were more musicologists and literary theorists than there were undergraduates who knew what those words meant. Interdisciplinarity also influenced the organization of faculty (if not necessarily the organization of studies and programs). As a "new social historian" with training in the social sciences as well as the humanities, I was hired and budgeted in the School of Arts and Humanities but for the founding year, I was housed in the School of Social and Behavioral Sciences. One historian of science officed in the School of Natural Science and Mathematics. A political theorist resided with Arts and Humanities. Anthropologists, linguists, and musicologists were also housed by research interests or approaches. Some of us, at least, found these relationships to be stimulating. There was a risk, however, of lessened contact with colleagues in major areas. After one year, all faculty were ordered back to their primary units, a matter of administrative and budgetary order, those of us who inquired were told.[16] This diminution of even symbolic commitment to interdisciplinarity difference was a sign of directions to come.

Despite UTD's avowed difference, most undergraduate concentrations or programs awarded degrees in disciplines like history or English, philosophy, economics, or political science. Undergraduates, who were primarily commuting students from the area, it was clear, were neither attracted to claims of interdisciplinarity nor often understood their differences or value.

There is reason to believe that both lack of departments (which over time troubled more faculty who saw it as a lack of something important that "real" universities had) and a rhetoric of inter- or perhaps non-disciplinarity were, on the one hand, part of economies of scale. On the other hand, they were useful for gaining approval of new programs at the state level and in appearing to reduce competition with other North Texas public universities.[17]

Interdisciplinarity also functioned as compensatory and as a narrative of sorts. It took the place of history and tradition in a new university, providing a thin narrative line in their place. It linked the institution to the present and future of higher education and the needs it would meet. In a new university that grew awkwardly from a graduate center in the sciences to an upper division and later a full university, interdisciplinarity also functioned to provide the appearance of covering more intellectual and pedagogical ground substantively. In theory, it took the place of more disciplines, disciplinary departments, and more faculty generally. In other words, there is an economics as well as a politics of interdisciplinarity. This was part of the construction of difference at UTD and other institutions that proclaimed a significant stance on distinctiveness via interdisciplinarity.

The use and abuse of interdisciplinarity, or of the language of inter-disciplinarity, had economic and political uses even when lacking in intellectual or educational ones. This was a huge lesson that I learned repeatedly but assimilated slowly. It would be some years before I was able to act directly on that learning. UTD's failings as well as its successes taught me a great deal.

At the level of graduate programs, matters seemed to differ. In the arts, humanities, and social sciences, there was what appeared to be one unifying Ph.D. program per college. Regardless of the disconnect with the tracks of the undergraduate majors, the School of Arts and Humanities offered M.A. and Ph.D. programs in Humanities (at some stages, a name change was proposed as Arts and Humanities but never enacted).[18] The School of Social and Behavioral Science's graduate program was Political Economy. The School of General Education offered a Master of Arts in Interdisciplinary Studies, indistinguishable from a liberal studies degree.

The Humanities graduate program was built explicitly on three areas of possible concentration: historical studies (originally history of ideas), literary studies (originally comparative literature), and aesthetic studies. The changes in the areas' names suggest the program's direction. Paralleling the generalizing and simplifying shifts in basic definitions of each area and contrasting (conflicting?) with the programmatic rhetoric on the institutional walls, many students and faculty saw these areas as little more than *not* too novel, different, or unconventional paths to more traditional ends: to programs of studies that resembled history, literature, *or* aesthetics. For many faculty and students—separately and together—that was a useful appropriation of the interdisciplinary.

Its legitimacy—if that is a fair word—is harder to assess. Difference had its uses, including its appeal as a qualification for teaching positions in community colleges. But for many reasons, difference also had its limits, including conflicts among the faculty over definitions of interdisciplinarity, student preparation, and faculty breadth and intellectual preparation for crossing major boundaries, melding approaches from distinct areas of knowledge, and commitment to intellectual and professional change.

Requirements that students work in at least two of the three major areas—whether history and literature or literature and aesthetics—were compatible with orientations that were more narrow or circumscribed than interdisciplinary or multidisciplinary are usually construed. Over time, interdisciplinarity and difference were increasingly distant objectives, other than for promotional value that included the self-promotion of some faculty, their areas, and *their* version of interdisciplinarity. Graduate student recruitment was a related goal. A series of new deans promised review, rededication, and restructuring but little of that took place or was successful. Each claimed to stabilize or redress the imbalances or excesses under their predecessors. With time, even the rhetoric of boundary crossing grew fainter.

Both underlying problems and limits to plans and action became clearer over time, some easier to resolve as a consequence but others no less difficult. Tales of battles past became a lesser part of the present. Faculty, of course, like to blame administrators (and *other* faculty) and administrators like to blame faculty (and *other* administrators) for program failures. Both are correct, up to a point. At UT-Dallas both were responsible for the limits and conflicts over interdisciplinary program development and commensurate support for research.

On the part of administrators—from college deans to VPAA and Provost—there was a lack of creativity, leadership, and material resources; an emphasis on similarity among programs; and an effort to control. Together, they probably constituted an insurmountable obstacle. But that does not absolve the faculty.

While often branded as acquiescent, faculty conflicted on multiple levels and in multiple ways over interdisciplinarity. There were problems of omission and those of commission, conception and execution. Some among the less helpful issues pertained to the boundaries of interdisciplinarity in the arts and humanities: *within* the humanities and/or *within* the arts; *across* the arts *and* the humanities, or *beyond* them, say, to the sciences and social sciences? The sense of a *bounded* interdisciplinary contradicts the spirit and practice of interdisciplinarity itself, however defined, unless, that is, it is defined by a fixed set of disciplines.

Failure to agree over definitions of interdisciplinarity is unavoidable given the long history of competing notions and ambiguous formulations from multi- to cross-, pluri-, inter-, and trans-disciplinary.[19] So too are squabbles over "how many disciplines does it take to be interdisciplinary" or "how hard it is" to be "truly interdisciplinary."[20] Those questions might function best as first steps rather than final ones. Exaggerated claims for difference and distinctiveness became another sign of a programmatic failure to develop and mature.

These difficulties do not fully explain the levels of conflict, which can go well beyond professional interests and descend into personal rivalry, self-promotion, and insult. Beginning with "I'm more interdisciplinary than you are," this carries into praise for one's "own unique" abilities especially when compared to the intellectual limits, narrowness, and parochialism of others. Not surprisingly, this level of hyper praise and criticism often exacerbates divisions among the faculty in the form of those in favor of (their version of) interdisciplinarity versus those opposed. Both positions are open to caricature, whether it involves the visionaries versus the old guard, or the grounded and solid versus the cavalier or fantastic. The controversy may then lose sight of intellectual and programmatic matters and degenerate into rival gangs warring over turf constructed by programs and student bodies. Too often students become the unfortunate pawns in the games of their seniors. The excesses of the "pro's" become grist for the mills of the "anti's." These tendencies reflect academia at its worse and can do irreparable damage to the mutual respect and collegial trust that interdisciplinary programs in particular require. They can give interdisciplinarity (much less often, disciplinarity) a bad name.[21] This is the stuff of professional narratives told best, I think, in the prose of academic novelists like Kingsly Amis, David Lodge, and Randall Jarrell.

For more than twenty years, from untenured assistant professor to tenured full professor, I labored in these groves of academe, trying to make interdisciplinary degree programs more successful especially at the graduate level, but also in the designated undergraduate courses. In part, this involved working toward greater truth in the advertising of the Humanities program and IS courses, and in part, designing possible additional programs in public history and public humanities. For many of those years, for better and for worse, I remained convinced that meeting my own goals as an interdisciplinary scholar meant working in a nontraditional, nondepartmental, avowedly if not fundamentally interdisciplinary institutional environment.

Any effort at reconciliation must be mixed. I took advantage of even limited interdisciplinarity in my teaching and research, in pioneering courses in Growing Up in America Past and Present, Reading and Writing the City, Dallas: The Course, and in required undergraduate and graduate interdisciplinary core courses, and books like *The Literacy Myth* and *Conflicting Paths: Growing Up in America*. Although I continued to write about literacy well into the 1980s, I taught related courses more often as a visiting professor in Canada than at home in Dallas. I also benefited enormously from a re-education in the arts and humanities. Along the way, I became recognized across the humanities, social sciences, and education, that is, in a variety of disciplines and interdisciplines. As a result, I was honored as the president of the Social Science History Association in 1999-2000, the 25th anniversary year, and awarded a Doctor of Philosophy *honoris causa* by the University of Linkoping, Sweden, in 2001.

I may have erred in some of my judgments about institutional environments. I will explore that later. But my experience at UT-Dallas, retrospectively, taught me a great deal. Particularly important was that the institutional and programmatic uses and abuses of interdisciplinarity unwittingly separated and segregated interdisciplinarity, however defined, instead of working to integrate it. In addition, the organization of colleges, disciplines, and major areas contributed to too great a separation of the arts and humanities, sciences, and social sciences from each other. No less importantly, interdisciplinarity too often meant nondisciplinary, undisciplinary, or a (pseudo)romantic predisciplinarity or even an anti-disciplinarity rather than a rigorously disciplined inter- or even multi-disciplinarity. What emerged as an informal sense of the history of the program was more destructive than constructive, another dimension of the experience that bears reflection.

Somewhat surprisingly, given the long years in Dallas, when it came time to relocate in pursuit of interdisciplinarity, it was to another Texas public institution, a few hundred miles down the road. In 1998, I accepted the position of Director of the Division of Behavioral and Cultural Sciences at the nondepartmental University of Texas at San Antonio, an institution in some ways very much like UT-Dallas and in other ways very different. Similarities included the rhetorical embrace and promotion of interdisciplinarity as well as recent founding as upper division universities. Differences grew from more humble origins and lesser pretentions in San Antonio and the absence of graduate programs in its first decades.

UTSA's lack of disciplinary departments, mixes of disciplines within divisions (within larger colleges), and supposed commitment to fuller interdisciplinary development, and the apparent quality of the faculty—and the city itself—were among the major reasons I accepted the position. The division director's position was more or less in between that of a dean and a department chair. My division, called BCS, included American studies, anthropology, history, and psychology. I was also attracted by the interest in my participation in new doctoral programs in

Bilingual and Bicultural Studies (literacy); English (literacy and children and youth), and Public Policy (urban studies).

I presumed—wrongly as it turned out—that from this position I could lead interdisciplinary program development and bring faculty together. It seemed that my own interdisciplinary experience and expertise, and scholarly stature were considered assets by both faculty and administration. But that proved to be truer in theory than in practice. I was also led to believe that relationships among these programs (which awarded degrees but lacked administrative independence) and their faculty were congenial. They were not. No more accurate was my impression that these programs had a real interest in working with each other and with other programs outside the Division. Should I have known better?

To make a story of six years short, when it became clear that the position in practice bore little resemblance to the one I thought I had accepted, I resigned after 15 months. I quickly learned that there was little to no trust among faculty in different disciplines. Competition was rife and inseparable from fears that one program might get some resource that others lacked. Never had I seen such extreme jealousies acted out professionally and personally. Or so little good will toward colleagues. It did not help that the new director—me—was a historian whereas my predecessor for many years had been a psychologist. It was expected, perhaps not surprisingly, that favors and advantages flowed to the director's disciplinary fellows. That was not my *modus operandi*, disappointing some historians. But to the non-historians, it really did not matter: a director from a different discipline was not a good thing.

In retrospect, I am struck more by how many of the signs that I initially read as supportive of interdisciplinary and nontraditional development proved to be just the opposite. This ranged from a relative lack of separating structures, need for cooperation based in part in limited resources, relative equality among programs (perceptions could vary more than realities), division-wide committee and governance structure, close physical proximity that promoted conversations among faculty and sometimes M.A. students, centralized services, relatively young and talented faculty. Much of which I had seen as potential advantages were, to others, not. That university leadership was unsettled during this period did not help.

Had I read into these signs what I was looking for? Or were the relationships between programs, faculty, organization and structures, and opportunities more complicated. No doubt. But I did not fabricate an emphasis (rhetorically, at least) on interdisciplinarity and development, or interest in what I brought to the institution. Clearly, I wanted another opportunity to put into practice an interdisciplinarity more broadly based and successful than was the case at UT-Dallas.

Regardless, the faculty desired disciplinary autonomy, at almost any cost, not integration. Divisions were yokes of administrative imprisonment and collegial constraint. "Reorganization," that academic catch-all of the late twentieth and early twenty-first century, at UTSA meant disciplinary departments no matter how small or underresourced. It did not mean interdisciplinarity. "Real" universities had departments, after all; a maturing university must replace cross- or multi-disciplinary units with separate disciplinary departments, ideally with as many as possible also offering Ph.D. degrees, regardless of larger, national or international trends or employment prospects for graduates.

Within a few years of my leaving the administrative office, disciplinary departments—often small and without adequate resources—rapidly became the norm. They quested after disciplinary graduate and doctoral programs. To differing degrees, both Texas public universities shared a lack of leadership and lacked the self-confidence required to be different. The reorganization of programs and colleges reduced the possibilities. They also lacked both faculty and administrative support and resources. Not for the first time, I wondered about my objectives and courses of action....

OSU Calling: Between Literacy Studies and Interdisciplinary Studies

When Ohio State contacted me in fall 2004, I was teaching in the new Department of History and in the graduate programs in English, Bilingual and Bicultural Studies, and Public Policy. Viewing what I saw as good for the department vis-à-vis the university, one senior colleague in history urged that I devote more time to committee work in the Department of History and less to interdisciplinary work beyond its boundaries.

Perhaps it was time for another, but a different change? That was not immediately clear when Ohio State's Department of English invited me to consider their new position. Nor was a return to literacy. I was ready for a change but never anticipated Ohio, Columbus, OSU, or literacy studies. Children and youth or urban studies seemed more likely. In recent years, I had considered moving to education and communication programs. I also liked to quip, not completely facetiously, that I had learned much more about what *not* to do in terms of interdisciplinary program development than what to do. But I may have been wrong about that, too. In retrospect, I now see that I had also learned a great deal from successful experiences working collaboratively, often connecting institutions, fields of expertise, approaches, audiences, and programming in what I call public history and public humanities. This included the Dallas Public Library, Dallas Historical Society, North Texas Phi Beta Kappa-Dallas Public Library lecture series on The City, City of Dallas historic landmarks, and related graduate and undergraduate courses. My return to the Midwest, perhaps, was foreshadowed by three years (2001-2004) of exciting work as principal advisor to the Chicago Historical Society's path-breaking Teen Chicago project. This work helped to shape the horizons—scale and scope—of my thinking about different kinds of programs for literacy studies at OSU.[22]

When I began seriously to consider moving to the Midwest, Ohio State University, and literacy studies, a sense of both difference and campus-wide experiment shaped my thinking, through a broad lens of interdisciplinarity. Moving to OSU in 2004 was a time for something new and different, including the sometime tensions and discomfits of being a social historian in an oversized English department in a huge university. I wanted to build a unique programs, test some theories about campus-wide and interdisciplinary program development, and answer questions that stemmed from my education, experience at other universities, and larger intellectual concerns, matters of theory and practice. Among them: can campus-wide interdisciplinarity be created and sustained? What are its limits, locations, connections, relationships? What would it look like? What were the relationships between the parts and the whole? Between professional schools and critical scholarship? My objectives did not include such common paths as launching a degree program or building a research center.

Much was attractive: clear interest in me (OSU had done its homework); freedom of my opportunity; welcoming constructive spirit; the quality of faculty colleagues; our friends and acquaintances at OSU; widespread interest in literacy; formal and informal support; a sense of a university in transition, a comprehensive *and* a research university; resources (within limits). My position gave me the gift of time (which I have overspent) to found and develop LiteracyStudies@OSU.

Constructing LiteracyStudies@OSU: Locations, Relationships, Integration

Being a historian in OSU's unusually diverse and large Department of English created a sense of difference, even liminality, that was mainly positive and constructive: Unlike my experience developing programs in other, avowedly non-traditional universities, both administrators and colleagues were very supportive (if not always very interested). Pursuit of difference was influenced strikingly by the simple fact—with complicated ramifications—that my professorship was separate from my home discipline. Although my cross-appointment in History was very important to me, the Ohio Eminent Scholar in Literacy Studies resided and was budgeted (along with most of the institutional funding for literacy studies) in the Department of English. I did not immediately realize the value of this liminal situation. The composition, concerns, core issues, organization, and conversations differed from those in history more than I had imagined. Although I was certainly welcomed, I felt a dissonance, distance, difference, separation, almost alienation. Not always but often, the tensions were creative; stimulating; suggestive of strategies, objectives, discourse, comparisons, constructive and not.

Location outside my primary or home discipline was very useful. Here was one missing piece in my continuing path. Among the messages sent by my prospective new colleagues: "if you come, you will change us. But you might change as well." How true. Individual as well as collective reciprocity and reflexivity, of oneself and others, was another piece. They were different with colleagues who did not share my disciplinary orientation or baggage. Both conflict and complementarity were different. The uses of location as well as integrative relationships were complicated but critical.[23]

Although I had no way to know this: I needed to be outside my primary discipline but still be part of or anchored in a stable and substantial disciplinary base. To some extent I needed disciplinary structures to move among, between, and against. One of interdisciplinarity's canonical questions has been: Can you have interdisciplinarity without disciplines? My response: Probably not. But that does not signify a simple, additive, or serial relationship along the lines of "take two or more disciplines and mix" or "mastering" at least two more or disciplines in order *to be interdisciplinary*. Overwhelmingly, interdisciplinarity tends to be driven by topics, problems, and questions that stimulate a search for answers that cross the usual boundaries between disciplines (which are themselves often in flux). In my view, interdisciplinarity mandates crossing significant boundaries or making clear connections across disciplinary areas.[24]

Regardless of whether interdisciplinarity requires disciplines, the normative language of disciplines and much of the vernacular of interdisciplines may confuse the understanding of interdisciplinarity. The locations, boundaries, and relationships of interdisciplines differ. We must consider interdisciplinarity and interdisciplines differently from disciplinarity and disciplines, despite their varying connections. For me to develop literacy studies, I needed to leave my home discipline of history to construct interdisciplinarity and interdisciplinary programs. I needed the freedom and the creative tension.[25] This was among the most valuable and powerful lessons I learned.

Contemplating working at OSU also led me to ponder what I call "the dialectics of size." Size interacts complexly with liminality. At approximately 55,000 students and countless faculty and staff, OSU is simply *too* big. Largeness is obstructive. It gets in the way, raising endless complications of organization, communication, and authority. Divided into 18 colleges of widely differing size combined with poor communication, cultures of separation not integration dominate the landscape of OSU. Development of a program both campus-wide *and* interdisciplinary is supposed to be all but impossible.

Huge disciplinary departments that influence boundaries for both intellectual pursuits and personal connections fill OSU's spaces. Known as "silos," that expression represents their size as well as their separation. My home department of English has 100 tenure track faculty plus other instructors; History, my other home, has more than 70. Departmental silos combine with the many distinct colleges that organize academic life at OSU. The perception or sense of silos and separate disciplinary departments is so strong that there are few broadly based attempts to cross them.

The arts and sciences, including social sciences and humanities, are poorly connected to each other. Even less well linked with either or among themselves are the professional colleges (with the partial exception of the health sciences). For example, the arts and sciences constituted five separate colleges of the "arts and sciences" federation (re-federated as one college with three divisions in 2008-09 after a prior effort "to federate" had failed). Before 2008, there were 18 biology departments across 3 colleges (human, animal, medical, including the Colleges of Biomedical Science, Biological Sciences, and Veterinary Medicine). As of 2009, federation and refederation had not stimulated interdisciplinary development. Nor had President Gordon Gee's rhetoric of "one university."

The phenomenon and the folklore of silos become self-fulfilling prophecies. Possible interdisciplinary developments typically become minors or majors safely within departments and colleges. There are few incentives to cross department or college lines. Unit budgets based on enrollments are a disincentive. Along with the usual competition and jealousies, enrollment battles spark "turf wars." Of this LiteracyStudies was not immune. It was attacked by members of the College of Education in April 2005 after only nine months of activity. They asserted "we 'own' literacy." To which the Department of English responded, to my dismay: "No you don't. We do." Several months later, the Office of Academic Affairs announced that literacy was a university-wide matter that no one owned, as LiteracyStudies wished. That, I strongly suspect, will not be the last chapter.

Other surprises were positive and stimulating. This included the striking interest in literacy studies by pediatric dentists, design faculty, health literacy across the health sciences, university outreach, and art education. But it also included the curious absence of social science faculty and students. Among the common consequences at OSU is that the parts seldom search for a whole. Regardless, there are important lessons here.

These circumstances follow from and contribute to a lack of communication, trust, transparency, and legibility in program development, on the one hand, and a lack of leadership, on the other hand. In the aggregate, they limit the cooperation and collaboration that might contribute to interdisciplinarity. It is hard to attract and even more difficult to retain interested students across departments and colleges without the complicity of their departments and programs and faculty advisors. This is one of the ways in which disciplinary departments retain their hegemony and, to my mind, constrain graduate education.

One unsurprising corollary is that the organization of knowledge—intellectual life, academic life—its bases in university and state history, and their expression in both ideology and everyday life—indirectly and directly, implicitly and explicitly, limit the possibilities for multi- and interdisciplinary discussion, planning, and development of teaching and research programs. Literacy Studies, I realized, needed to build its own space(s)—not only physical but also discursive and epistemological space.

There were more or less open spaces, I saw, among and between the silos. Building or occupying and maintaining spaces are enormously important, and not a little complicated. They impinge on matters of identity and identification, recognition, legibility, and logistics, as well as communication and funding.

For LiteracyStudies@OSU, a primary location has been the Institute for Collaborative Research and Public Humanities' Knight House, for both practical and symbolic reasons. Our office is there and most of our programs. Attempting to meet the challenge of constructing a campus-wide initiative demands multiple locations on different levels of university structures and hierarchies, from departmental and college bases to the Arts and Sciences college(s), departments and colleges across campus and their connections (for example, in the medical center/health sciences) and the professional schools. Our status as an "initiative" rather than a college-based center or institute facilitates these variable and flexible relationships. Occupying different spaces is also a matter of building, retaining, and integrating audiences. (See Fig. 8.2.)

With respect to graduate students who occupy a central place in the LiteracyStudies initiative, we have worked hard with students from a range of disciplines and specializations to build their own spaces. The success is noteworthy: Graduate Interdisciplinary Specialization (a minor); GradSem—graduate student monthly interdisciplinary seminar in literacy studies; GILSO—Graduate Interdisciplinary Literacy Studies Organization, registered university group; Expanding Literacy Studies conference; and time with visiting speakers. With respect to their opportunities taken together, integration may come in the form of connecting or "nesting" programs. In these and related ways, LiteracyStudies' concentration on graduate students constitutes one experimental model for a transformation of academic, preprofessional education. (See Fig. 8.3.)

Sometimes relationships and locations mean a collaborative association or integration between LiteracyStudies and one college, or several, for example, in the medical and health areas where we sparked and sponsored a graduate course in health literacy that was cross-listed in most of the health science colleges and in the Arts and Sciences. In 2009-10, LiteracyStudies joined with the Moritz College of Law to organize a day-long symposium on the Report of the Knight Commission on the Information Needs of Communities in a Democracy, directed by OSU law professor Peter Shane. We also cosponsored Youth and Social Media: A Symposium with *I/S: A Journal of Law and Policy for the Information Society*, the Justice for Children Project, and the Center for Interdisciplinary Law and Policy Studies in the law school.

Often the relationship and integration mean sharing the costs and promotion of a guest speaker. But it also includes informal talks and consultations on programs and curricula. It is our policy and practice to forge ongoing relationships including cosponsorships as broadly as possible. The variety of connections promotes our presence across campus. It also follows from our conviction that literacy is understood best when it is not separated from other subjects for which it holds importance or relevance. It also helps our moderate resources to go farther. It also argues for constructing more and clearer connections and relationships among departments, disciplinary clusters, and colleges, and additional efforts to balance size and relationships.

At OSU, it is hard to escape the manifestations of size. But size can cut two or more ways, I learned. While it obstructs, size simultaneously creates possibilities. Among the thousands of professors and researchers, I found many of the most talented scholars I have known. I had excellent advisors and informal guides who led me to make excellent contacts and connections. Many people responded to my queries about participating in a literacy studies initiative by saying that in the ten or twenty or more years they had worked at OSU, I was the first person outside their department or even their research group to contact them. Most signified an interest in learning more. My title—Ohio Eminent Scholar—perhaps helped with the response rate but is insufficient to explain more than that. Not only did this response confirm a general interest in interdisciplinarity, and in literacy. But it underscored my growing appreciation of OSU's rich resources …, if one troubled to search them out. My position afforded me the opportunity to do that.

Literacy has a powerful currency often rooted in an exaggerated sense of its independent impact, what I have called "the literacy myth."[26] (See chapters 3-4 in this book.) Literacy has certain peculiarities as well, not the least of which is the swamp of definitions and confusions. Currency also turns on a certain faddishness with respect to proliferating literacies, for example engineering or entomological literacy. Concerns over literacy, especially in a public university, cut in different ways. There can be great tensions, even contradictions, between the critical study of literacy and separate efforts to elevate mass literacy and specialized technical "literacies" to boost economic growth and general welfare. Critical studies confront threats of appropriation rooted in expectations aimed narrowly at improving literacy in Ohio. At the same time, they also risk being branded as negative if not dismissed out of hand. Not only was I aware of potential clashes between literacy educators (for lack of a better term) and literacy studies.[27] But any effort to escape them requires conveying some sense of the larger value of critical scholarly research into literacy to different branches of the university and the public.

There can be threats to critical independence and also risks in taking positions critical of literacy. Within the university, literacy studies also needs to deal with the ceaseless proliferation of new literacies and "many literacies," at times almost a caricature of every discipline claiming its own literacy. Indeed, not only does it seem that every discipline proclaims a literacy of its own but that literacy is in a crisis. Somehow that particular literacy will also save us!

This contradictory circumstance is simultaneously a help and a hindrance in building conversations and relationships with the sciences but even more with the professions.[28] An eye on OSU's twin roles as a research university and a comprehensive university helps in dealing with such conflicts and contradictions. In countless ways, it provides suggestions, if not guidelines, for constructing LiteracyStudies@OSU. That approach also demands greater attention.

LiteracyStudies@OSU in Theory and Practice[29]

When the Literacy Studies Working Group of the Institute for Collaborative Research and Public Humanities began to meet in autumn 2004, I wrote its first preamble or charge:[30]

> We live at a challenging time with respect to both literacy and literacy studies. On the one hand, many *different* literacies are proclaimed, from cyber to health and emotional literacy, mathematical to aesthetic literacy. The potential advance that this profusion might represent, however, is lost in the confusing clash of claims and counter-claims, and the persisting sense of doom due to fears of the decline of literacy skills and the consequent defeat of civilization as we have known it. A sense of crisis and despair contradictorily accompanies the assertion of many literacies. Talking clearly, knowledgeably, and critically about literacy is an inescapable need today. As we clarify our usage and our reflections about literacy(ies), we not only hold the potential to improve our communications and abilities to collaborate but we also have a rare opportunity to reinvigorate teaching and learning.

Drafting the proposal for the Graduate Interdisciplinary Specialization in Literacy Studies, I elaborated:

> Literacy, it has long been said, underlies and is part and parcel of modern society and civilization. Although that simple generalization has long influenced thinking, policy-making, and school building, literacy is no longer seen to be so powerful in and of itself. Reading and writing, along with other literacies, are now most often seen as cultural practices whose forms, functions, and influences take their shape and play their influence as part of larger contexts: social, cultural, political, economic, historical, material and ideological. The complexities of literacy as used by people in their daily lives take on greater importance as approaches, theories, and research focus more closely on the uses, abuses, and meanings of distinct literacies. The major topics now opened to debate include the "great debates" over literacy (orality v. literacy, writing v. print, illiteracy v. literacy/development/civilization/culture/progress); individual and social foundations of literacy; literacy and cognition;

literacy, schools, and families; multiple literacies, literacy and social action, uses and meanings of literacy.

With that as our mission and agenda; here was our initial plan:

> We are bringing together faculty, staff, and students who are seriously interested in the definition, conceptualization, and critique of literacy and literacies; developing comparative and historical perspectives on literacy; engaging in critiques and potential reconstructions of their own positions as well as others; beginning to re-conceptualize literacy within a collegial peer environment; who recognize the twenty-first-century imperative to integrate but also to go beyond the humanities, education, and social sciences to embrace the arts, sciences, engineering, technology, law, medicine, and more.

Two years later, under the heading: Creating a Cross-Disciplinary Model for Collaboration: LiteracyStudies@Ohio State University, I wrote:

> Developing since 2004, Literacy Studies @ OSU has been working to foster a critical, cross-campus conversation and collaborative investigation into the nature of literacy. The mission has been to bring together historical, contextual, comparative, and critical perspectives and modes of understanding, from the social and natural sciences to the arts and humanities, education, medicine, and law. Our goal has been to stimulate new institutional and intellectual relationships between different disciplinary clusters and their constituents. Literacy Studies @ OSU has grown in scope and scale of programs and activities. Literacy Studies has become a real cross-campus presence and is recognized broadly, not only across the Ohio State main campus but also nationally and even internationally. LiteracyStudies@OSU is an experiment in university-wide interdisciplinary program development.

Among the lessons I learned over many years was the importance of naming in the construction and acceptance of new programs, institutions, activities, and the like: "name it and claim it." I did not hesitate to promote an interdisciplinary field of "literacy studies," first as the work of the "literacy studies working group" and, then, when a more established vehicle was needed "LiteracyStudies@OSU."

The *Literacy Studies Working Group,* formed in 2004, following my appointment as the founding Ohio Eminent Scholar in Literacy Studies and Professor of English and History. With a steering group of six faculty from three colleges, we began by meeting and organizing activities with the goal of fostering a campus-wide conversation, or set of conversations, about literacy. From the beginning our work was supported by the Institute for Collaborative Research and Public Humanities, with programming funds from the College of Humanities and assistance from the Department of English. The founding group included faculty from Architecture, Education, English, and History. It now encompasses many OSU colleges and departments. We have achieved this with relatively modest resources.

In 2004-2005, the Literacy Studies Working Group initiated a series of public programs, along with a variety of special events and activities. The group organized the interests of faculty, staff, and student participants into several kinds of activities. We sought to develop overlapping but distinct audiences, or "publics," primarily across campus but also beyond its boundaries. I construe our efforts to spread literacy studies widely across campus as *horizontal*. Focus on distinct groups like graduate students or department chairs, college deans, or senior administrators can be considered *vertical*.

While Ohio State University has long been an intellectual leader in literacy studies, it quickly emerged as one of the most prominent universities at which a large number of scholars actively interrogate the nature of literacy from a variety of disciplinary perspectives. During the summer of 2005, LiteracyStudies was recognized as a university-wide initiative. In 2007, a University Council on Literacy Studies charged with promoting literacy studies and enhancing communication and coordination was appointed and looks forward to its work.

During 2005-2006, the group maintained interest and enhanced participation through focused public programs and discussion groups, including the History of the Book group, which began meeting in autumn of 2005. In addition, the Working Group launched a campus-wide monthly Graduate Student Interdisciplinary Seminar in Literacy Studies and proposed a Graduate Interdisciplinary Specialization in Literacy Studies (graduate minor). With these new programs, the range of exciting new courses and related opportunities for learning, discussion, and various activities increased rapidly. (See Figs. 8.2, 8.3, and 8.4.)

Operating with continuing annual funding, the Literacy Studies Working Group and LiteracyStudies@OSU have grown enormously in scope and scale of programs and activities. Literacy Studies became a real cross-campus presence and is recognized broadly, not only across the huge Ohio State main campus but also nationally and even internationally.

Summarizing schematically, LiteracyStudies@OSU's principal objectives are:

Figure 8.1
LiteracyStudies@OSU Principal Objectives

- Understanding literacy in its specific historical, social, cultural, political, and economic contexts
- Comprehending the uses, abuses, complexity, and contradictions of literacy as a social practice
- Exploring literacy's place in cognition and communication
- Developing critical approaches to common assumptions about the importance, power, and centrality of literacy
- Practicing the application of that critical perspective
- Evaluation, critiquing, and redeveloping communication and understanding across different literacies
- Exploring and evaluating both traditional—reading and writing—and multiple, "new" literacies
- Distinguishing and evaluating the literacies of academic disciplines for their commonalities and differences
- Studying *acquisition, uses, practice, and consequences of* literacy and literacies across age, gender, race, class, ethnicity, geography, media

LiteracyStudies@OSU: General Themes

A LiteracyStudies@OSU primer: *locations and relations; theory and practice; cross-campus, interdisciplinary program development; experiments; building spaces; making relationships; pursuing integration.*

LiteracyStudies@OSU as research, teaching, service—INTEGRAT-ED—with implications for academic careers for faculty and students, and program development for graduate students. (See below *LiteracyStudies and the Transformation of Graduate Education* and Fig. 8.3 for activities including seminars and conferences.)

Among the keys to LiteracyStudies@OSU:

- *Interdisciplinarity/interdisciplinary program development/*
- *Locations* physical & metaphysical, literal & metaphorical

  Institutional—OSU locations—multiple intersecting locations; also sites for integration. Some connections expected, some not: e.g., interest in arts, health sciences (including pediatric dentistry), law, Outreach, on one hand; lack of interest in social sciences; extent of territorial conflict with education, on the other hand

- *Relationships* in theory and practice; variable but aim to be complementary and constructive. Relationships aim at:

- *Integration* different levels and layers and their connections, epistemology and interpretation
- *Experimental. LS@OSU* explicitly as an experiment in university-wide interdisciplinarity
- *Building/Spaces*
- *Nodes/Intersections as in a web*

Literacy Studies as Interdisciplinary Studies

- Historical
- Comparative
- Critical

In other words: it matters that LS@OSU is headed by a social historian.

Literacy Studies is *not* a research center dependent on external grants. Nor a center for the teaching of literacy or training in that teaching. Rather, a flexible structure with many rooms on a number of levels, horizontal and vertical, many of which have connecting doors and direct elevators/escalators, to promote and enhance relationships and the integration of the many dimensions of literacy studies across disciplines, colleges, and other centers of interest.

Literacy Studies as Interdisciplinary[31]

As constructed and practiced in LiteracyStudies@OSU, interdisciplinarity is problem- and question-driven, not discipline-driven. It crosses and draws on many disciplines and departments.

Literacy Studies is not a discipline (and certainly not additive of disciplines); perhaps not an "interdiscipline."

Literacy Studies should not be a separate academic unit or have its own departments and degrees.

Literacy studies is a difficult, confusing, even contradictory subject that demands multiple and interdisciplinary approaches to its study and understanding from a number of standpoints.

Literacy needs to be included as an important aspect of all areas of inquiry in which "reading" and "writing"—across media and modes of understanding and communicating—play a part.

Some practitioners of literacy studies aspire to both disciplinary and interdisciplinary status.

Both potential benefits and serious risks, including confusion and conflicts, may follow from either confusion of disciplinary and interdisciplinary foundations or isolation within departments or colleges. LiteracyStudies's clash with the College of Education and Human Ecology represents certain dangers; the separation of interests in literacy in the health sciences from studies and conversations in the humanities and social sciences is another.

Discourses and traditions regarding different (presumed or asserted) literacies; with different claims attached to them underscore the need for interdisciplinarity.

Literacy studies demands an interdisciplinary approach. There are many possible.

One path led to LiteracyStudies@OSU, but with different streams within that path as shown here.

There are other paths at OSU and elsewhere. Some privilege reading, some writing, different media and modes, different disciplines, different targets of inquiry and questions.

Through the Graduate Interdisciplinary Specialization, conferences, interest groups, programs and other ways, we explore these issues and questions.

The seeds of literacy studies are found in several disciplines, especially anthropology, linguistics, psychology, and more recently in history. Lately, literacy studies are most often located in departments of English and departments or colleges of education. Academic and more general interests in literacy are far wider, the grounds for mutually beneficial relationships are broad.

The fields of Rhetoric, Composition, and English Studies more generally today reflect what we may we call "the lure of literacy," the appropriation of literacy to convey a higher status and greater immediate—at least—importance to the field.

The 1970s and after: the challenge of critical studies or the "New Literacy Studies" and historical studies.

The recent period in which LiteracyStudies@OSU developed has seen a shift from disciplinary to multi-disciplinary to interdisciplinary studies of literacy as a complicated "problem."

Major "players" at OSU: English/RCL, Disability Studies, Education, Folklore, History, Linguistics, Biology, Science Education, Architecture, Anthropology, Art Education, Design, Digital Media, Libraries, Music, Law, Outreach, Health Sciences including Public Health, Dentistry, Nursing, Allied Medicine, Medicine, Pharmacy.

Important parallels exist between the development of literacy studies and interdisciplinary studies.

The core curriculum of LiteracyStudies examines the rise of multi- and interdisciplinary studies of literacy and the historical bases of literacy studies: anthropology, linguistics, psychology, education. Similarly, the place of modernization theory and individual and collective ideologies of development are explored. The powerful spectre of notions of "Great Divides" between the literate and others, differences, dichotomies, and domination.

The recent history can be construed as a passage from Great Divides to disciplinary divides.

LiteracyStudies Integrated Program Development (Figure 8.2)

LiteracyStudies@OSU and the Transformation of Graduate Education (Figures 8.3-8.4)

The diversity of definitions, meanings, and approaches to literacy has stimulated a new awareness of the complexity of understanding and making meaning in diverse media and cultural contexts. Some commentators go so far as to deem this a "crisis." By providing an opportunity for graduate students to work with scholars from across the disciplines, the Graduate Interdisciplinary Specialization (GIS) in Literacy Studies prepares our students to pursue literacy-related research that will bring understanding informed by multiple disciplines to bear on challenges in a variety of cultural settings. Pursuit of this GIS will complement, ground, and extend graduate students' concentration in any discipline. It is integrative with other subjects under study and may also prove useful in career preparation and searching.

Constructing LiteracyStudies@OSU:
Lessons Learned and Limits Reached—Conclusions in Progress; or, From "My Students Can't Write" to Literacy Studies (changing discourse and understanding at OSU)

OSU taught me that my seemingly reasonable strategy of retaining positions at non-traditional, self-proclaimed interdisciplinary (or non-disciplinary) universities was probably wrong. Of course, I did not know that. And in their own ways, these institutions prepared me to function much more effectively and efficiently when I moved to a world with more stable structures and fewer personnel and organizational problems. There are lessons here, and issues of theory, too.

Figure 8.2
Literacy Studies Program Development: Major Activities Continuing[33]

- Established 2004 in association with the Institute for Collaborative Research and Public Humanities with additional funding from the College of Humanities
- Model for university-wide interdisciplinary studies and program development
- University Council on Literacy Studies (in development)
- 2004, 2005, 2006 funding from College of Humanities, Humanities Institute, support from Department of English
- 2007-2010 multi-year funding from College of Humanities, continuing funding from Humanities Institute, support from Department of English; Academic Program Coordinator; offices in Knight House
- An Executive Advisory Board of faculty, administrators, and graduate students whose membership includes most OSU units with strong interests in literacy studies--from Anthropology, Architecture, Art Education, Biology, Chemistry, Design, Education, English (main and regional campuses), Folklore, health and medical sciences, History, College of Law, Libraries, Linguistics, Music, Mathematics and Science Education Policy, Outreach and Community Partnerships, as well as the Office of Academic Affairs, the Arts and Sciences Colleges, Institute for Collaborative Research and Public Humanities, TELR, Teaching and Learning Center, and the Digital Union—has grown to 30 and encompasses most of OSU's colleges and many departments
- Quarterly and now bi-quarterly newsletter with national and international distribution
- Electronic listservs for faculty, staff, and graduate student literacy studies groups
- Web Site: http://literacystudies.osu.edu/
- Public programs 2 per quarter (2004-)—visiting scholars; OSU faculty, staff, students
- Different participants, audiences, constituencies, with different connections, and efforts at integration
- Annual major speaker (who also conducted required Workshops for graduate students in English, 2005- and informal sessions with graduate students), including Mike Rose, Shirley Brice Heath, Deborah Brandt, Ira Shor, Terri McCarty, and others
- Ohio-based researchers series (from 2005)
- Active co-sponsor of literacy-related events across campus, including East Asian Languages and Literatures, Disability Studies, Education, English: Rhetoric and Composition, Folklore, History, Humanities Institute, Law School, Medicine and Health Sciences, Medieval and Renaissance Studies, Sexuality Studies, Women's Studies, campus-wide events
- Campus-wide Graduate Students Interdisciplinary Seminar on Literacy Studies (The GradSem) monthly meetings, all year (2005-)
- History of the Book Group, faculty and graduate students (originally in association with the Department of History) (2005-)
- University wide curricular development—graduate, undergraduate, and interdisciplinary (2004-)

Figure 8.2 (cont.)

- University-wide announcement and promotion of literacy studies and closely related courses
- Graduate Interdisciplinary Specialization in Literacy Studies, a graduate minor (approved by the Council on Academic Affairs, June 2007)

   Redistributed a $15,000 grant from the Graduate School to faculty in the Colleges of Dentistry (for the Health Science colleges) for a graduate seminar on Health Literacy, Biology/Entomology for Science Literacy, Art for Visual Literacy, and Architecture for Spatial Literacy, to support the development of new basic graduate literacy studies seminars

- Graduate course on Health Literacies, first taught in Spring 2009 with cross-listing in the Colleges of Nursing, Medicine, Allied Medicine, Pharmacy, and the Arts and Science Colleges
- Assisting in development and promotion of undergraduate literacy studies courses for OSU's regional campuses
- Advisory to various OSU university initiatives and programs—advise on interdisciplinary activities, programs, curricula, literacy issues, recruitment of faculty and graduate students: McHale Committee on Undergraduate General Education, Arts and Sciences Colleges, Institute for Collaborative Research and Public Humanities, College of Engineering, College of Education, Department of Linguistics, School of Music, Weinland Park Child Study Center, Poverty Innovation Center, Moritz College of Law; College of Medicine; OSU Medical Center, Collaborative Translational and Clinical Studies (CCTS)
- Joint activities and conversations with Law and Medicine increasing
   - o   Day-long public symposium. Informing Ohio Communities: The Report of the Knight Commission on the Information Needs of Communities in a Democracy, organized by LiteracyStudies@OSU with co-sponsorship of the Moritz College of Law, November 2009
   - o   Youth and Social Media: a symposium cosponsored with *I/S: A Journal of Law and Policy for the Information Society*, Justice for Children Project, Center for Interdisciplinary Law and Policy Studies, Moritz College of Law, February 2010
   - o   College of Medicine: medical researchers and interdisciplinarity; Clinical and Translational Science and Medicine
- Advisor nationally and internationally on literacy studies programs and centers from Wyoming to Sweden; scholarly publications in literacy studies including journals and books
- Supportive relationships with outreach activities (from 2004)

   Mindy Wright from the ASC Outreach programs, Marcy Raymond, principal of the MetroSchool, and Sandy Cornett, Health Sciences have sat on our Executive Board, and other connections

- "Coming Out": sessions on LiteracyStudies@OSU at major professional meetings: Conference on College Composition and Communication in 2008, Society for the History of Children and Youth in 2009. Possible future venues include American Anthropological Association, American Educational Research Association, History of Education Society, Social Science History Association, etc.

Figure 8.2 (cont.)

Presentations on the theory and practice of establishing LiteracyStudies@OSU by Harvey Graff and doctoral students (who will be showcased along with the program, perhaps joined by other faculty, and critical reviews/responses by such noted scholars as Deborah Brandt, Mike Rose, Terri McCarty, John Duffy, and others

• Graduate Interdisciplinary Literacy Studies Organization (GILSO), an OSU registered student organization

• "Expanding Literacy Studies" International Interdisciplinary Graduate Student Conference on Literacy Studies, April 3-5 2009: an 18 month pedagogical experiment. Plenary sessions on the work of Shirley Brice Heath and the 30th anniversary of the publication of *The Literacy Myth* by Harvey J. Graff. OSU students from many disciplines and colleges, and students from 9 other major midwestern universities organized all aspects of the conference. More than 200 presentations; participants from 66 institutions and 6 countries. Approximately, 300 in attendance. (see website for more information)

On planning committees: graduate students from the universities of Illinois, Iowa, Kent State, Miami, Michigan, Michigan State, Penn State, Pittsburgh, Wisconsin, joined Ohio State students; approximately 45 students active in the process

Next graduate student conference is in planning.

• Working Group on Book Arts, the History of the Book, and the History of Reading and Writing, cosponsored with the Institute for Collaborative Research and Public Humanities and the University Library, 2007

• The Ohio State University Distinguished Lecture on Literacy Studies—visiting scholars, by invitation—at least one per year—the goal is to make this lecture *the* place for both well-established and younger scholars to present seminal work in progress or newly published major studies. This brings additional recognition to LiteracyStudies@OSU and OSU more generally. Beginning in 2007-08 with the support of funds from the Colleges of the Arts and Sciences, matched by the College of Dentistry, the College of Art, the College of Biological Sciences, the University Libraries, and the Department of Entomology

• 2008 John Duffy, University of Notre Dame

• 2009 Lesley Bartlett, Teachers College

• 2010 Wendy Griswold, Northwestern University

• Advise and develop programs for Sigma Tau Delta, English student honorary society

• Possible other future activities may include

   o public policy/literacy in public

   o research seminar for faculty and advanced students

   o one-day topical symposia combining visiting scholars, OSU faculty, and students

   o faculty "fellows" in literacy studies in cooperation with ICRPH

   o a triennial conference (with publication)

   o collaboration with Literacy Studies and Rhetoric, Composition, and Literacy graduate programs at other universities, especially but not solely in the Midwest. This might include student and/or faculty exchanges, graduate student conferences, and the like. Informal, preliminary conversations have begun with the University of Illinois, University of Wisconsin, Miami University, and University of Michigan

Figure 8.3
LiteracyStudies@OSU and the Transformation of Graduate Education

- Multiple layers of learning.
- Importance of location, relationships, integration: cross-campus, cross-colleges and departments
- Intellectual and professional development mutually informing and reinforcing each other
- Emphasis:
  - o learning the field and its leaders
  - o interdisciplinary
  - o collaboration & cooperation including interdisciplinary peer groups and joint faculty-student efforts
  - o theory and practice
  - o active participation/involvement
  - o connecting one's participation, learning, research with peers while advancing one's self
  - o integration
  - o responsibility
- Core courses on Literacy Studies
  - o historical, comparative, critical
  - o conceptual frames including theory and practice
- Special areas of involvement including peer groups: locations, relationships, integration
  - o Graduate Interdisciplinary Specialization (see Fig. 8.4)
  - o GradSem—graduate students monthly interdisciplinary seminar in literacy studies
  - o GILSO—Graduate Interdisciplinary Literacy Studies Organization, registered university group
  - o Expanding Literacy Studies conference *as professional training*
  - o LiteracyStudies public programs and visiting speakers
  - o History of the Book group
  - o Visitors/speakers—formal and informal meetings, and preparation in GradSem
  - o LiteracyStudies sessions at conferences—Conference on College Composition and Communication 2008, Society for the History of Children and Youth 2009, others planned
  - o Support for research and teaching
  - o Literacy Studies student service awards

Figure 8.4
Graduate Interdisciplinary Specialization in Literacy Studies

LiteracyStudies@OSU draws from and seeks to contribute to research in the humanities, education, social sciences, and arts most directly, but also the biological sciences and professional areas, such as medicine, dentistry, accounting, and law.

REQUIREMENTS
The GIS in Literacy Studies requires 21–23 hours of coursework. At least 14 hours must come from outside the student's home graduate program. Ohio State's strengths in literacy studies range widely. Students should work with their faculty advisors and the Advising Coordinators to determine how best to incorporate Literacy Studies into their program of study.

I. CORE COURSES 13 - 15 hours
The specialization includes 3 core courses. The first two core courses cover the foundations of literacy studies, the central questions, theories, approaches, methods, and history. The third core course provides an interdisciplinary perspective on particular forms of literacy and literacies and prepares students for their concentration.

A. FIRST CORE COURSE 5 hours

English 750 Introduce ion to Graduate Studies in Literacy

B. SECOND CORE COURSE 5 hours

English 884 Literacy Studies: Past and Present; cross-listed as History 775 History of Literacy

C. THIRD CORE COURSE 3 - 5 hours. Choose from:

Arts&Sci 709 Health Literacy 5 hours; cross-listed as AMP 710, MED COL 710, Nursing 710, and PHARMACY 709

EDU T&L 901 Changing Perspectives 3

EDU T&L 930 Literacy Research and Issues of Diversity 3

ENGLISH 789 Graduate Studies in Digital Media 5

ENGLISH 883 Studies in Literacy, topics vary 5

Additional hours in this category may count as electives

II. ELECTIVE COURSES 8 - 10 hours
There are four clusters of electives. The areas in which students might concentrate their elective courses include
- Reading, Writing, and Language Studies
- Social, Cultural, and Historical studies
- Science, Technology, Health, and Medicine
- Visual, Spatial Arts and Performance Studies

The GIS in Literacy Studies is open to all graduate and professional students at Ohio State. Students do not need to apply for enrollment.

Students may establish a focus for their elective coursework from the list and select courses for electives from those associated with that focus. A second option is to develop a focus for the elective coursework in consultation with their faculty advisor that extends their main course of study or anticipates career goals.

Building literacy studies program in early 21st century: foundations

- mutual suspension of disbelief
- serendipity and luck
- timeliness and currency: "the historical moment"
- interests to build on
- interests in many literacies, both multiple literacies and disciplines claiming literacies of their own
- the special position of Ohio Eminent Scholar in Literacy Studies
- Graff's need to answer basic questions about the prospects and possibilities for cross-campus interdisciplinary studies programs
- an overall sense of plan or vision—an "interdisciplinary dream"
- agency *and* legitimacy/authority, from will to various kinds of support
- resources, beginning with well-placed advice/advisers
- moderate material resources
- support and encouragement of administrators and peers
- interest and energy of students
- form approaches that are: comparative, historical, and critical
- in meeting potential participants across disciplines: avoid correction, negativism, derogation in responses to others—especially regarding definitions of literacy and their uses/abuses
- build on more or less "common denominators" (even if fictitious) respecting interests, definitions, condition of literacy, etc.
- build locations, relationships, integration
- strategy of interdisciplinary development with more emphasis on breadth than depth (at least at first). As a choice or strategy, "loose integration"—building in locations, building on relationships
- strategy of many activities and affiliations on many levels horizontal and vertical, and relationships both within and between/across layers and levels: integration in part through points and styles of contacts and interactions.
  By horizontal, I mean developments, activities, programs organized among relative peers and/or by common topics, themes, questions, for example, people interested in visual perspectives, and the like, across departments, colleges, campus.
  By vertical, I refer to developments, activities, programs more of a hierarchical organization: graduate and on occasion undergraduate students, graduate chairs, department chairs, college deans, senior administrators, off-campus
- build a variety of paths to interdisciplinary literacy studies
- construct interdisciplinary locations

In addition, presence and personal power of Ohio Eminent Scholar (OES) and program founder/director. In classical social theory, Weber's charisma and the challenge of the routinization of charisma. Related danger: over-identification with leader; identification with Department of English or College of Humanities.

From literacy studies working group 2004 to LiteracyStudies@OSU
2007-: Basic tasks and beyond

- assemble building blocks, individual and institutional
- networking[32]
- develop interdisciplinarity piece by piece, locating and linking, and lumping related elements, for example, visual, spatial, performance literacy
- take risks intellectually and institutionally
- power of naming/claiming including Literacy Studies Working Group and LiteracyStudies@OSU
- establish locations and identity, create a base (special location at Institute for Collaborate Research and Public Humanities [Humanities Institute]), decision to locate literacy studies at historic core of university—liberal arts and sciences
- create developing spaces and linking spaces
- importance of in-between, intermediate spaces
- build relationships and integration
- interdisciplinarity, including the OES position, mandates both creative energies and generative conflicts
- locate, identify, solicit, bring together faculty, staff, students—across many lines including disciplines, also kinds and levels of literacy(ies): bring together in order to change and create larger more integrated developments
- develop continuing support that also crosses departmental, college, and other lines
- engage in a process of differentiating and integrating—as intellectual, curricular, theoretical processes to develop and maintain distinct but overlapping audiences and active participants
- bring different audiences together (and keeping them)
- balance size and relationships
- the power of the free lunch at OSU: to bring people together

Limits: From Rhet-Comp to RCL, and from Literacy Studies Working Group to LiteracyStudies@OSU, from English to College of Humanities to The Ohio State University

- limits: attracting faculty and students but keeping them, getting programs and units, not just individuals, to buy in
- to get students, advisers must be open—we can draw students and faculty out, but how to keep them? [funding formula questions]
- at OSU, roles of graduate studies chairs, advisers; communications; funding
- disciplines/departments dominate and influence graduate students activities in both general and specific ways
- manage conflicts (as with College of Education, School of Communication)

- OSU's poor communications
- competition, turf and territoriality struggles with other programs, units
- bring different audiences together and keeping them
- the need for more and clearer connections, relationships among departments, disciplinary clusters, colleges
- balance size and relationships
- from participation at various levels of intellectual engagement relating to literacy studies to pursuit of individual or collective research in a collaborative setting
- the boundaries of an initiative?

The future?

Notes

1. On the relationships and certain similarities between literacy studies and interdisciplinary studies, see Harvey J. Graff, "Literacy Studies and Interdisciplinary Studies: Reflections on History and Theory," in *The Scope of Interdisciplinarity*, ed. Raphael Foshay, forthcoming, 2010-11, and *"The Literacy Myth* at 30," *Journal of Social History*, 43 (Spring, 2010), included in this book as chapters 7 and 4, respectively..

    For LiteracyStudies@OSU more generally, see http://literacystudies.osu.edu/.

    I want to acknowledge my major debts in the successful construction of LiteracyStudies@OSU. Very special thanks to Susan Hanson, who served from 1st Graduate Administrative and Research Assistant to Academic Program Coordinator and Assistant Program Director. Her contribution essential, Susan has been there all along.

    In addition, special appreciation to colleagues Ed Adelson, Steve Acker, Marcia Farr, Susan Fisher, Kay Bea Jones, Susan Metros, Beverly Moss, Steve Pentak, Randy Smith, Chris Zacher; and also Nan Johnson, Valerie Lee, and John Roberts. Thanks, too, to graduate assistants: Kelly Bradbury, Shawn Casey, Lindsay Dicuirci, Michael Harker, Karin Hooks, Kate White.

    For further perspectives on my research, see the essays in Graff, *The Labyrinths of Literacy* (Pittsburgh: University of Pittsburgh Press, Composition, Literacy, and Culture Series, 1995); "The Shock of the '"New" Histories': Social Science Histories and Historical Literacies," Presidential Address, Social Science History Association, 2000, *Social Science History*, 25, 4 (Winter 2001), 483-533; *Conflicting Paths: Growing Up in America* (Cambridge, MA: Harvard University Press, 1995); *The Dallas Myth: The Making and Unmaking of an American City* (Minneapolis: University of Minnesota Press, 2008).

2. My work on literacy and the history of literacy had been concentrated in the 1970s mid-1980s: *The Literacy Myth: Literacy and Social Structure in the Nineteenth-Century City* (New York and London: Academic Press, Studies in Social Discontinuity Series, 1979), *Children and Schools in Nineteenth-Century Canada/L'école canadienne et l'enfant au dix-neuvième siècle,* with Alison Prentice (Ottawa: National Museum of Civilization, Canada's Visual History Series, 1979; rev. CD-Rom ed., 1994), *Literacy and Social Development in the West,* editor and contributor (Cambridge: Cambridge University Press, Studies in Oral and Literate Culture, 1981). *The Legacies of Literacy: Continuities and Contradictions in Western Society and*

Culture (Bloomington: Indiana University Press, 1987; paper, 1991), *The Labyrinths of Literacy: Reflections on Literacy Past and Present* (Sussex: Falmer Press, 1987), *National Literacy Campaigns: Historical and Comparative Perspectives*, co-editor with Robert F. Arnove (New York: Plenum Publications, 1987), *The Literacy Myth: Cultural Integration and Social Structure in the Nineteenth Century,* new ed.(New Brunswick, NJ: Transaction Publishers, 1991), *The Labyrinths of Literacy* rev. and exp. ed. (Pittsburgh: University of Pittsburgh Press, Composition, Literacy, and Culture Series, 1995).

3. *The Dallas Myth: The Making and Unmaking of an American City (Minneapolis: University of Minnesota Press, 2008).* The study of interdisciplinarity is tentatively entitled *Undisciplining Knowledge: Pursuing the Dream of Interdisciplinarity in the 20th Century. A Social History.*

4. In this usage, "silo" is apparently a Midwestern term also used at University of Alberta, Canada, and elsewhere.

5. The Arts and Sciences Colleges are undergoing reorganization again, beginning in 2008.

6. On the field and its development, see below. In English departments, literacy is sometimes tagged on to Rhetoric and Composition, making for RCL programs (or Composition and Rhetoric). See Graff, "Literacy Studies and Interdisciplinary Studies: Reflections on History and Theory," in *The Scope of Interdisciplinarity*, ed. Raphael Foshay, forthcoming, 2010, included as chapter 7 in this book.

7. Jessica Zacher now teaches at California State University, Long Beach.

8. See Graff, "The Shock of the '"New" Histories': Social Science Histories and Historical Literacies," Presidential Address, Social Science History Association, 2000, *Social Science History*, 25, 4 (Winter 2001), 483-533 (reprinted in *Looking Backward and Looking Forward: Perspectives in Social Science History*, ed. Harvey J. Graff, Leslie Page Moch, and Philip McMichael (Madison: University of Wisconsin Press, 2005), 13-56), and the literature cited there. See also William H. Sewell, Jr., *Logics of History: Social Theory and Social Transformations* (Chicago: University of Chicago Press, 2005), and Graff, *Conflicting Paths: Growing Up in America* (Cambridge, MA: Harvard University Press, 1995); *The Dallas Myth: The Making and Unmaking of an American City* (Minneapolis: University of Minnesota Press, 2008). For other historians, see James M. Banner, Jr. and John R. Gillis, eds. *Becoming Historians* (Chicago: University of Chicago Press, 2009).

9. See also Michael B. Katz, *Reconstructing American Education* (Cambridge: Harvard University Press; 1987)) and *Improving Poor People: The Welfare State, the "Underclass," and Urban Schools as History*. (Princeton, N.J.: Princeton University Press, 1995).

10. Graff, "The Shock of the '"New" Histories,'" 494.

11. See "The Shock of the '"New" Histories.'" On Katz's Canadian Social History Project, see Michael B. Katz, *The People of Hamilton, Canada West: Family and Class in a Mid-Nineteenth-Century City.* (Cambridge: Harvard University Press; 1975) and with Michael J. Doucet and Mark J. Stern. *The Social Organization of Early Industrial Capitalism.* (Cambridge: Harvard University Press; 1982). For a sense of the moment and its politics, see Graff, "Towards 2000: Progress and Poverty in the History of Education," *Historical Studies in Education*, 3 (1991), 191-210. For literacy, see the two editions of Graff, *The Labyrinths of Literacy* and the new introduction to the 1995 edition, cited above.

12. Taking my Ph.D. in 1975, the odds that I would find a tenure track position in British history were not good.

13. They included, in addition to Katz, Edward Shorter, Natalie Zemon Davis, Jill Ker Conway, Maurice Careless, and Ian Winchester.

14. See Graff, *The Literacy Myth: Literacy and Social Structure in the Nineteenth-Century City* (New York and London: Academic Press, Studies in Social Discontinuity Series, 1979) and *The Literacy Myth: Cultural Integration and Social Structure in the Nineteenth Century,* new ed.(New Brunswick, NJ: Transaction Publishers, 1991), "Towards 2000: Progress and Poverty in the History of Education," *Historical Studies in Education,* 3 (1991), 191-210, *The Labyrinths of Literacy,* "The Shock of the '"New" Histories,'" "Literacy Studies and Interdisciplinary Studies: Reflections on History and Theory," in *The Scope of Interdisciplinarity,* ed. Raphael Foshay, forthcoming, 2010-11, and *"The Literacy Myth at 30,"* *Journal of Social History,* 43 (Spring, 2010),.

15. In general, see discussion in *The Dallas Myth* and references there.

16. There is some limited evidence that initial distance from hiring and reviewing units may have worked against retention of some of these faculty.

17. Part of the graduate program in Humanities was shared jointly with the humanities faculty at UT-Arlington, but this was seldom mentioned or discussed.

18. The politics of combining both rubrics into one program and degree name were endless. On some levels they mocked the interdisciplinary pretentions. I recall that some of the arts faculty felt estranged by the Humanities nomenclature and sense of hierarchy. In the arts and creative writing areas, the divides among history, theory, and practice were never resolved, and sometimes not much acknowledged. Some of the constraints followed from the circumstances in which the program was founded jointly with two campuses, UTD and UT-Arlington.

19. I am at work on a social history of interdisciplinarity tentatively entitled, *Undisciplining Knowledge: Pursuing the Dream of Interdisciplinarity in the 20th Century. A Social History.* See also Graff, "Literacy Studies and Interdisciplinary Studies: Reflections on History and Theory," in *The Scope of Interdisciplinarity,* ed. Raphael Foshay, forthcoming, 2010-11, chapter 7 in this book.

20. Stanley Fish, "Being Interdisciplinary Is So Very Hard to Do," *Profession 89* (MLA), 1989, 15-22.

21. See, for example, Julie Thompson Klein, *Interdisciplinarity: History, Theory, and Practice* (Detroit: Wayne State University Press, 1990) and *Crossing Boundaries: Knowledge, Disciplinarities, and Interdisciplinarities* (Charlottesville: University of Virginia Press, 1996). Compare with Neil J. Smelser, "Interdisciplinarity in Theory and Practice," in *The Dialogical Turn: New Roles for Sociology in the Postdisciplinary Age,* ed. Charles Camic and Hans Joas (Lanham, MD: Rowman and Littlefield, 2004), 43-64, Dean R. Gerstein, R. Duncan Luce, Neil J. Smelser, and Sonja Sperlich, eds., *The Behavioral and Social Sciences: Achievements and Opportunities.* Committee on Basic Research in the Behavioral and Social Sciences/Commission on Behavioral and Social Sciences and Education. National Research Council, 1988. There is a large but not always illuminating literature between the "pro's" and the "anti's."

22. See "Teen Chicago," special issue *Chicago History,* 33, 2 (2004). The Chicago Historical Society was renamed the Museum of Chicago History.

23. I do not mean to exaggerate my difference from many English faculty or the degree of similarity among historians.

24. See Graff, "Literacy Studies and Interdisciplinary Studies," *Undisciplining Knowledge,* in progress.

25. See Graff, "Literacy Studies and Interdisciplinary Studies," syllabus for ENG 750 Introduction to Graduate Study in Literacy. See also Andrew Abbott, *Chaos of Disciplines* (University of Chicago Press, 2001).

26. See Graff and John Duffy, "Literacy Myths," *Encyclopedia of Language and Education,* 2nd ed., Vol. 2 Literacy, ed. Brian V. Street and Nancy Hornberger (Berlin and

New York: Springer, 2007), 41-52, Graff, "*The Literacy Myth* at 30," *Journal of Social History*, 43 (Spring, 2010). They appear as chapters 3 and 4 in this book.

27. Not the least of the confusion and complications is over the difference between literacy and literacy studies, and teaching reading and writing versus critical study of literacy.

28. When an administrator in the College of Engineering came to see me for help in planning a concentration in "engineering literacy" for non-majors, in part to increase enrollments, he was not pleased with my questioning the existence of a unique engineering literacy or my effort to suggest that what he had in mind might be better developed as part of other programs rather than as a separate area.

29. Widely recognized for its scholarship and contributions to the field, OSU Department of English's Rhetoric and Composition faculty has embraced Literacy Studies, revising its program to include Literacy as a third component of inquiry and changing its name to RCL, Rhetoric, Composition, and Literacy. This shift is important symbolically and substantively. It carries significant potential for interdisciplinary learning and teaching and for inquiry into the fields of composition and rhetoric more generally. The relationships are complicated and it may be most accurate to see Literacy as sometimes part of RCL but often as (semi-)autonomous.

30. The original group included Mollie Blackburn (Education/Teaching and Learning), Marcia Farr (Education/Teaching and Learning), Kay Bea Jones (Architecture), Beverly Moss (English/RCL), Amy Shuman (English/Folkore), and myself.

31. See Graff, "Literacy Studies and Interdisciplinary Studies."

32. Constructing literacy studies across campus: Within the first year, my department chair Valerie Lee was asked by people outside the department if she'd met me; Dean of the College of Humanities John Roberts was told by others including chairs and deans that they are thinking about literacy differently than they had before my initiative.

33. For specific events, see LiteracyStudies website: http://literacystudies.osu.edu/.

9

Bibliography of the History of Literacy in Western Europe and North America

This bibliography is comprehensive in scope but makes no claims to completeness. For additional guides to the literature, see my *Literacy in History: An Interdisciplinary Research Bibliography* (New York: Garland, 1981); *The Legacies of Literacy: Continuities and Contradictions in Western Society and Culture* (Bloomington: Indiana University Press, 1987); and *The Labyrinths of Literacy* (revised and expanded edition, Pittsburgh: University of Pittsburgh Press, 1995); and the new introduction to the paperback edition of *The Literacy Myth* (New Brunswick, NJ: Transaction, 1991, originally, 1979). In addition, see Graff, Leslie Page Moch, and Philip McMichael, eds., *Looking Backward and Looking Forward: Perspectives on Social Science History* (Madison: University of Wisconsin Press, 2005); Robert F. Arnove and Harvey J. Graff, eds., *National Literacy Campaigns and Movements: Historical and Comparative Perspectives* (New Brunswick, NJ: Transaction Publishers, 2008, originally 1987); and Graff, ed., *Literacy and Historical Development* (Carbondale: Southern Illinois University Press, 2007). See also Rab Houston, *Literacy in Early Modern Europe,* 2nd ed. (London: Longman, 2002) and David Vincent, *The Rise of Mass Literacy: Reading and Writing in Modern Europe* (Cambridge: Polity, 2000). For related work in the field of the history of the book, see the publications of the Society for the History of Authorship, Reading, and Publishing (SHARP).

References

Abrams, Philip (1980) "History, Sociology, Historical Sociology," *Past & Present* 87: 3-16.
"Adult Literacy" (1990) Special issue. *Comparative Education Review* 34, 1.

Allen, James Smith. (1979) "Toward a Social History of French Romanticism," *Journal of Social History*, 13: 253-276.

Allen, James Smith. (1983) "History and the Novel," *History & Theory*, 22: 233-252.

Allen, James Smith (1991) *In the Public Eye: A History of Reading in Modern France.* Princeton: Princeton University Press.

Altick, Richard. (1957) *The English Common Reader.* Chicago: University of Chicago Press.

Amodio, Mark C. (2004) *Writing the Oral Tradition.* Notre Dame: University of Notre Dame Press.

Amory, Hugh and David D. Hall, eds. (2000) *A History of the Book in America: The Colonial Book in the Atlantic World.* Vol I. American Antiquarian Society/Cambridge: Cambridge University Press.

Andersen, Jennifer and Elizabeth Sauer, eds. (2002) *Books and Readers in Early Modern England.* Philadelphia: University of Pennsylvania Press.

Armbruster, Carol, ed. (1993) *Publishing and Readership in Revolutionary France and America.* Greenwood: Greenwood Press.

Arnove, Robert F. (1981) "The Nicaraguan National Literacy Crusade of 1980," *Comparative Education Review,* 25: 244-260.

Arnove, Robert F. (1986) *Education and Revolution in Nicaragua.* Westport, CT: Praeger Publishers.

Arnove, Robert F. (1994) *Education as Contested Terrain: Nicaragua, 1979-1993.* Boulder: Westview Press.

Arnove, Robert F., and Graff, Harvey J., eds. (1987) *National Literacy Campaigns: Historical and Comparative Perspectives.* New York: Plenum.

Aronowitz, Stanley, and Giroux, Henry (1985) *Education Under Siege: The Conservative, Liberal, and Radical Debate Over Schooling.* South Hadley, Mass.: Bergin & Garvey.

Aronowitz, Stanley, and Giroux, Henry (1988) "Schooling, Culture, and Literacy in the Age of Broken Dreams: A Review of Bloom and Hirsch," *Harvard Educational Review* 58: 172-194.

Aston, Margaret. (1977) "Literacy and Lollardy," *History,* 62: 347-371.

Augst, Thomas. (2003) *The Clerk's Tale: Young Men and Moral Life in Nineteenth-Century America.* Chicago: University of Chicago Press.

Bailey, Peter. (1978) *Leisure and Class in Victorian England.* Oxford: Taylor & Francis Group.

Bailyn, Bernard and John B. Hench, eds. (1980) *The Press and the American Revolution.* Worcester, Mass.: American Antiquarian Society.

Barrett, Michael J. (1990) "The Case for More Schooling," *The Atlantic,* November: 78-106.

Bartoli Langeli, A., and Petrucci, A., eds. (1978) "Alfabetismo e cultura scritta." *Quaderni Storici* 38.

Bartoli Langeli, A., and Toscani, X., eds. (1991) *Istruzione, alfabetismo, scrittura: Saggi di storia dell'alfabetizzione in Italia.* Milan: Franco Angeli.

Barton, David. (1994, 2006) *Literacy: An Introduction to the Ecology of Written Language.* Oxford: Blackwell.

Barton, David, and Ivanic, Roz, eds. (1991) *Writing in the Community*. Written Communication Annual, vol. 6. Newbury Park, Calif.: Sage.

Barton, David and M. Hamilton (1998) *Local Literacies: Reading and Writing in One Community*. London: Routledge.

Barton, David, Mary Hamilton, and Roz Ivanic, eds. (2000) *Situated Literacies: Reading and Writing in Context*. London: Routledge.

Baumann, Gerd, ed. (1986) *The Written Word*. Oxford: Oxford University Press.

Bauml, Franz (1980) "Varieties and Consequences of Medieval Literacy and Illiteracy," *Speculum*, 55: 237-265.

Baym, Nina (1984) *Novels, Readers and Reviewers: Responses to Fiction in Antebellum America*. Ithaca: Cornell University Press.

Berlin, Gordon, and Andrew Sum (1988) *Toward a More Perfect Union: Basic Skills, Poor Families, and Our Economic Future*. New York: Ford Foundation Project on Social Welfare and the American Future.

Besnier, Niko (1993) "Literacy and Feelings: The Encoding of Affect in Nukulaelae Letters," in *Cross-Cultural Approaches to Literacy*, ed. Brian V. Street. Cambridge: Cambridge University Press: 62-86.

Besnier, Niko (1995) *Literacy, Emotion and Authority: Reading and Writing on a Polynesian Atoll*. Cambridge: Cambridge University Press.

Bhola, H. S. (1990) "Literature on Adult Literacy: New Directions in the 1990s," *Comparative Education Review* 34: 139-144.

Biller, Peter and Anne Hudson, eds. (1994) *Heresy and Literacy, 1000-1530*. Cambridge: Cambridge University Press.

Birkerts, Sven (1994) *The Gutenberg Elegies*. Winchester, MA: Faber and Faber.

Bloch, Maurice (1989) "Literacy and Enlightenment." In *Literacy and Society*, ed. Karen Schouseboe and Moges Trolle Larsen, pp. 15-37. Copenhagen: Akademisk Forlag.

Bloch, R. Howard and Carla Hesse, eds. (1995) *Future Libraries*. Berkeley: University of California Press.

Boone, Elizabeth Hill and Walter D. Mignolo, eds. (1966) *Writing Without Words: Alternative Literacies in Mesoamerica and the Andes*. Durham: Duke University Press.

Bossy, John (1970) "The Counter Reformation and the People of Catholic Europe," *Past and Present*, 47: 51-70.

Botstein, Leon (1990) "Damaged Literacies and American Democracy," *Daedalus* 119, 2: 55-84.

Bottero, Jean et al. (1992) *Ancestors of the West*. Chicago: University of Chicago Press.

Boyarin, Jonathan, ed. (1993) *The Ethnography of Reading*. Berkeley and Los Angeles: University of California Press.

Brandt, Deborah (1990) *Literacy as Involvement: The Acts of Writers, Readers, and Texts*. Carbondale: Southern Illinois University Press.

Brandt, Deborah (2001) *Literacy in American Lives*. New York: Cambridge University Press.

Brantlinger, Patrick (1998) *The Reading Lesson: The Threat of Mass Literacy in Nineteenth-Century British Fiction*. Bloomington: Indiana University Press.

Briggs, Asa and Peter Burke (2002) *A Social History of the Media.* Cambridge: Polity Press.

Brodhead, Richard H. (1993) *Cultures of Letters: Scenes of Reading and Writing in Nineteenth-Century America:* Chicago: University of Chicago Press.

Brooks, Jeffrey (1985) *When Russia Learned to Read: Literacy and Popular Literature, 1861-1917.* Princeton: Princeton University Press.

Brown, Gillian (2001) *The Consent of the Governed: The Lockean Legacy in Early American Culture.* Cambridge, Mass.: Harvard University Press.

Brown, Richard D. (1989) *Knowledge Is Power: The Diffusion of Information in Early America, 1700-1865.* New York: Oxford University Press.

Brown, Richard D. (1996) *The Strength of a People: The Idea of an Informed Citizenry in America, 1650-1870.* Chapel Hill: University of North Carolina Press.

Bruckner, Martin (2006) *The Geographic Revolution in Early America: Maps, Literacy, and National Identity.* Chapel Hill: University of North Carolina Press.

Burke, Peter (1972) *Culture and Society in Renaissance Italy.* London: Batsford.

Burke, Peter (1978) *Popular Culture in Early Modern Europe.* New York: Harper and Row.

Burke, Peter (1987) *The Historical Anthropology of Early Modern Italy.* Cambridge: Cambridge University Press.

Burke, Peter (2000) *A Social History of Knowledge.* Cambridge: Polity Press.

Burke, Peter (2004) *Languages and Communities in Early Modern Europe.* Cambridge: Cambridge University Press.

Burke, Peter and Roy Porter, eds. (1987) *The Social History of Language.* Cambridge: Cambridge University Press.

Calhoun, Daniel H. (1969) "The City as Teacher," *History of Education Quarterly* 9: 312-325.

Calhoun, Daniel H. (1973) *The Intelligence of a People.* Princeton: Princeton University Press.

Capp, Bernard (1979) *Astrology and the Popular Press.* London: Faber and Faber.

Carceles, Gabriel (1990) "World Literacy Prospects at the Turn of the Century," *Comparative Education Review* 34: 4-20.

Carpenter, Kenneth, ed. (1983) *Books and Society in History.* New York: Bowker, 1983.

Casper, Scott et al, eds. (2002) *Perspectives on American Book History.* Amherst, Mass.: University of Massachusetts Press.

Cavallo, Guglielmo and Roger Chartier, eds. (1999) *A History of Reading in the West.* Amherst, Mass.: University of Massachusetts Press.

Cayton, Mary Kupiec (1987) "The Making of An American Prophet: Emerson, His Audiences, and the Rise of the Culture Industry in Nineteenth-Century America," *American Historical Review* 92: 597-620.

Chartier, Roger (1985) "Text, Symbols, Frenchness," *Journal of Modern History,* 57: 682-695.

Chartier, Roger (1987) *The Cultural Uses of Print in Early Modern France.* Princeton: Princeton University Press.

Chartier, Roger (1989a) "Texts, Printing, Readings." In *The New Cultural History,* ed. Lynn Hunt, pp. 154-175. Berkeley and Los Angeles: University of California Press.

Chartier, Roger, ed. (1989b) *The Culture of Print.* Princeton: Princeton University Press.

Chartier, Roger (1994) *The Order of Books.* Stanford: Stanford University Press.

Chartier, Roger (1995) *Forms and Meanings.* Philadelphia: University of Pennsylvania Press.

Chartier, Roger (1996) *On the Edge of the Cliff.* Baltimore: Johns Hopkins University Press.

Chisick, Harvey (1980) *The Limits of Reform in the Enlightenment.* Princeton: Princeton University Press, 1980.

Cintron, Ralph (1997) *Angels' Towns: Chero Ways, Gang Life, and Rhetorics of the Everyday.* Boston: Beacon Press.

Cipolla, Carlo (1969) *Literacy and Development in the West.* Harmondsworth: Penguin.

Clammer, J. R. (1976) *Literacy and Social Change: A Case Study of Figi.* Leiden: Brill.

Clanchey, Michael T. (1979, 1993) *From Memory to Written Record: England, 1066-1307.* Cambridge, Mass.: Harvard University Press; revised ed., Oxford: Blackwell.

Cohen, Patricia Cline (1982) *A Calculating People: The Spread of Numeracy in Early America.* Chicago: University of Chicago Press.

Coleman, Janet (1981) *Medieval Readers and Writers, 1350-1400.* New York: Columbia University Press.

Coleman, Janet (1996) *Public Reading and the Reading Public in Late Medieval England and France.* Cambridge: Cambridge University Press.

Cook-Gumperz, Jenny, ed. (1986) *The Social Construction of Literacy.* Cambridge: Cambridge University Press.

Cope, Bill and Mary Kalantzis, eds. (2000) *Multiliteracies: Literacy Learning and the Design of Social Futures.* London: Routledge.

Cornelius, Janet D. (1983) "We Slipped and Learned to Read: Slave Accounts of the Literacy Process, 1830-1860," *Phylon* 44: 171-186.

Cornelius, Janet D. (1991) *When I Can Read My Title Clear: Literacy, Slavery, and Religion in the Antebellum South.* Columbia: University of South Carolina Press.

Cranfield, G.A. (1978) *The Press and Society.* London: Longman.

Cremin, Lawrence (1970) *American Education: The Colonial Experience.* New York: Harper and Row.

Cressy, David (1980) *Literacy and the Social Order: Reading and Writing in Tudor and Stuart England.* Cambridge: Cambridge University Press.

Crick, Julia and Alexandra Walsham, eds. (2004) *The Uses of Script and Print.* Cambridge: Cambridge University Press.

Cushman, Ellen, Eugene R. Kintgen, Barry M. Kroll, and Mike Rose, eds. (2001) *Literacy: A Critical Sourcebook.* New York: Bedford/St. Martins.

Damon-Moore, Helen (1994) *Magazines for the Millions: Gender and Commerce in the Ladies' Home Journal and the Saturday Evening Post, 1880-1910.* Albany: SUNY Press.

Danky, James P. and Wayne A Wiegand, eds. (1998) *Print Culture in a Diverse America.* Urbana: University of Illinois Press.

Danky, James P. and Wayne A. Wiegand, eds. (2006) *Women in Print: Essays on the Print Culture of American Women from the Nineteenth and Twentieth Centuries.* Madison: University of Wisconsin Press.

Darnton, Robert (1972) "Reading, Writing, and Publishing in Eighteenth-century France." In *Historical Studies Today,* ed. Felix Gilbert and Stephen R. Graubard, pp. 238-250. New York: Norton.

Darnton, Robert (1979) *The Business of Enlightenment.* Cambridge, Mass.: Harvard University Press.

Darnton, Robert (1982) *The Literary Underground of the Old Regime.* Cambridge, Mass.: Harvard University Press.

Darnton, Robert (1983) "What is the History of Books?" In *Books and Society in History,* ed. Kenneth E. Carpenter, pp.: 3-28. New York: Bowker.

Darnton, Robert (1984a) *The Great Cat Massacre and Other Episodes in Cultural History.* New York: Basic Books.

Darnton, Robert (1984) "Readers Respond to Rousseau: The Fabrication of Romantic Sensitivity." In *The Great Cat Massacre and Other Episodes in French Cultural History,* pp. 215-256. New York: Basic Books.

Darnton, Robert (1986) "The Symbolic Element in History," *Journal of Modern History,* 58: 218-234.

Darnton, Robert (1990) *The Kiss of Lamourette: Reflections on Cultural History.* New York: Norton.

Davidson, Cathy N. (1986) *Revolution in the Word: The Rise of the Novel in America.* New York: Oxford University Press.

Davidson, Cathy N., ed. (1989) *Reading in America.* Baltimore: Johns Hopkins University Press.

Davis, Natalie Z. (1975) "Printing and the People." In *Society and Culture in Early Modern France,* pp. 189-226. Stanford: Stanford University Press.

Davis, Natalie Z. (1975) *Culture and Society in Early Modern France.* Stanford: Stanford University Press.

De Certaux, Michael (1984) "'Walking in the City" and "Spatial Stories." In *The Practice of Everyday Life.* Berkeley and Los Angeles: University of California Press.

Denning, Michael (1987) *Mechanic Accents: Dime Novels and Working-Class Culture in America.* London: Verso.

Diebert, Ronald J. (1997) *Parchment, Printing, and Hypermedia: Communication in World Order Transformation.* New York: Columbia University Press.

diSessa, Andrea A. (2000) *Changing Minds: Computers, Learning, and Literacy.* Cambridge, Mass.: MIT Press.

Dobranki, Stephen B. (2005) *Readers and Authorship in Early Modern England.* Cambridge: Cambridge University Press.

Docherty, Linda J. (1997) "Women as Readers: Visual Representations," *Proceedings of the American Antiquarian Society*, 107: 335-388.

Douglas, Ann (1977) *The Feminization of American Culture.* New York: Knopf.

Dyson, Anne Haas (1997) *Writing Superheroes.* New York: Teachers College Press.

Dyson, Anne Haas (2003) *The Brothers and Sisters Learn to Write: Popular Literacies in Childhood and School Cultures.* New York: Teachers College Press.

Edelsky, Carole (1991) *With Liberty and Justice for All: Rethinking the Social in Language and Education.* London: Falmer.

"Education as Transformation: Identity, Change, and Development" (1981) Special issue. *Harvard Educational Review* 51, 1.

Eisenstein, Elizabeth (1979) *The Printing Press as an Agent of Change: Communications and Cultural Transformations in Early Modern Europe.* 2 vols. Cambridge: Cambridge University Press.

Eklof, Ben (1986) *Russian Peasant Schools, 1861-1914.* Berkeley: University of California Press.

Eldred, Janet Carey and Peter Mortensen (2002) *Imagining Rhetoric: Composing Women of the Early United States.* Pittsburgh: University of Pittsburgh Press.

Elfenbein, Andrew (2006) "Cognitive Science and the History of Reading," *PMLA*, 121: 484-502.

Engelsing, Rolf (1973) *Analphabetentum und lekture.* Stuttgart.

Engelsing, Rolf (1974) *Der berger als leser: Lesergeschichte in Deutschland, 1500-1800.* Stuttgart.

Esrock, Ellen J. (1994) *The Reader's Eye: Visual Imaging as Reader Response.* Baltimore: Johns Hopkins University Press.

Ezell, Margaret J. M. (1999) *Social Authorship and the Advent of Print.* Baltimore: Johns Hopkins University Press.

Feather, John (1980) "Cross-Channel Currents: Historical Bibliography and *L'histoire du livre*," *The Library,* 2: 1-15.

Feather, John (1985) *The Provincial Book Trade in Eighteenth-Century England.* Cambridge: Cambridge University Press.

Febvre, Lucien, and Henri-Jean Martin (1958) *L'apparition du livre.* Paris: Editions Albin Michel.

Febvre, Lucien, and Henri-Jean Martin (1976) *The Coming of the Book.* London: New Left Books.

Ferdman, Bernardo (1990) "Literacy and Cultural Identity," *Harvard Educational Review* 60:181-204.

Ferguson, Eugene (1977) "The Mind's Eye: Nonverbal Thought in Technology," *Science* 197: 827-836.

Ferguson, Eugene (1992) *Engineering and the Mind's Eye.* Cambridge, Mass.: MIT Press.

Ferguson, Margaret W. (2003) *Dido's Daughters: Literacy, Gender, and Empire in Early Modern England and France.* Chicago: University of Chicago Press.

Fernandez, James (1988) "Historians Tell Tales," *Journal of Modern History* 60: 113-127.

Fernandez, Ramona (2001) *Imagining Literacy*. Austin: University of Texas Press.

Finkelstein, David and Alistair McCleery, eds. (2000) *Book History Reader.* London: Routledge.

Finnegan, Ruth (1973) "Literacy Versus Non-literacy: The Great Divide," in *Modes of Thought,* ed. Robin Horton and Finnegan. London: Faber and Faber: 112-144.

Finnegan, Ruth (1988) *Literacy and Orality.* Oxford: Blackwell.

Fleury, M., and P. Valmary (1957) "Les progrès de l'instrucion élèmentaire de Louis XIV à Napoléon III," *Population* 12: 71-92.

Flint, Kate (1993) *The Woman Reader 1837-1914.* Oxford: Oxford University Press.

Flint, Kate (2006) "Women and Reading," *Signs,* 31: 511-536.

Fox, Adam (2000) *Oral and Literate Culture in England 1500-1700.* Oxford: Oxford University Press.

Fox, Adam and Daniel Woolf, eds. (2002) *The Spoken Word ... Britain 1500-1800.* Manchester: Manchester University Press.

Frankel, Oz (2006) *States of Inquiry: Social Investigations and Print Culture in Nineteenth-Century Britain and the United States.* Baltimore: Johns Hopkins University Press.

Frasca-Spada, Marina and Nick Jardine, eds. (2000) *Books and the Sciences in History.* Cambridge: Cambridge University Press.

Freebody, Peter, and Anthony R. Welch, eds. (1993) *Knowledge, Culture and Power: International Perspectives on Literacy as Policy and Practice.* Pittsburgh: University of Pittsburgh Press.

Freedman, David (1999) "African-American Schooling in the South Prior to 1861," *Journal of Negro History,* 84: 147.

Freire, Paulo (1985) *The Politics of Education: Culture, Power and Liberation.* Boston: Bergin and Garvey.

Freire, Paulo, and Donaldo Macedo (1987) *Literacy: Reading the Word and the World.* South Hadley, Mass.: Bergin & Garvey.

Fullerton, Ronald (1977) "Creating a Mass Book Market in Germany," *Journal of Social History* 10: 265-283.

Fullerton, Ronald (1979) "Toward a Popular Culture in Germany," *Journal of Social History,* 12: 265-83.

Furet, Francois and Jacques Ozouf (1976) "Literacy and Industrialization: The Case of the Department du Nord," *Journal of European Economic History,* 5: 5-44.

Furet, Francois and Jacques Ozouf (1977) *Lire et écrire.* 2 vols. Paris: Editions de Minuit.

Furet, Francois and Jacques Ozouf (1983) *Reading and Writing.* Cambridge: Cambridge University Press.

Furtwangler, Albert (2005) *Bringing Indians to the Book.* The Emil and Kathleen Sick Lecture Book Series in Western History and Biography. Seattle: University of Washington Press.

Gagnon, Paul, and the Bradley Commission on History in Schools, ed. (1989) *Historical Literacy: The Case for History in American Education.* New York: Macmillan.

Galenson, David (1977) "Immigration and the Colonial Labor System: An Analysis of the Length of Indenture," *Explorations in Economic History* 14: 360-77.

Galenson, David (1979) "Literacy and the Social Origins of Some Early Americans," *Historical Journal* 22: 75-91.

Galenson, David (1981a) "Literacy and Age in Pre-industrial England," *Economic Development and Cultural Change* 29: 815-829.

Galenson, David (1981b) "The Market Evaluation of Human Capital: The Case of Indentured Servitude," *Journal of Political Economy* 89: 446-67.

Galenson, David (1984) "The Rise and Fall of Indentured Servitude in the Americas: An Economic Analysis," *Journal of Economic History* 44: 1-26.

Galenson, David (1989) "Labor Market Behavior in Colonial America: Servitude, Slavery, and Free Labor," *Markets in History: Economic Studies of the Past* Cambridge: 52-96.

Galenson, David (1994) "The Rise of Free Labor: Economic Change and the Enforcement of Service Contracts in England, 1351-1875," *Capitalism in Context: Essays on Economic Development and Cultural Change in Honor of R. M. Hartwell*, ed. John A. James and Mark Thomas. Chicago: 114-37.

Galenson, David (1995) "Educational Opportunity on the Urban Frontier: Nativity, Wealth, and School Attendance in Early Chicago," *Economic Development and Cultural Change*, 43: 551-63.

Galenson, David (1996) "The Rise and Fall of Indentured Servitude in the Americas: An Economic Analysis," in *Trade and the Industrial Revolution, 1700-1850*, ed. Stanley L. Engerman. Elgar Reference Collection. Growth of the World Economy series, vol. 2. Elgar: 331-56.

Galenson, David (1997) "Neighborhood Effects on the School Attendance of Irish Immigrants' Sons in Boston and Chicago in 1860," *American Journal of Education*, 261-93.

Galenson, David (1998a) "Ethnic Differences in Neighborhood Effects on the School Attendance of Boys in Early Chicago," *History of Education Quarterly*, 17-35.

Galenson, David (1998b) "Ethnicity, Neighborhood, and the School Attendance of Boys in Antebellum Boston," *Journal of Urban History*, 603-26.

Gallego, Margaret A. and Sandra Hollingsworth, eds. (2000) *What Counts as Literacy: Challenging the School Standard*. New York: Teachers College.

Gallegos, Bernardo P. (1992) *Literacy, Education, and Society in New Mexico, 1693-1821*. Albuquerque: University of New Mexico Press.

Gallman, Robert E. (1988) "Changes in the Level of Literacy in a New Community of Early America," *Journal of Economic History*, 48: 567-582.

Gamble, Henry (2003) *Books and Readers in the Early Church*. New Haven: Yale University Press.

Garvey, Ellen Gruber (1996) *The Adman in the Parlor: Magazines and the Gendering of Consumer Culture, 1889s to 1910*. New York: Oxford University Press.

Gee, James (1990) *Social Linguistics and Literacies: Ideology in Discourses*. London: Falmer.

Gee, James Paul, Glynda Hull, and Colin Lankshear (1996) *The New Work Order.* Boulder: Westview.

Gerber, David A. (2006) *Authors of their Lives: The Personal Correspondence of British Immigrants to North America.* New York: New York University Press.

Gere, Anne Ruggles (1997) *Intimate Practices: Literacy and Cultural Work in U.S. Women's Clubs, 1880-1920.* Champaign: University of Illinois Press.

Gilmore, William J. (1989) *Reading Becomes a Necessity of Life: Material and Cultural Life in Rural New England, 1780-1835.* Knoxville: University of Tennessee Press.

Ginzburg, Carlo (1980) *The Cheese and the Worms.* Baltimore: Johns Hopkins University Press.

Giroux, Henry A. (1988) "Literacy and the Pedagogy of Voice and Political Empowerment," *Educational Studies* 38: 61-76.

Giroux, Henry A., and Harvey J. Kaye (1989) "The Liberal Arts Must Be Reformed to Serve Democratic Means," *Chronicle of Higher Education,* 29 March: A44.

Gitelman, Lisa (1999) *Scripts, Grooves, and Writing Machines: Representing Technology in the Edison Era.* Stanford: Stanford University Press.

Goodman, Dena (2002) "L'ortografe des Dames: Gender and Language in the Old Regime," *French Historical Studies,* 25: 191-223.

Goody, Jack (1977) "What's in a List?" in *Literacy,* ed. Goody, 32-51 [reprinted from Goody, *The Domestication of the Savage Mind.* Cambridge: Cambridge University Press. 74-111].

Goody, Jack (1977) *The Domestication of the Savage Word.* Cambridge: Cambridge University Press.

Goody, Jack (1986) *The Logic of Writing and the Organization of Society.* Cambridge: Cambridge University Press.

Goody, Jack (1987) *The Interface Between the Written and the Oral.* Cambridge: Cambridge University Press.

Goody, Jack and Ian Watt (1968) "The Consequences of Literacy," in *Literacy in Traditional Societies,* ed. Jack Goody. Cambridge: Cambridge University Press (originally published in 1963): 27-68.

Gough, Kathleen (1968) "Implications of Literacy in Traditional China and India," in *Literacy in Traditional Societies,* ed. Jack Goody. Cambridge: Cambridge University Press: 69-84.

Gowen, Sheryl (1992) *The Politics of Workplace Literacy: A Case Study.* New York: Teachers College Press.

Graff, Harvey J. (1978) "Literacy Past and Present: Critical Approaches in the Literacy/Society Relationship," *Interchange* 9: 1-21.

Graff, Harvey J. (1979, 1991) *The Literacy Myth: Literacy and Social Structure in the Nineteenth-Century City.* New York and London: Academic Press. Reprinted with a new introduction. New Brunswick, N.J.: Transaction.

Graff, Harvey J. (1981a) *Literacy in History: An Interdisciplinary Research Bibliography.* New York: Garland.

Graff, Harvey J. ed. (1981b) *Literacy and Social Development in the West.* Cambridge: Cambridge University Press.

Graff, Harvey J. (1981c) "Reflections on the History of Literacy: Overview, Critique, and Proposals," *Humanities in Society,* 4: 303-333.

Graff, Harvey J. (1987a) *The Legacies of Literacy: Continuities and Contradictions in Western Culture and Society.* Bloomington: Indiana University Press.

Graff, Harvey J. (1987b) *The Labyrinths of Literacy: Reflections on Past and Present.* London: Falmer.

Graff, Harvey J. (1988) "Whither the History of Literacy? The Future of the Past," *Communication* 11: 5-22.

Graff, Harvey J. (1989) "Critical Literacy versus Cultural Literacy: Reading Signs of the Times," *Interchange* 20: 46-52.

Graff, Harvey J. (1993a) "Literacy Patterns in Historical Perspective." In *Reading Across the Life Span: Recent Research in Psychology,* ed. Steven R. Yussen and M. Cecil Smith, pp. 73-94. New York and Berlin: Springer-Verlag.

Graff, Harvey J. (1993b) "Literacy, Myths, and Legacies: Lessons from the Past—Thoughts for the Future." *Interchange* 24: 271–86.

Graff, Harvey J. (1994) Literacy, Myths, and Legacies: "Lessons from the History of Literacy," pp. 37-60. In *Functional literacy: Theoretical Issues and Educational Implications,* ed. Ludo Verhoeven. Amsterdam: John Benjamins.

Graff, Harvey J. (1995a) "Assessing the History of Literacy in the 1990s: Themes and Questions," in *Escribir y Leer en Occidente,* ed. Armando Petrucci and M. Gimeno Blay. Valencia, Spain: Universitat de Valencia: 5-46.

Graff, Harvey J. (1995b) *The Labyrinths of Literacy: Reflections on Literacy Past and Present,* rev. and exp. ed. Pittsburgh: University of Pittsburgh Press.

Graff, Harvey J. (1995c) *Conflicting Paths: Growing Up in America* Cambridge, Mass.: Harvard University Press.

Graff, Harvey J. (1999a) "Interdisciplinary Explorations in the History of Children, Adolescents, and Youth—For the Past, Present, and Future." *Journal of American History* 85: 1538–47.

Graff, Harvey J. (1999b) "Teaching and Historical Understanding: Disciplining Historical Imagination with Historical Context," in B. A. Pescosolido and R. Aminzade (eds.) *The Social Worlds of Higher Education: Handbook for Teaching in a New Century.* Thousand Oaks, CA: Pine Forge Press: 280–93.

Graff, Harvey J. (2001) "The Shock of the '"New" Histories': Social Science Histories and Historical Literacies," Presidential Address, Social Science History Association, 2000, *Social Science History,* 25, 4, 483-533.

Graff, Harvey J., Alison Mackinnon, Bengt Sandin, and Ian Winchester (2003) "Introduction to Historical Studies of Literacy," special double issue, *Interchange,* ed. Harvey J. Graff, Alison Mackinnon, Bengt Sandin, and Ian Winchester, 34, 2-3: 117-122.

Graff, Harvey J. (2003) "Understanding Literacy in its Historical Contexts: Past Approaches and Work in Progress," special double issue, *Interchange,* ed. Harvey J. Graff, Alison Mackinnon, Bengt Sandin, and Ian Winchester, 34. 2-3: 123-131.

Graff, Harvey J. and John Duffy (2007) "The Literacy Myth," *Encyclopedia of Language and Education,* Vol. 2 Literacy, ed. Brian Street; Nancy Hornberger, general editor. Berlin and New York: Springer.

Grafton, Anthony T. (1980) "The Importance of Being Printed," *Journal of Interdisciplinary History,* 11: 265-286.

Grafton, Anthony T. et al. (2002) "How Revolutionary Was the Print Revolution," *American Historical Review,* 107: 84-128.

Gray, Edward G. (1999) *New World Babel: Languages and Nations in Early America.* Princeton: Princeton University Press.

Gregory, Eve and Ann Williams (2000) *City Literacies: Learning to Read Across Generations and Cultures.* London: Routledge.

Grendler, Paul (1989) *Schooling in Renaissance Italy: Literacy and Learning, 1300-1600.* Baltimore: Johns Hopkins University Press.

Griswold, Wendy, Terry McDonnell, and Nathan Wright (2005) "Reading and the Reading Class in the Twenty-First Century," *Annual Reviews in Sociology,* 31, 127-141.

Gross, Robert A. (1988) *Books and Libraries in Thoreau's Concord: Two Essays.* Worcester, Mass.: American Antiquarian Society.

Gross, Robert A. (1988b) *Much Instruction from Little Reading: Books and Libraries in Thoreau's Concord.* Charlottesville: University of Virginia Press.

Gross, Robert A. (1989) "Printing, Politics, and the People," *Proceedings of the American Antiquarian Society* 99: 375-397.

Gross, Robert A. (1996) "Reading Culture, Reading Books," *Proceedings of the American Antiquarian Society* 106: 59-78.

Grubb, Farley (1987) "Colonial Immigrant Literacy: An Economic Analysis of Pennsylvania-German Evidence, 1727-1775," *Explorations in Economic History,* 24: 63-76.

Grubb, Farley (1990) "Growth of Literacy in Colonial America: Longitudinal Patterns, Economic Models, and the Direction of Future Research," *Social Science History,* 14: 451-481.

Grubb, Farley (1992) "Educational Choice in the Era Before Free Public Schooling: Evidence from German Immigrant Children in Pennsylvania, 1771-1817," *Journal of Economic History,* 52: 363-375.

Grubb, W. Norton and Marvin Lazerson (1982) *Broken Promises: How Americans Fail Their Children.* New York: Basic Books.

Gustafson, Sandra M. (2000) *Eloquence Is Power: Oratory and Performance in Early America.* Chapel Hill: University of North Carolina Press.

Hackenberg, Michael, ed. (1987) *Getting the Books Out.* Papers of the Chicago Conference on the Book in 19th-Century America. Washington, D.C.: Library of Congress.

Hall, David D. (1979) "The World of Print and Collective Mentality in Seventeenth-Century New England." In John Higham and Paul Conkin, eds., *New Directions in American Intellectual History.* pp. 166-180. Baltimore: Johns Hopkins University Press.

Hall, David D. (1983) "The Uses of Literacy in New England, 1600-1850." In William Joyce, et al, eds., *Printing and Society in Early America.* pp. 1-47. Worcester, MA: American Antiquarian Society.

Hall, David D. (1992) *Worlds of Wonder, Days of Judgment: Popular Religious Belief in Early New England.* Cambridge, Mass: Harvard University Press.

Hall, David D. (1996) *Cultures of Print.* Amherst: University of Massachusetts Press.

Hall, David D. and John Hench, eds. (1987) *Needs and Opportunities in the History of the Book: America, 1639-1876.* Worcester, Mass.: American Antiquarian Society.

Hall, Oswald and Richard Carlton (1977) *Basic Skills at School and Work: The Study of Albertown.* Toronto: Ontario Economic Council.

Harman, David (1974) *Community Fundamental Education.* Lexington, Mass.: Lexington Books.

Hautecoeur, Jean-Paul, ed. (1990) *Alpha 90: Current Research in Literacy.* Quebec: Unesco Institute for Education.

Havelock, Eric (1963) *Preface to Plato.* Cambridge, Mass.: Harvard University Press.

Havelock, Eric (1973) *Prologue to Greek Literacy.* Cincinnati: University of Cincinnati.

Havelock, Eric (1976) *Origins of Western Literacy.* Toronto: Ontario Institute for Studies in Education.

Havelock, Eric (1977) "The Preliteracy of the Greeks," *New Literary History* 8: 369-392.

Havelock, Eric (1986a) *The Literate Revolution in Greece and Its Cultural Consequences.* Princeton: Princeton University Press.

Havelock, Eric (1986b) *The Muse Learns to Write.* New Haven: Yale University Press.

Harris, William V. (1989) *Ancient Literacy.* Cambridge, Mass.: Harvard University Press.

Haywood, Ian (2004) *The Revolution in Popular Literature: Print, Politics, and the People 1790-1860.* Cambridge: Cambridge University Press.

Headrick, Daniel R. (2002) *When Information Came of Age: Technologies of Knowledge 1700-1850.* Oxford: Oxford University Press.

Heath, Shirley Brice (1983) *Ways with Words: Language, Life, and Work in Communities and Classrooms.* Cambridge: Cambridge University Press.

Hebrard, Jean (1980) "Ecole et alphabétisation au XIXe sièle (approche psychologique de documents historiques)," *Annales: e.s.c.* 35: 66-80.

Henkin, David (1998) *City Reading: Written Works and Public Spaces in Antebellum New York.* New York: Columbia University Press.

Hesse, Carla (2001) *The Other Enlightenment: How French Women Became Modern.* Princeton: Princeton University Press.

Higham, John and Paul Conkin, eds. (1979) *New Directions in American Intellectual History.* Baltimore: Johns Hopkins University Press.

Hilliard, Christopher (2006) *To Exercise Our Talents: The Democratization of Writing in Britain.* Cambridge, Mass.: Harvard University Press.

Hindman, Sandra L., ed. (1991) *Printing the Written Word: The Social History of Books, circa 1450-1520.* Ithaca: Cornell University Press.

Hirsch, E. D., Jr. (1987) *Cultural Literacy.* Boston: Houghton Mifflin.

Hirsch, E. D., Jr. (1988) *The Dictionary of Cultural Literacy.* Boston: Houghton Mifflin.

Hirsch, Rudoph (1978) *The Printed Word.* London: Variorum Editions.

Hobbs, Catherine (1995) *Nineteenth-Century Women Learn to Write.* Charlottesville: University of Virginia Press.

Hobsbawm, E. J. (1980) "The Revival of Narrative: Some Comments," *Past & Present* 86: 3-8.

Hoggart, Richard (1958) *The Uses of Literacy.* Harmondsworth: Penguin.

Horowitz, Helen (1992) "Nous Autres: Reading, Passion, and the Creation of M. Carey Thomas," *Journal of American History* 79: 68-95.

Houston, Rab (1982a) "The Development of Literacy: Northern England, 1640-1750," *Economic History Review,* 35: 199-216.

Houston, Rab (1982b) "The Literacy Myth? Illiteracy in Scotland, 1630-1760," *Past and Present,* 96: 81-102.

Houston, Rab (1983) "Literacy and Society in the West, 1500-1800," *Social History* 8: 269-293.

Houston, Rab (1985) *Scottish Literacy and the Scottish Identity: Illiteracy and Society in Scotland and Northern England, 1600-1800.* Cambridge: Cambridge University Press.

Houston, Rab (2002) *Literacy in Early Modern Europe: Culture and Education, 1500-1800.* London: Longman.

Hudson, Nicholas (1994) *Writing and European Thought 1600-1830.* Cambridge: Cambridge University Press.

Hull, Glynda and Katherine Schultz, eds. (2002) S*chool's Out! Bridging Out-of-School Literacies with Classroom Practice.* New York: Teachers College Press.

Hunter, Michael (1979) "The Impact of Print," *The Book Collector,* 28: 335-352.

Hunter, Jane (2002) *How Young Ladies Became Girls: The Victorian Origins of American Girlhood.* New Haven: Yale University Press.

Hyde, J.K. (1979) "Some Uses of Literacy in Venice and Florence in the Thirteenth and Fourteenth Centuries," *Transactions,* Royal Historical Society, 5th series, 29: 109-129.

Illich, Evan and Barry Sanders (1988) *The Alphabetization of the Popular Mind.* San Francisco: North Point Press.

Innes, Matthew. (1998) "Memory, Orality and Literacy in an Early Medieval Society," *Past and Present.* 158: 3-36.

Isaacs, Rhys (1976a) "Dramatizing the ideology of revolution: Popular mobilization in Virginia, 1774 to 1776," *William and Mary Quarterly* 33: 357-385.

Isaacs, Rhys (1976b) "Preachers and patriots: Popular culture and the revolution in Virginia." In *The American Revolution,* ed. Alfred F. Young, Dekalb: Northern Illinois University Press: 125-156.

Isaacs, Rhys (1982) *The Transformation of Virginia.* Chapel Hill: University of North Carolina Press.

Ivins, William (1969) *Prints and Visual Communications.* Cambridge, Mass.: MIT Press.

Jackson, H. J. (2005) *Romantic Readers: The Evidence of Marginalia.* New Haven: Yale University Press.

James, Louis (1963) *Fiction for the Working Man.* Oxford: Oxford University Press.

Johansson, Egil (1977) *The History of Literacy in Sweden.* Educational Reports No. 12. Umea, Sweden: Umea University and School of Education.

Johansson, Egil (1981) "The History of Literacy in Sweden." In *Literacy and Social Development in the West,* ed. Harvey J. Graff, pp. 151-182. Cambridge: Cambridge University Press.

Johansson, Egil (1985) "Popular Literacy in Scandinavia about 1600-1900," *Historical Social Research* 34: 60-64.

Johansson, Egil (1998) *Alphabeta Varia. Orality, Reading and Writing in the History of Literacy.* Festschrift in honour of Egil Johansson on the occasion of his 65th birthday. Album Religionum Umense 1. Umea University.

Johns, Adrian (1998) *The Nature of the Book: Print and Knowledge in the Making.* Chicago: University of Chicago Press.

Johnson, Richard (1976) "Notes on the Schooling of the English Working Class," in *Schooling and Capitalism,* ed. R. Dale, G. Esland, and M. MacDonald. London: Routledge & Kegan Paul: 44-55.

Jordan, John O. and Robert L Patten, eds. (1995) *Literature in the Marketplace.* Cambridge: Cambridge University Press.

Joyce, William L., David D. Hall, Richard D. Brown, and John B. Hench, eds. (1983) *Printing and Society in Early America.* Worcester, Mass.: American Antiquarian Society.

Justice, Steven (1994) *Writing and Rebellion: England in 1381.* Berkeley: University of California Press.

Kaestle, Carl F. (1976) "Between the Scylla of Brutal Ignorance and the Charybdis of a Literary Education: Elite Attitudes Toward Mass Schooling ...," in *Schooling and Society,* ed. Lawrence Stone. Baltimore: Johns Hopkins University Press: 77-191.

Kaestle, Carl F. (1983) *Pillars of the Republic.* New York: Hill & Wang.

Kaestle, Carl F. (1985) "The History of Literacy and the History of Reading." *Review of Educational Research* 12: 11-53.

Kaestle, Carl F., Helen Damon-Moore, Lawrence C. Stedman, Katherine Tinsley, and William Vance Trollinger, Jr. (1991) *Literacy in the United States: Readers and Reading Since 1880.* New Haven: Yale University Press.

Kaestle, Carl F. and Maris Vinovskis (1980) *Education and Social Change in Nineteenth Century.* Massachusetts: Cambridge: Cambridge University Press.

Kammen, Michael, ed. (1980) *The Past Before Us.* Ithaca: Corneal University Press.

Kaplan, Steven L., ed. (1984) *Understanding Popular Culture: Europe from the Middle Ages to the Nineteenth Century.* Berlin: Mouton.

Kasson, John (1984) "Civility and Rudeness: Urban Etiquette and the Bourgeois Social Order in Nineteenth-Century America," *Prospects* 9: 143-167.

Kates, Susan (2006) "Literacy, Voting Rights, and the Citizenship Schools in the South, 1957-1970," *CCC* 57: 479-502.

Katz, Michael B. (1976) "The Origins of Public Education," *History of Education Quarterly,* 16: 381-408.

Katz, Michael B. (1988) "The New Educational Panic," in *America in Theory*, ed. Leslie Berlowitz, Denis Donohue, and Louis Menand, pp. 178-194. New York: Oxford University Press.

Katz, Michael B. (1989) *Reconstructing American Education*. Cambridge, Mass.: Harvard University Press.

Kelley, Mary (1996) "Reading Women/Women Reading: The Making of Learned Women in Antebellum America," *Journal of American History* 83: 401-424.

Kelley, Mary (2006) *Learning to Stand and Speak: Women, Education, and Public Life in America's Republic*. Chapel Hill: University of North Carolina Press.

Kett, Joseph F. (1994) *The Pursuit of Knowledge Under Difficulties: From Self-Improvement to Adult Education in America, 1759-1990*. Stanford: Stanford University Press.

Kett, Joseph F. and Patricia A. McClung (1984) *Book Culture in Post-Revolutionary Virginia*. Worcester, Mass.: American Antiquarian Society.

Kirsch, Irwin S., Ann Jungeblut, Lynn Jenkins, and Andrew Kolstad (1993) *Adult Literacy in America*. Educational Testing Service under Contract with National Center for Education Statistics, Office of Educational Research and Improvement, U.S. Department of Education.

Klaus-Joachim, Lorenzen-Schmidt, and Bjorn Poulsen, eds. (2002) *Writing Peasants: Studies on Peasant Literacy in Early Modern Northern Europe*. Iceland: Landbohistorisk Selskab.

Kozol, Jonathan (1965) *Amazing Grace: The Lives of Children and the Conscience of a Nation*. New York: Crown.

Kozol, Jonathan (1978a) *Children of the Revolution*. New York: Delacorte.

Kozol, Jonathan (1978b) "A New Look at the Literacy Campaign in Cuba," *Harvard Educational Review*, 48: 341-377.

Kozol, Jonathan (1981) "Education as Transformation: Identity, Change, and Development." Special Issue, *Harvard Educational Review*, 52: 54-60.

Kozol, Jonathan (1985) *Illiterate America*. Garden City: Doubleday.

Kozol, Jonathan (2000) *Ordinary Resurrections: Children in the Years of Hope*. New York: Crown.

Krug, Rebecca (2002) *Reading Families: Women's Literate Practice in Late Medieval England*. Ithaca: Cornell University Press.

LaCapra, Dominick (1985a) "The Cheese and the Worms: The Cosmos of a Twentieth-Century Historian," in his *History and Criticism*. Ithaca: Cornell University Press: 45-69.

LaCapra, Dominick (1985b) *History and Criticism*. Ithaca: Cornell University Press: 87-94.

LaCapra, Dominick (1988) "Chartier, Darnton, and the Great Symbol Massacre," *Journal of Modern History*, 60: 95-112.

LaCapra, Dominick and Steven L. Kaplan, eds. (1982) *Modern European Intellectual History*. Ithaca: Cornell University Press.

Lanehart, Sonja (2002) *Sista Speak! Black Women Kinfolk Talk about Language and Literacy*. Austin: University of Texas Press.

Lankshear, Colin, with Moira Lawler (1987) *Literacy, School and Revolution.* London: Falmer.

Lankshear, Colin, and Peter McLaren, eds. (1993) *Critical Literacy: Politics. Praxis, and the Postmodern.* Albany, N.Y.: SUNY Press.

Laqueur, Thomas W. (1976a) "Working-Class Demand and the Growth of English Elementary Education, 1750-1850," in *Schooling and Society,* ed. Lawrence Stone. Baltimore: Johns Hopkins University Press: 192-205.

Laqueur, Thomas W. (1976b) "The Cultural Origins of Popular Literacy in England, 1500-1800," *Oxford Review of Education* 2: 255-275.

Lee, A.J. (1974) *The Origins of the Popular Press.* London: Croom Helm.

Lehuu, Isabel (2000) *Carnival on the Page: Popular Print Media in Antebellum America.* Chapel Hill: University of North Carolina Press.

Leith, James (1973) "Modernization, Mass Education, and Social Mobility in French Thought," *Eighteenth Century Studies,* 2: 223-238.

Leith, James (1977) "Introduction: Unity and Diversity in Education During the Eighteenth Century," in "Facets of Education in the Eighteenth Century," ed. Leith, *Studies on Voltaire and the Eighteenth Century:* 13-28.

Leith, James (1983) "The Hope for Moral Regeneration in French Educational Thought," in *City and Society in the Eighteenth Century*, ed. Paul Fritz and David Williams. London: Hakkert: 215-229.

Leonard, Thomas (1995) *News for All: America's Coming of Age with the Press.* New York: Oxford University Press.

LeRoy Ladurie, Emmanuel (1978) *Montaillou: Promised Land of Error.* New York: Braziller.

Levine, David (1979) "Education and Family Life in Early Industrial England," *Journal of Family History* 4: 368-380.

Levine, David (1980) "Illiteracy and Family Life during the First Industrial Revolution," *Journal of Social History* 14: 25-44.

Levine, David and Zubedeh Vahed (2001) "Ginzburg's Menocchio: Refutations and Conjectures," *Histoire Sociale* 34: 437-464.

Levine, David P. (2005) "The Birth of the Citizenship Schools: Entwining the Struggles for Literacy and Freedom," *History of Education Quarterly,* 44: 388-414.

Levine, Kenneth (1982) "Functional Literacy: Fond Illusions and False Economies," *Harvard Educational Review* 52: 249-266.

Levine, Kenneth (1985) *The Social Context of Literacy.* London: Routledge and Kegan Paul.

Levine, Lawrence W. (1978) *Highbrow/Lowbrow: The Emergence of Cultural Hierarchy in America.* New York: Oxford University Press.

Lindblom, Charles (1990) *Inquiry and Change.* New Haven: Yale University Press; New York: Russell Sage Foundation.

Lindblom, Charles and David Cohen (1979) *Usable Knowledge.* New Haven: Yale University Press.

Lindblom, Charles (1988) "Literacy, Culture, and the Dilemmas of Schooling," *Journal of Education* 170, 1.

"Literacy in America" (1990) *Daedalus* 119, 2.

Lockridge, Kenneth A. (1974) *Literacy in Colonial New England.* New York:

Norton.

Long, Elizabeth (2002) *Book Clubs.* Chicago: University of Chicago Press.

Luebke, David M. (2004) "Signatures and Political Culture in Eighteenth-Century Germany," *Journal of Modern History,* 76: 497-530.

Lunsford, Andrea A., Helene Moglen, and James Slevin, eds. (1990) *The Right to Literacy* New York: Modern Language Association.

Luria, Keith (1986) "The Paradoxical Carlo Ginzburg," *Radical History Review* 35: 80-87.

Lyons, Martyn (2001) *Readers and Society in Nineteenth-Century France: Workers, Women, Peasants.* London: Palgrave.

Mace, Jane (1988) *Playing With Time: Mothers and the Meaning of Literacy.* London: University College London.

Machor, James L., ed. (1993) *Readers in History: Nineteenth-Century American Literature and the Contexts of Response.* Baltimore: Johns Hopkins University Press.

MacKenzie, D.F. (1999) *Bibliography and the Sociology of Texts.* Cambridge: Cambridge University Press.

MacKenzie, D.F. (2002) *Making Meaning.* Amherst, Mass.: University of Massachusetts Press.

Mackinnon, A., C. Batson, and J. Peterson Grey (2007) "'But I'm So Embarrassed I Said, If It's Another Baby!': Schooling, Girls and Declining Fertility in Urban South Australia in the Late Nineteenth and Early Twentieth Century." In *Gendering the Fertility Decline in the Western World.* Ed. Angelique Janssens. Bern: Peter Lang.

Mah, Harold (1998) "Suppressing the Text: The Metaphysics of Ethnographic History in Darnton's Great Cat Massacre," *History Workshop* 31: 1-20.

Main, Gloria L. (1991) "An Inquiry into When and Why Women Learned to Write in Colonial New England," *Journal of Social History* 24: 579-89.

Manguel, Albert (1996) *A History of Reading.* New York: Viking.

Marchesini, Daniele (1987) *Il Bisogno di Scrivere: Usi Dela Scrittura Nell'Italia Modera.* Rome: Laterza.

Marcus, Steven (1973) "Reading the Illegible." In *The Victorian City,* ed. H. J. Dyos and Michael Wolf. pp. 257-276. London: Routledge.

Marcus, Steven (1974) *Engels, Manchester, and the Working Class.* New York: Random House.

Martin, Henri-Jean (1968-70) *Le livre et la civilisation écrite.* 3 vols. Paris: Ecole nationale supérieure des bibliothèques.

Martin, Henri-Jean (1975) "Culture écrite et culture orale, culture savante et culture populaire dans la France d'Ancien Régime," *Journale des Savants:* 225-282.

Martin, Henri-Jean (1977) "Pour une histoire de la lecture," *Revue française d'histoire du livre* 16: 583-609.

Martin, Henri-Jean (1978) "The Bibliotheque Bleue," *Publishing History,* 3: 70-102.

Martin, Henri-Jean (1994) *The History and Power of Writing.* Chicago: University of Chicago Press.

Martin, John (1992) "Journeys to the World of the Dead: The Work of Carlo Ginzburg," *Journal of Social History* 25: 613-626.

Martinez, Pedro Luiz Moreno (1989) *Alfabetizacion y cultura impresa en Lorca (1760-1860).* Murcia: Universidad de Murcia.

Marvin, Carolyn (1988) *When Old Technologies Were New: Thinking About Communications in the Late Nineteenth Century.* New York: Oxford University Press.

Maynes, Mary Jo (1979) "The Virtues of Archaism," *Comparative Studies in Society and History* 21: 611-625.

Maynes, Mary Jo (1980) "Work or School?" in "The Making of Frenchmen," *Historical Reflections*, 7: 115-134.

Maynes, Mary Jo (1985a) *Schooling for the People: Comparative Local Studies of Schooling History in France and Germany, 1750-1850.* New York: Holmes and Meier.

Maynes, Mary Jo (1985b) *Schooling in Western Europe.* Albany: State University of New York Press.

Maynes, Mary Jo (1995) *Taking the Hard Road: The Life Course in French and German Workers' Autobiographies in the Era of Industrialization.* Chapel Hill: University of North Carolina Press.

Mayor, A. Hayett (1981) *Prints and People.* Princeton: Princeton University Press.

McCloud, Scott (1993) *Understanding Comics: The Invisible Art.* New York: A Kitchen Sink Book for Harper Perennial.

McHenry, Elizabeth (2002) *Forgotten Readers: Recovering the Lost History of African American Literary Societies.* Durham, NC: Duke University Press.

McHenry, Elizabeth and Shirley Brice Heath (1994) "The Literate and the Literary: African Americans as Writers and Readers—1830-1940," *Written Communication,* 11: 419-444.

McKitterick, David (2003) *Print, Manuscript and the Search for Order.* Cambridge: Cambridge University Press.

McKitterick, Rosamond (1989) *The Carolingians and the Written Word.* Cambridge: Cambridge University Press.

McKitterick, Rosamond, ed. (1991) *The Uses of Literacy in Early Medieval England.* Cambridge: Cambridge University Press.

McKitterick, Rosamond (2004) *History and Memory in the Carolingian World.* Cambridge: Cambridge University Press.

McLaren, Peter L. (1988) "Culture or canon? Critical pedagogy and the politics of literacy," *Harvard Educational Review* 58: 213-234.

McNeely, Ian F. (2003) *The Emancipation of Writing: German Civil Society in the Making.* Berkeley: University of California Press.

Melton, James Van Horn (1988) *Absolutism and the Eighteenth-Century Origins of Compulsory Schooling in Prussia and Austria.* Cambridge: Cambridge University Press.

Melton, James Van Horn (2001) *The Rise of the Public in Enlightenment Europe.* Cambridge: Cambridge University Press.

Messaris, Paul (1994) *Visual Literacy: Image, Mind, and Reality.* Boulder: Westview.

Mignolo, Walter D. (1995) *The Darker Side of the Renaissance: Literacy, Territoriality, and Colonization.* Ann Arbor: University of Michigan Press.

Miller, Arthur I. (2000) *Insights of Genius: Imagery and Creativity in Science and Art* Cambridge, Mass.: MIT Press.

Miller, Susan (1998) *Assuming the Position: Cultural Pedagogy and the Politics of Commonplace Writing.* Pittsburgh: University of Pittsburgh Press.

Milner, Henry (2002) *Civic Literacy.* Hanover, N.H.: University Press of New England.

Mitch, David (1992) *The Rise of Popular Literacy in Victorian England.* Philadelphia: University of Pennsylvania Press.

Mitch, David. (1992b) "The Rise of Popular Literacy in Europe," in *The Political Construction of Education,* ed. Bruce Fuller and Richard Rubinson. Praeger: 31-46.

Mitch, David. (1999) "The Role of Skill and Human Capital in the British Industrial Revolution." In *The British Industrial Revolution. An Economic Perspective.* 2nd edition. ed. Joel Mokyr. Boulder: Westview: 241-279.

Mitchell, Candace, and Kathleen Weiller, eds. (1991) *Rewriting Literacy.* New York: Bergin and Garvey.

Mitchell, Sally (1977) "Sentiment and Suffering: Women's Recreational Reading," *Victorian Studies* 21: 29-45.

Mitchell, Sally (1981) *The Fallen Angel: Chastity, Class and Women's Reading, 1835-1880.* Bowling Green, Ohio: Popular Press.

Monaghan, E. Jennifer (1988) "Literacy Instruction and Gender in Colonial New England," *American Quarterly,* 40: 18-41.

Monaghan, E. Jennifer (1990) "'She Loved to Read in Good Books': Literacy and the Indians of Martha's Vinyard," *History of Education Quarterly, 30*: 492-521.

Monaghan, E. Jennifer (1991) "Family Literacy in Early 18th-Century Boston: Cotton Mather and His Children," *Reading Research Quarterly,* 26: 342-370.

Monaghan, E. Jennifer (1998) "Reading for the Enslaved, Writing for the Free: Reflections on Liberty and Literacy," *Proceedings,* American Antiquarian Society, 108: 308-341.

Monaghan, E. Jennifer (2005) *Learning to Read and Write in Colonial America.* Amherst, Mass.: University of Massachusetts Press in Association with the American Antiquarian Society.

Moran, Jo Ann Hoeppner (1985) *The Growth of English Schooling, 1340-1548: Learning, Literacy, and Laicization in Pre-Reformation York Diocese.* Princeton: Princeton University Press.

Morgan, Teresa (1998) *Literate Education in the Hellenistic and Roman Worlds.* Cambridge: Cambridge University Press.

Morris, Robert C. (1976) *Reading, Riting, and Reconstruction: The Education of Freedmen in the South, 1861-1871.* Chicago: University of Chicago Press.

Moylan, Michele and Lane Stiles, eds. (1996) *Reading Books: Essays on the Material Text and Literature in America.* Amherst, Mass.: University of Massachusetts Press.

Muchembled, Robert (1985) *Popular Culture and Élite Culture in France,*

1400-1750. Baton Rouge: Louisiana State University Press.

Munck, Thomas (2004) "Literacy, Educational Reform and the Uses of Print in Eigthteenh-Century Denmark," *European History Quarterly,* 34: 275-303.

Murray, John (1995) "Human Capital in Religious Communes: Literacy and Selection of Nineteenth Century Shakers," *Explorations in Economic History,* 32: 217-235.

Murray, John (1997) "Generation(s) of Human Capital: Literacy in American Families, 1830-1875," *Journal of Interdisciplinary History,* 27:413-435.

Murray, John (2000) "Literacy and Industrialization in Modern Germany," in *The Industrial Revolution in Comparative Perspective,* ed. Christine Rider and Michéal Thompson. Krieger Publishing: 17-32.

Murray, John (2003) "Fates of Orphans: Poor Children in Antebellum Charleston," *Journal of Interdisciplinary History,* 33: 519-545.

Murray, John (2004a) "Family, Literacy, and Skill Training in the Antebellum South: Historical-Longitudinal Evidence from Charleston," *Journal of Economic History,* 64: 773-99.

Murray, John (2004b) "Literacy Acquisition in an Orphanage: A Historical-Longitudinal Case Study," *American Journal of Education,* 110: 172-195.

Neuberg, Victor (1973) "The Literature of the Streets," in *The Victorian City,* ed. H.J. Dyos and Michael Wolff. London: Routledge and Kegan Paul. I: 191-210.

Neuberg, Victor (1977) *Popular Literature.* Harmondsworth: Penguin.

New London Group (2000) "A Pedagogy of Multiliteracies Designing Social Futures," in *Multiliteracies: Literacy Learning and the Design of Social Futures,* ed. Bill Cope and Mary Kalantzis. London: Routledge: 9-37 (also *Harvard Educational Review,* 1996).

Newbury, Michael (1997) *Figuring Authorship in Antebellum America.* Stanford: Stanford University Press.

Newcomb, Lori Humphrey (2002) *Reading Popular Romance in Early Modern England.* New York: Columbia University Press.

Newman, Charles (1985) *The Post-Modern Aura.* Evanston: Northwestern University Press.

Nicholas, Stephen, ed. (1988) *Convict Workers: Reinterpreting Australia's Past.* Cambridge: Cambridge University Press.

Nicholas, Stephen J and Jacqueline M. Nicholas (1992) "Male Literacy, 'Deskilling', and the Industrial Revolution," *Journal of Interdisciplinary History.* 23: 1-18.

Nicholas, Stephen J and Deborah Oxley (1993) "The Living Standards of Women During the Industrial Revolution, 1795 - 1820," *Economic History Review,* 2nd ser., 46: 723-49.

Nicholas, Stephen J and Deborah Oxley (1996) "Living Standards of Women in England and Wales, 1785–1815: New Evidence from Newgate Prison Records," *Economic History Review,* 2nd ser., 49: 591-99.

Nicholas, Stephen J and Richard H. Steckel (1991) "Heights and Living Standards of English Workers During the Early Years of Industrialization, 1770 - 1815," *Journal of Economic History,* 51: 937-57.

Nilsson, Anders (1999) "What Do Literacy Rates Really Signify? New Light on an Old Problem from Unique Swedish Data," *Paedagogica Historica*, 35: 275-96.

Nilsson, Anders and Birgitta Svard (1994) "Writing Ability and Agrarian Change in Early Nineteenth Century Rural Scania," *Scandinavian Journal of History*, 19: 251-74.

Nilsson, Anders et al. (1999) "Agrarian Transition and Literacy: The Case of Nineteenth Century Sweden," *European Review of Economic History*. No. 3.

Noakes, Susan (1981) "The Development of the Book Market in Late Quattrocento Italy," *Journal of Medieval and Renaissance Studies* 11: 23-55.

Nord, David (2001) *Communities of Journalism: A History of American Newspapers and Their Readers*. Champaign: University of Illinois Press.

Nord, David (2004) *Faith in Reading: Religious Publishing and the Birth of Mass Media in America*. New York: Oxford University Press.

Nunberg, Geoffrey, ed. (1996) *The Future of the Book*. Berkeley: University of California Press. OECD (1992) *Adult Illiteracy and Economic Performance*. Paris: Centre for Educational Research and Development, OECD.

Ohmann, Richard (1996) *Selling Markets: Magazines, Markets, and Class at the Turn of the Century*. London: Verso.

Olson, David (1977) "The Languages of Instruction: On the Literate Bias of Schooling," in *Schooling and the Acquisition of Knowledge*, ed. Richard C. Anderson and William E. Montague. Hillsdale, N.J.: Lawrence Erlbaum.

Olson, David (1994) *The World on Paper: The Conceptual and Cognitive Implications of Writing and Reading*. Cambridge: Cambridge University Press.

Ong, Walter (1958) *Ramus, Method, and the Decay of Dialogue*. Cambridge, Mass.: Harvard University Press.

Ong, Walter (1967) *The Presence of the Word*. New Haven: Yale University Press.

Ong, Walter (1977) *Interface of the Word*. Ithaca: Cornell University Press.

Ong, Walter (1982) *Orality and Literacy*. London: Methuen.

Pauwels, Luc, ed. (2006) *Visual Cultures of Science: Rethinking Representational Practices in Knowledge Building and Science Communication*. Hanover, N.H.: Dartmouth College Press.

Pawley, Christine (2001) *Reading on the Middle Border*. Amherst, Mass.: University of Massachusetts Press.

Pearson, Jacqueline (1999) *Women's Reading in Britain, 1750-1835: A Dangerous Recreation*. Cambridge: Cambridge University Press.

Pelizzari, Maria Rosaria, ed. (1989) *Sulle vie della scrittura: Alfabetizzazione, cultura scritta e istitzioni in eta moderna*. Naples: Edizioni Scientifiche Ialiane.

Perlmann, Joel and Dennis Shirley (1991) "When Did New England Women Acquire Literacy?" *William and Mary Quarterly*, 48: 18-41.

Perlmann, Joel, Silvana R. Siddali, and Keith Whitescarver (1997) "Literacy, Schooling, and Teaching Among New England Women, 1730-1820," *History of Education Quarterly*, 37: 117-39.

Peters, Kate (2005) *Print Culture and the Early Quakers*. Cambridge: Cambridge University Press.

Peterson, Glen (1997) *The Power of Words: Literacy and Revolution in South China 1949-95.* Vancouver: University of British Columbia Press.

Petrucci, Armando (1987) *Scrivere e no: Politche della scrittura e analfabetismo nel mondo d'oggi.* Rome: Riuniti.

Petrucci, Armando (1995a) *Public Lettering.* Chicago: University of Chicago Press.

Petrucci, Armando (1995b) *Writers and Readers in Medieval Italy.* New Haven: Yale University Press.

Phillipps, K C. (1984) *Language and Class in Victorian England.* London: Blackwell.

Plumb, J.H. (1972) "The Public, Literature & the Arts in the 18th Century." *The Triumph of Culture: Eighteenth Century Perspectives.* Eds. Paul Fritz and David Williams. Toronto: A.M. Hakkert. 27-48.

Plumb, J.H. (1975) "The New World of Children in Eighteenth Century England," *Past and Present,* no. 67: 64-95.

Poster, Mark (1986) "Darnton's Historiography," *The Eighteenth Century,* 27: 87-92.

Poster, Mark (2001) *What's the Matter with the Internet?* Minneapolis: University of Minnesota Press.

Prendergast, Catherine (2002) "The Economy of Literacy: How the Supreme Court Stalled the Civil Rights Movement," *Harvard Educational Review* 72: 206-229.

Prendergast, Catherine (2003) *Literacy and Racial Justice: The Politics of Learning after Brown v. Board of Education.* Carbondale: Southern Illinois University Press.

Purcell-Gates, Victoria (1995) *Other People's Words: The Cycle of Low Literacy.* Cambridge, Mass.: Harvard University Press.

Rabb, Theodore K. and Robert I. Rotberg, eds. (1982) *The New History: 1980s and Beyond.* Princeton: Princeton University Press.

Radway, Janice A. (1983) "Women Read the Romance," *Feminist Studies, 9:* 53-78.

Radway, Janice A. (1984a) "Interpretive Communities and Variable Literacies," *Daedalus* 113: 49-73.

Radway, Janice A. (1984b) *Reading the Romance: Women, Patriarchy, and Popular Literature.* Chapel Hill: University of North Carolina Press.

Radway, Janice A. (1986a) "Identifying Ideological Seams: Mass Culture, Analytic Method, and Political Practice," *Communication* 9: 93-123.

Radway, Janice A. (1986b) "Reading is Not Eating: Mass-Produced Literature and the Theoretical, Methodological, and Political Consequences of a Metaphor," *Book Research Quarterly* 2: 7-29.

Radway, Janice A. (1989) "The Book of the Month Club and the General Reader: On the Uses of Serious Fiction," in *Reading,* ed. Davidson: 259-284.

Radway, Janice A. (1997) *A Feeling for Books: The Book-Of-The-Month Club, Literary Taste, and Middle-Class Desire.* Chapel Hill: University of North Carolina Press.

Raven, James, Helen Small, and Naomi Tadmor, eds. (1996) *The Practice and Representation of Reading in England.* Cambridge: Cambridge University Press.

Rawski, Evelyn (1979) *Education and Popular Literacy in Ch'ing China.* Ann Arbor: University of Michigan Press.

"Reading Old and New" (1983) *Daedalus,* Winter.

Richardson, Brian (1994) *Print Culture in Renaissance Italy.* Cambridge: Cambridge University Press.

Roche, Daniel (1987) *The People of Paris.* Berkeley and Los Angeles: University of California Press.

Rollo, David (2000) *Glamorous Sorcery: Magic and Literacy in the High Middle Ages.* Minneapolis: University of Minnesota Press.

Rose, Jonathan (1992) "Rereading the English Common Reader," *Journal of the History of Ideas,* 53: 47-70.

Rose, Jonathan (2001) *The Intellectual Life of the British Working Classes.* New Haven: Yale University Press.

Rose, Mike (1989) *Lives on the Boundary: The Struggles of America's Underprepared.* New York: Free Press.

Rose, Mike (1995) *Possible Lives: The Promise of Public Education in America.* Boston: Houghton Mifflin.

Rose, Mike (2004) *The Mind at Work: Valuing the Intelligence of American Workers.* New York: Viking.

Royer, Daniel J. (1994) "The Process of Literacy as Communal Involvement in the Narratives of Frederick Douglass," *African American Review* 28: 363-374.

Royster, Jaqueline Jones (2000) *Traces of a Stream: Literacy and Social Change Among African American Women.* Pittsburgh: University of Pittsburgh Press.

Rubin, Joan Shelly (1983) "'Information, Please!' Culture and Expertise in the Interwar Period," *American Quarterly, 35*: 499-517.

Rubin, Joan Shelly (1985) "Self, Culture and Self-Culture in Modern American: The Early History of the Book-of-the-Month Club," *Journal of American History* 71: 782-806.

Rubin, Joan Shelly (1992) *The Making of Middle Brow Culture.* Chapel Hill: University of North Carolina Press.

Ryan, Barbara and Amy M. Thomas, eds. (2002) *Reading Acts: U.S. Readers' Interactions with Literature 1800-1950.* Knoxville: University of Tennessee Press.

Saenger, Paul (1977) *Space Between Words: The Origins of Silent Reading.* Stanford: Stanford University Press.

Saljo, Roger, ed. (1988) *The Written World: Studies in Literate Thought and Action.* Berlin: Springer-Verlag.

Sanderson, Michael (1972) "Literacy and Social Mobility in the Industrial Revolution in England," *Past and Present,* 56: 75-104.

Schenda, Rudolf (1970) *Volk ohne buch ... 1770-1910.* Frankfurt.

Schenda, Rudolf (1976) *Die lesestoffe der kleinen leute.* Munich: Beck.

Schofield, Roger S. (1968) "The Measurement of Literacy in Pre-industrial England," in *Literacy in Traditional Societies,* ed. Jack Goody, pp. 311-325. Cambridge: Cambridge University Press.

Schofield, Roger S. (1973) "The Dimensions of Illiteracy in England, 1750-1850," *Explorations in Economic History* 10: 437-454.

Schudson, Michael (1978) *Discovering the News.* New York: Basic Books.

Schutte, Anne Jacobson (1976) "Carlo Ginzburg: Review Article," *Journal of Modern History* 48: 296-315.

Schutte, Anne Jacobson (1981) "Printing, Piety, and the People in Italy," *Archive for Renaissance History,* 71: 5-19.

Scribner, R. W. (1981) *For the Sake of Simple Folk: Popular Propaganda for the German Reformation.* Cambridge: Cambridge University Press.

Scribner, R. W. (1984) "Oral Culture and the Diffusion of Reformation Ideas," *History of European Ideas* 5: 237-256.

Scribner, Sylvia and Michael Cole (1973) "Cognitive Consequences of Formal and Informal Education," *Science* 182: 553-559.

Scribner, Sylvia and Michael Cole (1981) *The Psychology of Literacy.* Cambridge, Mass.: Harvard University Press.

Scribner, Sylvia and Michael Cole (1981) "Unpacking Literacy" In *Writing: The Nature, Development, and Teaching of Written Communication,* ed. Marcia Farr Whiteman. Lawrence Erlbaum Associates: 123-137.

"Scientific Literacy" (1983) *Daedalus,* Spring.

Searle, John (1990) "The storm over the university," *New York Review of Books,* 6 December: 34-42.

Selfe, Cynthia L. (1999) *Technology and Literacy in the 21st Century.* Carbondale: Southern Illinois University Press.

Sewell, William H., Jr. (1985) *Structure and Mobility: The Men and Women of Marseille, 1820-1870.* Cambridge: Cambridge University Press.

Sharpe, Kevin (2000) *Reading Revolutions: The Politics of Reading in Early Modern England.* New Haven: Yale University Press.

Sheridan, Dorothy, Brian Street, and David Bloome, eds. (2000) *Writing Ourselves: Mass-Observation and Literacy Practices.* Cresskill, NJ: Hampton Press.

Shor, Ira (1922) *Empowering Education: Critical Teaching for Social Change.* Chicago: University of Chicago Press.

Sicherman, Barbara (1989) "Sense and Sensibility: A Case Study of Women's Reading in Late-Nineteenth-Century America," in *Reading in America,* ed. Davison, 201-225.

Sicherman, Barbara (1993) "Reading and Ambition: M. Carey Thomas and Female Heroism," *American Quarterly,* 45: 73-103.

Sicherman, Barbara (1995) "Reading Little Women: The Many Lives of a Text," in *U.S. History as Women's History,* ed. Linda K. Kerber et al. Chapel Hill: University of North Carolina Press: 245-266.

Singh, Michael Garbutcheon (1989) "A Counter-Hegemonic Orientation to Literacy in Australia," *Journal of Education,* 171: 35-56.

Siskin, Clifford (1998) *The Work of Writing: Literature and Social Change in Britain 1700-1830.* Baltimore: Johns Hopkins University Press.

Slights, William W E. (2001) *Managing Readers: Printed Marginalia and English Renaissance Books.* Ann Arbor: University of Michigan Press.

Soltow, Lee and Edward Stevens (1977) "Economic Aspects of School Participation in the U.S.," *Journal of Interdisciplinary History,* 8: 221-244.

Soltow, Lee and Edward Stevens (1981) *The Rise of Literacy and the Common
School in the United States.* Chicago: University of Chicago Press.

Spufford, Margaret (1979) "First Steps in Literacy: The Reading and Writing
Experiences of the Humblest Seventeenth-Century Spiritual Autobiogra-
phers," *Social History* 4: 407-435.

Spufford, Margaret (1981) *Small Books and Pleasant Histories: Popular Fiction
and Its Readership in Seventeenth-Century England.* London: Methuen.

St. Clair, William (2004) *The Reading Nation in the Romantic Period.* Cambridge: Cambridge University Press.

Starkey, Kathryn (2004) *Reading the Medieval Book.* Notre Dame: University
of Notre Dame Press.

Starr, Paul. (2004) *The Creation of the Media.* New York: Basic Books.

Stearns, Peter. (1991) "The Challenge of 'Historical Literacy.'" *Perspectives:
American Historical Association Newsletter* 29: 21–23.

Stearns, Peter. (1993) *Meaning Over Memory: Recasting the Teaching of Culture
and History.* Chapel Hill: University of North Carolina Press.

Steedman, Carolyn (1987) *The Tidy House.* London: Virago.

Stephens, W.B. (1987) *Education, Literacy, and Society, 1830-1870.* Manchester: Manchester University Press.

Stephens, W.B., ed. (1983) *Studies in the History of Literacy: England and
North America.* Educational Administration and History Monographs
No. 13. Leeds: Museum of the History of Education, University of
Leeds.

Stevens, Edward (1985) "Literacy and the Worth of Liberty," *Historical Social
Research* 34: 65-81.

Stevens, Edward (1988) *Literacy, Law, and Social Order.* DeKalb: Northern
Illinois University Press.

Stevens, Edward (1995) *The Grammar of the Machine: Technical Literacy
and Early Industrial Expansion in the United States.* New Haven: Yale
University Press.

Stevenson, Louise L. (1990-1991) "Prescription and Reality: Reading Advisors
and Reading Practice, 1860-1880," *Book Research Quarterly,* 6: 43-61.

Stock, Brian (1983) *The Implications of Literacy: Written Language and Models
of Interpretation in the Eleventh and Twelfth Centuries.* Princeton: Princeton
University Press.

Stock, Brian (1990) *Listening for the Text.* Baltimore: Johns Hopkins University Press.

Stock, Brian (1996) *Augustine the Reader.* Cambridge, Mass.: Harvard University Press.

Stock, Brian (2001) *After Augustine.* Philadelphia: University of Pennsylvania
Press.

Stone, Lawrence (1969) "Literacy and Education in England, 1640-1900," *Past
& Present* 42: 69-139.

Stone, Lawrence (1979) "The Revival of Narrative: Reflections on a New Old
History," *Past & Present* 85: 3-24.

Stout, Harry S. (1977) "Religion, Communications, and the Ideological Origins of the American Revolution," *William and Mary Quarterly* 34: 519-541.

Strauss, Gerald (1978) *Luther's Home of Learning*. Baltimore: Johns Hopkins University Press.

Strauss, Gerald (1984) "Lutheranism and Literacy: A Reassessment." In *Religion and Society in Early Modern Europe,* ed. Kaspar Von Greyerz, pp. 109-123. London: Allen and Unwin.

Strauss, Gerald, and Richard Gawthrop (1984) "Protestantism and Literacy in Early Modern Germany," *Past & Present* 104: 31-55.

Street, Brian (1984) *Literacy in Theory and Practice.* Cambridge: Cambridge University Press.

Street, Brian (1993) *Cross-cultural approaches to literacy.* Cambridge: Cambridge University Press.

Street, Brian (1995) *Social Literacies: Critical Approaches to Literacy in Development, Ethnography, and Education.* London: Longman.

Street, Brian (2001) "The New Literacy Studies." In *Literacy: A Critical Sourcebook,* eds. Ellen Cushman, Eugene R. Kintgen, Barry M. Kroll, and Mike Rose. Boston: Bedford/St. Martin's: 430-442.

Stuckey, Elspeth (1991) *The Violence of Literacy.* Portsmouth N.H.: Boynton/Cook.

Svenbro, Jesper (1993) *Phrasikleia: An Anthropology of Reading in Ancient Greece.* Ithaca: Cornell University Press.

Swearingen, Jan (1991) *Rhetoric and Irony: Western Literacy and Western Lies.* New York: Oxford University Press.

Tannen, Deborah, ed. (1982) *Spoken and Written Language: Exploring Orality and Literacy.* Norwood, N.J.: Ablex.

Thomas, Keith (1986) "The Meaning of Literacy in Early Modern England," in *The Written Word: Literacy in Transition,* ed.: Gerd Baumann, pp, 97-131. Oxford: Oxford University Press.

Thomas, Rosalind (1989) *Oral Tradition and Written Record in Classical Athens.* Cambridge: Cambridge University Press.

Thomas, Rosalind (1992) *Literacy and Orality in Ancient Greece.* Cambridge: Cambridge University Press.

Thompson, Paul (1975) *The Edwardians.* Bloomington: India University Press.

Thompson, Paul (1978) *The Voice of the Past: Oral History.* Oxford: Oxford University Press.

Thornton, Tamara Plakins (1996) *Handwriting in America: A Cultural History.* New Haven: Yale University Press.

Todd, Emmanuel (1987) *The Causes of Progress.* Oxford: Blackwell.

Tuman, Myron C. (1987) *A Preface to Literacy: An Inquiry into Pedagogy, Practice, and Progress.* Tuscaloosa: University of Alabama Press.

Tuman, Myron (1993) *Word Perfect.* Pittsburgh: University of Pittsburgh Press.

Tompkins, Jane (1985) *Sensational Designs: The Cultural Work of American Fiction, 1790-1860.* New York: Oxford University Press.

Tortella, Gabriel, ed. (1990) *Education and Economic Development Since the Industrial Revolution.* Valencia: Generalitat Valencia.

Toth, Istvan Gyorgy (2000) *Literacy and Written Culture in Early Modern Europe.* Budapest: Central European University Press.

Van Slyck, Abigail A. (1995) *Free to All: Carnegie Libraries and American Culture 1890-1920* Chicago: University of Chicago Press.

Vinao, Frago A., ed. (1989) "Alfabetizacion," *Revista de educacion,* 288.

Vincent, David (1981) *Bread, Knowledge, and Freedom: A Study of Nineteenth-Century Working class Autobiography.* London: Europa.

Vincent, David (1989) *Literacy and Popular Culture: England 1750-1914.* Cambridge: Cambridge University Press.

Vincent, David (2000) *The Rise of Mass Literacy: Reading and Writing in Modern Europe.* Cambridge: Polity.

Wagner, Daniel A. (1990) "Literacy Assessment in the Third World: An Overview and Proposed Schemes for Survey Use," *Comparative Education Review* 34: 112-138.

Walvin, James (1978) *Leisure and Society.* London: Longman.

Warner, Michael (1990) *The Letters of the Republic: Publication and the Public Sphere in Eighteenth-Century America.* Cambridge, Mass.: Harvard University Press.

Warner, William B. (1998) *Licensing Entertainment: The Elevation of Novel Reading 1684-1750.* Berkeley: University of California Press.

Watt, Teresa (1991) *Cheap Print and Popular Piety, 1550-1640.* Cambridge: Cambridge University Press.

Webb, Robert K. (1955) *The British Working Class Reader.* London: Allen and Unwin.

Webber, Thomas (1978) *Deep Like the Rivers: Education in the Slave Quarter Community.* New York: Norton.

Weber, Eugen (1976) *Peasants into Frenchmen.* Stanford: Stanford University Press.

Welch, Kathleen E. (1999) *Electric Rhetoric: Classical Rhetoric, Oralism, and a New Literacy.* Cambridge, Mass.: MIT Press.

West, E.G. (1975) *Education and the Industrial Revolution.* London: Batsford.

West, E.G. (1978) "Literacy and the Industrial Revolution," *Economic History Review,* 31: 369-83.

Wheale, Nigel (1999) *Writing and Society ... Britain 1590-1660.* London: Routledge.

Whiteman, Marcia Farr, ed. (1981) *Writing: The Nature, Development and Teaching of Written Composition,* Vol. 1: *Variation in Writing.* Hillsdale, N.J.: Lawrence Erlbaum.

Wiles, R.M. (1968) "Middle Class Literacy in Eighteenth Century England," in *Studies in the Eighteenth Century,* ed. R.F. Brissenden. Camberra: Australian National University Press: 49-66.

Wiles, R.M. (1972) "Provincial Culture in Early Georgian England," in *The Triumph of Culture,* ed. Paul Fritz and David Williams. Toronto: Hakkert: 49-68.

Williams, Heather Andrea (2005) *Self-Taught: African American Education in Slavery and Freedom.* Chapel Hill: University of North Carolina Press.

Williams, Susan S. (1990) "Widening the World: Susan Warner, Her Readers, and the Assumption of Authorship," *American Quarterly,* 42: 565-586.

Willinsky, John (1990) *The New Literacy: Redefining Reading and Writing in the Schools.* New York: Routledge.

Winchester, Ian (1978) "How Many Ways to Universal Literacy?" Paper presented to the Ninth World Congress of Sociology, Uppsala, and Seminar on the History of Literacy in Post-Reformation Europe, University of Leicester.

Winchester, Ian (1990a) "Beyond the Revised Standard Picture of Literacy." Paper presented to the Social Science History Association, Minneapolis, 1990.

Winchester, Ian (1990b) "The Standard Picture of Literacy and its Critics," *Comparative Education Review* 34: 21-40.

Wormald, Patrick (1977) "The Uses of Literacy in Anglo-Saxon England and its Neighbours," *Transactions*, Royal Historical Society, 5th series, 27: 47-80.

Wrightson, Keith and David Levine. (1979) *Poverty and Piety.* New York and London: Academic Press.

Wyss, Hilary E. (2000) *Writing Indians: Literacy, Christianity, and Native Community in Early America.* Amherst: University of Massachusetts Press.

Young, Morris (2004) *Re/Visions: Asian American Literacy Narratives as a Rhetoric of Citizenship.* Carbondale: Southern Illinois University Press.

Zambelli, Paola (1985) "From Menocchio to Piero Della Francesa: The Work of Carlo Ginzburg," *Historical Journal,* 28: 983-999.

Zaret, David (2000) *Origins of Democratic Culture.* Princeton: Princeton University Press.

Zboray, Ronald (1993) *A Fictive People: Antebellum Economic Development and the American Reading Public.* New York: Oxford University Press.

Zboray, Ronald J. and Mary Saracin Zboray (2005) *Literary Dollars and Social Sense: A Peoples History of the Mass Market Book.* New York: Routledge.

Zboray, Ronald J. and Mary Saracin Zboray (2006) *Everyday Ideas: Socioliteracy Experiene Among Antebellum New Englanders.* Knoxville: University of Tennessee Press.